PRESIDENT AND POWER IN NIGERIA

Kaduna   September 1983.

Portrait photograph by Paul Kaye F.I.I.P. F.R.P.S. of London.

PRESIDENT SHEHU SHAGARI

With kind permission of the Department of Information, Executive Office of the President, Federal Republic of Nigeria.

PRESIDENT AND POWER
IN NIGERIA

The Life of
Shehu Shagari

DAVID WILLIAMS

with a Foreword by
KURT WALDHEIM

FRANK CASS

First published 1982 in Great Britain by
FRANK CASS AND COMPANY LIMITED
Gainsborough House, 11 Gainsborough Road,
London, E11 1RS, England

and in the United States of America by
FRANK CASS AND COMPANY LIMITED
c/o Biblio Distribution Centre
81 Adams Drive, P.O. Box 327, Totowa, N.J. 07511

British Library Cataloguing in Publication Data

Williams, David
    President and power in Nigeria: the life of Shehu
    Shagari.
    1. Shagari, Shehu   2. Statement—Nigeria—
    Biography
    I. Title
    996.9'05'0924   DT515.6.S/

    ISBN 0-7146-3182-5 (Case)

    ISBN 0-7146-4036-0 (Paper)

Typeset by John Smith, London
Printed and bound in Great Britain by
Robert Hartnoll Ltd, Bodmin, Cornwall

To the memory of
ALHAJI SIR ABUBAKAR TAFAWA BALEWA
Prime Minister of the Federation of Nigeria

and

ALHAJI SIR AHMADU BELLO,
SARDAUNA OF SOKOTO
Premier of the Northern Region of Nigeria

CONTENTS

LIST OF ILLUSTRATIONS

FOREWORD

There has been a considerable growth in studies of the Third
World in recent years. However, one area where scarcity
still prevails, is the biographies of leaders and statesmen of
large, populous developing countries. Apart from the theme
of personal struggle through difficult conditions inherent in
them, accounts of the experiences of these leaders can vividly
portray the effort to modernize economies, evolve civilian
rule and representative government and, in societies like that
of Nigeria with complex ethnic compositions, establish the
Federal principle as a basis of national unity. I believe this
multi-dimensional effort to be of crucial importance for the
stability and social progress of the Third World countries and
also for narrowing the gap between them and the longer
established political societies of the industrialized world.

I am glad that we have now a biography of Alhaji Shehu
Usman Aliyu Shagari. I have had the pleasure of meeting
President Shehu Shagari on several important occasions,
including the Summit Conferences of the Organization of
African Unity and the one convened at Cancun in 1981 to
stimulate a more purposeful dialogue between the North and
the South. President Shehu Shagari's forceful address to
the 35th General Assembly of the United Nations and his
contributions to discussions of the great issues of our time
showed his profound personal dedication to the aims of peace
and progress and his keen understanding of the need for a
rational accommodation of diverse interests which alone can
yield enduring agreements. I would recommend a reading of

his biography to all who are interested in Nigeria, in Africa and in the vast endeavour now taking place in the Third World to make up for centuries of neglect and underdevelopment. President Shehu Shagari has, of course, not yet concluded his high political mission, but even an interim presentation like this one tells us more than academic expositions can about the conditions of an important and influential country like Nigeria. The events described in this biography have a significance far beyond that country's borders.

Kurt Waldheim

PREFACE

The man who leads the world's fourth largest democracy is perhaps the least well known, outside his own country, of any statesman of his rank. Even inside his country he was, until his election as President in 1979, largely unknown; he was variously described as of "humble origin" or as a "Fulani feudalist". This book is an attempt to present Nigeria's President as an individual who has had a long and varied public career; not as a representative of a party, of a class, or of an ethnic group.

It is an "interim" presentation, although I hope it does not look like a hasty one. In early 1982 he is still only 56, and has many years of service to his country ahead. Nor do I claim that the book is a complete account of a career which has been far fuller than is generally realised. It does not attempt, either, to be a political, social or economic history of Nigeria in the years since Shehu Shagari first appeared on the national scene in 1954; that history is already well covered by numerous works, to many of which I am indebted. Events are recorded only because of their importance for the subject of the biography; although I hope that I give enough background to explain the significance of these events, not only for him but for Nigeria. Perhaps I should add that I have myself followed that country's fortunes closely since 1949, when I became editor of the weekly *West Africa*.

My thanks are due, above all, to the President himself. For some eighteen months he has given his time to me generously – though never in "official" hours, a restriction about which he has been punctilious. I have interviewed him in his Lagos State House, in his own home in Sokoto, on his farm at Shagari, in the house of his High Commissioner in London in Kensington Palace Gardens. He has talked to me in the Presidential Lodge in Yankari Game Reserve in Bauchi State. There the then Bauchi State Commissioner for Trade, Industry and Tourism, Alhaji Ibrahim Magaji Abubakar, and his officers ensured my comfort.

For much of his earlier life, Alhaji Shehu Shagari himself, or his papers, are virtually the only source for an author who has no research team. He has given me access to his personal papers and has himself patiently filled in many gaps. Two of the men who might have given the most valuable information about him were murdered in 1966 – Sir Abubakar Tafawa Balewa, Nigeria's first Prime Minister, in whose governments Alhaji Shehu served for six years, and Sir Ahmadu Bello, Sardauna of Sokoto, his party leader for many years. This, therefore, has some characteristics of autobiography. Yet, while he has helped me greatly in supplying and check- ing dates, names, places and the like, the President has refrained from comment on my judgments and has not himself suggested that any event should be emphasised or that any- thing should be played down or omitted. This makes him an ideal subject; but it makes this, too, a book for whose sub- stance and for whose deficiencies, of which I am well aware, I alone am responsible.

My thanks are due secondly to Alhaji Shehu Malami, Sarkin Sudan, Wurno. Although a personal friend of the Presi- dent, he plays no direct part in Nigerian politics. Without his generous sponsorship this book would not have been possible. The President insisted that this must be a purely private enterprise, for which the Nigerian taxpayer should have no responsibility. Without Alhaji Shehu Malami's con- stant assistance, including the provision of transport and accommodation in Nigeria, I could not have done my work. In all this he, I know, is concerned only that a great leader should receive some of the recognition which is his due, and which so far has been given him inadequately. I am grateful, too, for assistance from West Africa Publishing Company, of which I am a director.

I have received – as I have for over thirty years – incidental assistance from the Federal and State information services in Nigeria. This was given to me in the ordinary way as a visiting journalist.

I am particularly grateful to Alhaji Dosumu, Head of Press at the Federal Department of Information, who can skilfully find a Presidential speech even while he exchanges pleasantries with you. I am grateful, too, to Chief J. K. Bodunde, for finding photographs in the Information Ministry's archives. I received help in Sokoto from the Governor's Adviser on Information, Alhaji Shehu Aliyu, and from one of his young officers, Yusuf Attahir, who briefly acted as my interpreter. The President's Press Secretary, Charles Igoh, and his ADC, Colonel Usman, have always been ready to assist this importunate visitor, as has been Alhaji Ahmadu Suka, a Presidential Assistant.

Among private individuals I am particularly grateful to the President's elder brother, Muhammadu Magajin Shagari, and his elders who at Shagari patiently answered my questions about their village and its history. Allison Ayida, now an industrial consultant, who was for some years closely associated with Alhaji Shehu Shagari as his Permanent Secretary, was a valued informant about those years. I am grateful, too, for my discussions with Malam Aminu Kano, for decades both personal friend and political adversary of the President; and I owe thanks to very many of Alhaji Shehu Shagari's political associates and opponents. For over thirty years I have learnt much from talking to Nigerian journalists, to many of whom I acknowledge my debt. Nigerian friends, too numerous to mention, have helped me to understand their country and its people.

I am pleased that the book is appearing under the imprint of Frank Cass who has been publishing books about Nigeria for 25 years. Many have become and remain standard works.

Averill McGarvey, editor of *Nigeria Newsletter*, has helped me greatly at all stages of my work. Mrs Gwen Chilton has typed and re-typed drafts and re-drafts with unfailing patience, speed and accuracy.

Finally my wife has allowed our whole house to be turned into a study and research office. She has even tolerated the occasional loss of her dining table, swamped by books, papers and reports. I cannot find words to express gratitude for such forbearance.

INTRODUCTION

After thirteen and a half years of military rule Nigeria returned to civilian government on October 1, 1979. Alhaji Shehu Shagari was on that day sworn in as President by the Chief Justice at an open-air ceremony in front of tens of thousands of his fellow-countrymen in the great Tafawa Balewa Square, in the centre of Lagos. The return to civilian government transformed the political face of West Africa, which the world had long regarded as an area of military or one-party regimes. Now Nigeria, with some eighty million people, or over half the population of the whole region, was adopting a multi-party, American-type, presidential system. A little earlier Ghana, too, had returned to civilian rule under a similar system. The great majority of West Africans were once more living under multi-party democracy.

Civilian rule did not survive in Ghana, where a military regime was again established in December 1981. The attachment of Nigerians to democracy seems to be more determined; and their success in maintaining democratic institutions concerns democrats everywhere. Nigeria is now the fourth biggest democracy in the world; she could, if her democracy thrives, become the second, after India. UN projections give her a population of 153 million by the year 2000; and make her third in population among the nations some time in the next century, after China and India. Nigeria is already the sixth most populous country; and although her income per head remains low because of her vast population, as the world's sixth most important oil exporter, and in recent years the second most important supplier of oil to the United States, she is Black Africa's economic giant.

For Britain Nigeria is the most important market outside Western Europe and North America; and with no country does Britain have a more favourable balance of payments. Indeed to a large degree the colonial relationship is now reversed. Britain buys very little from Nigeria, but depends heavily on the Nigerian market. Rumours during the military regime that Nigeria might withdraw her reserves held in Britain were thought to have weakened sterling. Nigeria's own naira, which was valued at 50 UK pence when it was introduced, is now, although probably overvalued, officially worth £0.75; and the price of UK North Sea oil is geared to that of Nigeria's oil.

The military regime which in 1975 had removed General Gowon, who had been in power for nine years, and his military governors and lieutenants, made meticulous preparation for the return to civilian government. It was not forced, as were the regimes in Ghana, and earlier in Sierra Leone, to hand over to civilians. The new regime laid down a careful timetable, covering over three years, which was rigorously observed. The soldiers, indeed, were providing an answer to Henry Hallam, who wrote of the Cromwellian regime: "it is not in general difficult for an armed force to destroy a government; but something else than the sword is required to create one."

A new constitution was drafted inside a year by a representative civilian committee under the chairmanship of Chief Rotimi Williams, QC. It was then considered by a largely elected Constituent Assembly, of which Alhaji Shehu Shagari was a prominent member, and which first met in 1977. An electoral register was prepared and constituencies were delimited for the Federal House of Representatives, the Federal Senate, and the State Houses of Assembly. Some 47.5 million voters – all citizens over 18 years of age – were registered.

The supremacy of the Northern Region, both in area and population, over the other three together had been generally regarded as one cause of the breakdown of civilian administration in 1966. The Gowon military regime, on the eve of the civil war, divided up the Regions into twelve "states", enjoying the same powers as had the Regions. In 1976 a further seven states were created to meet what the new military regime felt to be legitimate demands for "self-determination". The boundaries of all states were also examined and in some cases re-drawn.

In 1976, too, a new system of local government was introduced, to be a democratic basis for the coming civilian government. In northern states women were able, in most for the first time, both to vote and to stand for election in the polling for these new authorities. A beginning was made in the running down of the numbers of the armed forces, swollen because of the civil war. A site was chosen for a new federal capital – Abuja, right in the middle of the country. This would allow the Federal Government and its agencies, and the National Assembly, to escape the traffic jams and other inconveniences of Lagos. It would also help to establish the Federal Government's character as the country's "central" authority, which would no longer be based on a remote, essentially Yoruba, city in the country's far south-west.

The soldiers made other preparations. The previously chaotic trade union movement was reformed and unified. The customary courts were reorganised, a controversial new arrangement was announced for the use of land; marketing boards for export produce were reconstructed to ensure that the producers, not the politicians, benefitted from them; new marketing boards were set up for domestic food crops.

At all levels, however, the bureaucracy President Shehu Shagari inherited was weak. The public services, notably electricity supply, were strained by the demands of an expanding economy. Inflation was, and has remained, serious. Agriculture was stagnant, and rising prices of local food were the most significant factor in inflation. Violent crime was widespread. The trade unions, after years of restriction by the soldiers, were expected to be anxious to show their strength in the new conditions. The soldiers, in spite of occasional forays, had proved no more able than had the civilian politicians to deal with corruption, even in their own ranks.

So the legacy for the new President was not entirely healthy. Public finances were in reasonably good condition; but both federal and state budgets were showing deficits. By 1979 the soldiers had long overstayed their welcome, which in 1966, when civilian rule was overthrown, had been genuine. During almost six years of civilian rule which followed independence, which came in 1960, a significant degree of democracy was maintained at the centre, where Shehu Shagari was a Minister. This was not matched, however, in the Regions. In all of them the governments, if not virtually one-party, were authoritarian; political thuggery, too, had been widespread. Military rule, however, proved to be far less stable than had civilian rule; it finally plunged the country into civil war.

One of the most encouraging developments ever seen in the world was, however, General Gowon's enlightened stance towards the Biafrans after that war; "no victors, no vanquished". Now, one hopes, nobody in Nigeria sees military rule as an alternative to the present democratic government, or looks to self-appointed saviours to solve any of the multiplicity of problems which the present administration faces, some short-term and man-made, many arising out of the country's nature. President Shehu Shagari, however, felt obliged to warn one of his more vociferous political opponents, soon after his own installation: "in this country now, there are in the end only two parties; the civilians and the soldiers".

The country which Alhaji Shehu Shagari now leads is one of the most complex in the world. Perhaps only India offers a greater variety of peoples. Nigeria has ten major and hundreds of lesser languages. She still uses English as her official language and as the language of higher education, commerce and national politics (the constitution provides for the use of Hausa, Ibo and Yoruba in the National Assembly "when adequate arrangements have been made" and of other Nigerian languages, as well as of English, in State Assemblies). In some northern states, however, Hausa, which is spoken by perhaps twenty-five million Nigerians, and by millions more elsewhere in West Africa and in the Sudan, is also an official language; for over two centuries there has been a written Hausa literature and Shehu Shagari himself is a well-known Hausa poet.

Nigeria's present frontiers are less than a century old. They were created by European colonial powers, and for most of their length divide closely related peoples. Nigeria was a British creation, dating from the day in 1861 when the Royal Navy occupied Lagos in the campaign against the slave trade. The very name Nigeria had not then been invented; but piecemeal British expansion into the interior was to create a country of over 350,000 square miles, as big as France and Italy together. The furthest point on the northern frontier is 1,000 miles from Lagos; the eastern frontier is 600 miles away.

These frontiers enclose many venerable kingdoms, such as the Emirates of the north, coastal Opobo, and Benin and Ife, whose ancient art has earned the world's admiration for decades. Although Nigeria's national political institutions are all new, there is abundant and growing evidence of the existence in the past of many high cultures, some flourishing a thousand or more years ago, in the area of modern Nigeria. There is evidence, too, of much closer relations in past centuries, particularly through trade, between the communities which were to form Nigeria than was once supposed. There was warfare between them, too; but even that implies communication.

Some so-called "tribes" – an inappropriate word for ethnic or linguistic groups often numbering many millions – are numerous enough to be called "nations". Yet other quite distinct groups, with their own languages, may number only thousands. The Yoruba of the western and northern states, according to the last census, held in 1963*, then numbered some eleven and a half million, the Ibo of the eastern states and Bendel numbered some nine million, and the Fulani, Alhaji Shehu Shagari's people, almost five millions. The Kanuri of

---

*The 1973 census was repudiated by the military regime as being unreliable. Until a new census is held, the 1963 figures, which themselves were hotly disputed, are used officially, with the addition of an annual increase of 2.5 per cent.

the north-east numbered about two and a half million, the Ibibio of the south-east some two million, and the Ijaw of the south-east over one million. Perhaps half a dozen other groups now exceed a million in number, and over a score exceed 100,000.

Some traditional chiefs, who are still an expression of group identity, represent communities of millions; some only collections of villages. Today no Nigerian can forget that he belongs to one or other of his country's ethnic groups. The social and political consequences of these divisions is often exaggerated. Yet they do affect the country's life at many points; for example, it is assumed that anybody in a position to hire workers tends to hire people from his own group, if he can. It is for this reason that the constitution constantly emphasises the need, in the making of official appointments, etc., to "have regard to the federal character of Nigeria and the need to promote national unity". The constitution even places on the state a duty to "encourage intermarriage among persons from different places of origin, or of different religions, ethnic or linguistic associations and ties" – although it is not explained how this duty can be discharged. The President, too, who is directly elected by the whole electorate acting as "one constituency", is, unlike the ceremonial President of the years before 1966, the nation's "chief executive", and expected to be the focus of national unity for all Nigerians, regardless of party.

Nigeria is a secular state whose constitution forbids the adoption of any religion as a state religion. But Nigerians are a religious people. According to the 1963 census there were then twenty-six million Muslims, twenty million Christians and ten million people of other religions, nearly all those indigenous to Nigeria. The great majority of people in the most northerly states are Muslims, as is the President himself. There are few Muslims among the Ibo or in the south-east states. But Islam is strong among the Yoruba of the western states, and in Lagos itself, where mosques may outnumber the Christian places of worship, including the Anglican and Catholic cathedrals. Most denominations are represented among the Christians and there are a number of indigenous Christian churches.

Only Chad and the Lebanon among the nations of the world show such an even balance between the adherents of Islam and Christianity. But while both these countries have suffered from dissension between Muslims and Christians, in Nigeria followers of the two faiths are remarkably tolerant of each other. Shehu Shagari's Vice-President, for example, is a devout Christian, and it was on the President's invitation that the Pope visited Nigeria in 1982. Indeed, it is the growth of discord among different persuasions inside Islam that now gives concern, rather than relations between the supporters of the two great faiths.

Yet Nigeria would be much poorer without her diversity. It is shown, for example, in the colour and splendour of traditional dress, in music and dancing, and in indigenous architecture. This diversity can be one of the country's greatest assets. If perverted by politicians it can be destructive.

The land itself does not show the same variety as the people. Yet although Nigeria lies entirely in the tropics, there are significant variations in terrain and climate. The most northerly areas, with average rainfall of as little as 50 centimetres a year, are in general flat and very dry. Nigeria lies between latitudes 4° and 14° north and in recent years the area above 13° north has suffered from the droughts which have affected the whole of what is called the Sahel area of West Africa. In much of the south, however, rainfall is heavy, averaging some 180 centimetres a year in the west and as much as 430 centimetres in some eastern areas. In contrast to the savannah of the northern states or the rocky hills of the northern plateau, there is much high forest in the south, and there are mangrove swamps along the coast.

Nigeria is by far the most populous country in Africa, but she is only tenth in area. So the average density of population, some 60 per square kilometre, is high by the standards of Africa although low compared with the UK's 230. Nigeria still has abundant undeveloped land. Yet two states, Anambra and Imo, in the south east, are probably the most densely populated parts of Africa outside the Nile Valley and Rwanda. In other areas there is population pressure on the land. In Kwara and Niger states, however, in the middle of the country, population is particularly sparse. This creates problems for the state governments, since it makes provision of services so expensive. Yet states with a land surplus do not welcome farmer immigrants even from highly populated states. Everywhere, however, there is a drift from the land in a search, usually unsuccessful, for urban jobs. So agriculture is starved of the labour of young men. The proportion of children of school age in the population grows, placing an increasing burden on those of working age.

Standards of living also vary widely, both between individuals and social classes, and between areas, regions and communities. But while disparities among the latter, which are the disparities which still matter in Nigeria politically and socially, are slowly diminishing as development proceeds, disparities in income between individuals and social classes are probably growing. The establishment by the National Assembly of a legal minimum wage of ₦125 a month gives many Nigerians an income which workers in other countries of the Third World might envy; it does not help millions of small farmers, herdsmen and fishermen – which the majority of Nigerians still are – or employees of the thousands of very small private establishments which are a feature of the Nigerian economy. Indeed the new minimum, because it raises market prices, particularly of food, and requires heavier taxation to allow governments to meet it, and higher charges to allow statutory corporations to pay it, may actually affect adversely those who do not receive it.

Nigeria has a mixed economy and Nigerians in all parts of the country, and of both sexes, readily and successfully engage in trade – often as a sideline to a salaried job. The growing class of rich, sometimes very rich, businessmen and businesswomen are not drawn from any particular part of the country or any particular group. The great majority of them are "self-made" and they often come from poor families. The Nigerian owner of a large flat in London's Mayfair may be the son of a small farmer.

Many professional people, particularly lawyers, are also rich. Senior civil servants and officials of the legion of state enterprises are now as well paid as some of their counterparts in Western Europe; but their salaries do not compare with those offered by private industry – which is the fastest growing section of the economy – banks, or private professional practices.

The most important development for equalising living standards between different parts of the country has been the introduction, beginning in 1976, of Universal Primary Education (UPE). This was one of the biggest social revolutions ever attempted in a poor country. For Nigeria the most significant social division has long been that between the educated – in the Western sense – and the uneducated (millions are literate in simple Arabic). For the Western-educated, whatever their family background, there have been luxurious prizes. For peasant farmers or herdsmen, the unskilled labourers, or the urban unemployed, life has been much harder.

Until UPE some northern states, such as President Shehu Shagari's own state of Sokoto, had a school enrollment of under 10 per cent. The enrollment now is not complete, the standard of teaching in primary schools has fallen, and there is little hope of work or salaried employment for the millions who will end their education at the primary schools. But there is no longer a great divide educationally between north and south, although it will be years before the equalisation in primary education works through into secondary, technical and university education. Nigeria now also has almost twenty universities (and the number is growing), and many other institutions of higher education. Thousands of Nigerian students still go abroad, often on scholarships from home or host governments; there remains, however, a serious shortage of trained people.

Oil revenues, some 80 per cent of total government revenues, have enabled the Federal Government to affect the daily lives of people everywhere in Nigeria – and not only through UPE, the cost of which has been met by that government. In contrast, in the first years of independence the government in Lagos seemed infinitely remote to millions of Nigerians, for whom "the government" was the regional government, or even the chiefdoms. And whatever the deficiencies of military rule, it established clearly the pre-eminence of federal power. President Shehu Shagari is the first Nigerian to be voted directly into office by the whole nation. Today Nigerians everywhere, whether they voted for him or not, recognise him as the nation's leader.

1

A PLACE CALLED SHAGARI

Alhaji Shehu Usman Aliyu Shagari takes his name from the old village of Shagari, which lies in the broad arid savannah of north-western Nigeria, forty kilometres south of the city of Sokoto. Once Shagari was a convenient night-stop for trading caravans of many tribes, with their camels, horses and donkeys, travelling to and from Sokoto, capital of the Caliphate which for almost a century before the British occupation in 1903 dominated most of what was to become Northern Nigeria. Now, bypassed by the great concrete and tarmac motorway leading to the south and Lagos, it is a backwater in Sokoto State and in the Sultan of Sokoto's emirate.

The modest two-storey house Shehu Shagari built here for himself twenty years ago was already, apart from the mosque, the village's main building. Now it has been expanded, though still modestly, to become a presidential rural retreat, with its own small mosque with a copper-coloured dome.

The future President was born in the house of his father, then Shagari's Village Head, in the middle of the village. It was built of sun-baked clay, reinforced by scantlings from fan-palms, which are uniquely resistant to white ants, was decorated with traditional motifs, and had a thatched roof. His elder brother, Alhaji Muhammadu Bello, Magajin Shagari, now himself Village Head, still lives in this traditional edifice.

Shagari has some 3,000 people and the area over which the Village Head holds jurisdiction has some 8,000 farmers and cattle-herders. From these surroundings come people austere and dignified; qualities which even his critics concede to the

1

President, a devout Muslim, always dressed in traditional robes.

He was the fifth child and third son of Magaji Aliyu and Mairamu, daughter of Sarkin Kebbi Riskuwa, District Head of Yabo, which lies some ten kilometres north of Shagari. Other brothers and sisters followed, and all have homes in the village. He puts his birthday at February 25, 1925, a different date from that given in reference books, but carefully calculated according to information from his mother and the guidance of Malam Bello of the Islamic Research Bureau, Benin.

Shagari, we have said, is now a backwater. But it once played a significant part in one of the most important episodes in the history of West Africa.

In the last decades of the eighteenth and first years of the nineteenth century the Hausa states, most of which were later to form part of Nigeria's Northern Region, were the scene of a remarkable religious and social reform movement. This was intent on the purification of Islam, which had come to these states – if only, often superficially, to their rulers – some three centuries earlier. The movement culminated in 1804 in the Jihad or Holy War. This removed most of the Hausa rulers of the states, the Emirs, who were replaced with "flagbearers" of the movement's leader, the pious and learned Shehu Uthman dan Fodio, the "Shaikh". It also led to the establishment of the Sokoto* Caliphate, which, in its religious aspect, under its Sultans, survives to this day.

The Hausa kingdoms were separate, independent, states, whose peoples, though sharing a common language and

---

*The Jihad is sometimes called "the Sokoto Jihad" and the system which the Shaikh established, the "Sokoto Empire". But the building of Sokoto City did not begin until 1809, when the Jihad was almost completed; and Wurno, not Sokoto, was the residence of the Sultans and their courts for most of the nineteenth century. In 1903, as the biggest town of the area, and then residence of the Sultan, Sokoto was made by the British the headquarters of a Province named after it; and in 1976 it became the capital of the new Sokoto State of Nigeria. The Sultan of Sokoto is, in Hausa, Sarkin Musulmi, "Commander of the Faithful"; and his spiritual leadership is still recognised by Muslims far beyond Nigeria's borders.

aspects of culture, and having ancient trade links, had distinctive national histories and tribal names. In spite of intermittent warfare among them no state established hegemony over all the others. Hausa was then, and should still be, used as a linguistic rather than an ethnic term, although of the many diverse cultures which have been brought together to shape modern Nigeria, the Hausa culture is among the most important. Even the Caliphate did not unite all the Hausa states politically; a few remained outside it, and the system was administratively loose and often challenged.

For thirty years before the Jihad, the Shaikh had been preaching reform. His home at Degel, in the north of what was to become Sokoto State, was a centre for scholarship and spiritual guidance. He did not, however, seek conflict with the Hausa temporal rulers; the Jihad in fact started as a defensive movement against the harassment of the Shaikh and his followers by those rulers.

The Shaikh was a Fulani. This people then, as now, lived throughout the savannah areas of West Africa, from Senegal to the north of the Cameroon Republic. They are called variously Fulani, Peul, Fulbe, Fourah, etc. Their origin is uncertain, although, whether or not it lay in Egypt or the Arab lands as has been suggested, they were established in the Futa Toro of Senegal well over a millenium ago. By the middle of the eighteenth century large numbers had migrated to and settled in the Hausa states. Many were largely integrated politically with the Hausa-speaking peoples, although maintaining a separate identity because of their longer adherence to Islam and their superior education. Others remained, as they still do, nomadic cattle owners and herders, sometimes in conflict with the long-settled Hausa farmers over grazing and water.

The Shaikh's principal lieutenants, who included members of his family, were also Fulani, as were most of his "flag-bearers", whom he sent to replace so many Hausa rulers. So it has often been asserted that the Jihad was a revolt, religiously inspired, of Fulani against their oppressive Hausa overlords, resulting in a system which in time made the Fulani them-

3

selves oppressive overlords of the Hausa peasantry.

Scholars now, however, emphasise that during the Jihad combatants from all ethnic groups in the area could be found on both sides. There was little "ethnic" about the movement which the scholarly Shaikh inspired. Nor was the Jihad simply a war between Muslims and non-Muslims; it represented a revolutionary movement *inside* a traditional society which was Islamic in character. And in the sometimes fierce resistance against British occupation of Hausaland at the beginning of this century, people of all races joined.

Now Nigerian scholars prefer to emphasise the social and religious ideas behind the Jihad; the conception of an ideal society, even if it was never achieved, and the belief that science requires knowledge of God's law.

The nature of the Jihad is significant for Nigeria's modern history. Sir Frederick Lugard, who was Britain's first High Commissioner in Northern Nigeria, and later first Governor-General of Nigeria, frequently used the theory that the Fulani liberators had turned into oppressors of the Hausa peasantry to justify Britain's own occupation of the northern Nigerian emirates in 1901-3. But even if the rule of the Fulani Emirs had by then degenerated, the main reasons for the British occupation sprang from trade and great-power rivalry.

Lugard also used the view that the Fulani had originally, after the Jihad, shown themselves to be unusually able administrators, to justify his support, after the British occupation, for continuation of the highly developed Emirate system. This the Fulani had maintained, although they had not created it. Lugard used it as the basis, suitably reformed and controlled, of "indirect rule" in Northern Nigeria, the system under which a handful of British administrative officers exercised authority through traditional rulers and institutions. Some Nigerian politicians, too, have attacked what they called "Fulani imperialist domination", particularly in the days between 1951 and 1966 when the Northern Peoples Congress, based in the Emirates and enjoying the patronage of most traditional rulers in the then Northern Region, particularly in Sokoto itself, dominated Nigerian politics.

4

Alhaji Shehu visits his Fulani relations at an encampment near Shagari in January 1973. *Photos by courtesy of Mr Jim Boyd.*

At Shagari in 1972. *Photo by courtesy of Mr Jim Boyd.*

Today, although the earlier Hausa-Fulani division is not forgotten, and nobody denies that there were Hausa revolts against the new Fulani rulers at the beginning of the last century, this division is not significant politically.

The cattle-Fulani continue their nomadic existence and retain their language, and many their own religion. Their attachment to the nomadic life and their need of children to herd their stock creates obvious problems, for example for those administering Universal Primary Education, which was introduced throughout Nigeria in 1976. But the nomad and the semi-nomad Fulani, who number perhaps ten million in Nigeria and throughout West Africa, represent the world's biggest nomadic community. And as main custodians of Nigeria's livestock population, perhaps over ten million cattle, twenty million goats, and millions of sheep, they play a significant part in the agricultural economy.

The settled Fulani, however – although a high proportion of traditional rulers, Emirate notables and politicians in the Hausa-speaking states, as well as President Shehu Shagari himself, can today claim Fulani descent – have, with the exception of those of Adamawa, lost their language. They have adopted Hausa, now the language in widest use in West Africa. Their dress is Hausa, as are their Emirate titles, and intermarriage and the former institution of concubinage have eroded Fulani identity.

Whatever the origin of the Fulani people, those Fulani who finally settled in the area which was to become Sokoto and the southern areas of the modern Niger Republic, and from whom Alhaji Shehu Shagari himself is descended – the Toronkawa, or people of the Toronke clan – were among those who came from Senegal. From there they migrated slowly across the Sahel as far as what was to become North Cameroon. In Futa Toro an Arab missionary called Ukba ben Yasir had been married to a Taurudo wife called Bajamangu and by her had four sons, who had developed the Fulfulde language, neither Arabic nor Toro. Some Fulani became Islamic teachers and missionaries, some herdsmen.

The Toronkawa were the descendants of Musa Jokollo, a

5

grandson of Ukba ben Yasir. Famous as Islamic scholars throughout West Africa they moved eastwards to what is now Sokoto State. Today the name is applied only to descendants of the Shaikh, who, born in 1754 at Marata, which is now in the Niger Republic, was eleventh descendant of Musa Jokollo who led the migration eastwards from Senegal.

Among leaders of Fulani clans in the Sokoto area was Namoda, whose headquarters, Kaura Namoda in the now extinct kingdom of Zamfara, was some hundred miles north-east of what was to become Sokoto, and who gave the Shaikh notable support in the Jihad. In Namoda a member of the ruling family, Muhammadu, head of the long-settled village of Kungurki, found himself passed over for the succession. He decided, around the year 1810, to leave the area and to seek service with the Shaikh, now "Commander of the Faithful" and Caliph.

Muhammadu was rich by the standards of the time; when he set out on the 120 mile journey to join the Shaikh he took with him many people – his wives and children, his servants and herdsmen, and his "berebere" slaves from Borno. He had, too, many cattle, and flocks of goats and sheep as well as horses.

At that time the Shaikh resided at Sifawa, some twenty miles south of the site of Sokoto, where his son, Sultan Bello, was to build a capital for the eastern part of the newly founded Caliphate, responsibility for administering which had been given to him by Uthman dan Fodio. The site was so exposed and bleak that the pious Shaikh hoped that it would deter all but dedicated followers from settling there, so that it would become a place of learning and devotion, not of commerce.

Muhammadu of Kungurki learnt, however, that the Shaikh, who still constantly taught and preached, was then, during a return journey from a visit to Gwandu, at a village called Sala, some 28 miles to the south of Sifawa. There Muhammadu took his caravan and met the Shaikh; and from there the two set out for Sifawa.

On the way the party stopped to pray under a huge baobob tree in an area with many such trees. When the prayers were completed the Shaikh turned to his new disciple and suggested to him that, because his people and animals were so numerous, it might be wiser for him to travel no more. Here was an ideal site for a settlement. There appeared to be grazing and water; there was certainly firewood. And although dye-pits suggested that people had once lived in the area, there was now no sign of habitation. Led by the Shaikh's scholar brother Abdullahi, whose own residence was at Bodinga, near Sifawa, the men of the party eagerly cleared a site for the settlement and Abdullahi himself suggested a plan for it.

Before he continued on his own journey to Sifawa, now only some ten miles to the north, the Shaikh told Muhammadu; "here you can sit and drink for ever your 'gari' ". In other words – and to this day the people of the small town believe it to be true – there would never be famine in the village which was to be named Shagari, after the nickname by which Muhammadu came to be known. ("Gari" in Hausa means guinea corn "flour", which Hausa people mixed with water. The Fulani adopted this staple food, but mixed it with milk.)

Unhappily within a month Shagari was dead. His people took his body for burial to the Shaikh's town, Sifawa, which he had never seen. The Shaikh led prayers for him, and he was buried between two ancient trees on the edge of the town, in a simple grave kept in perfect order to this day, with a small place for prayer adjoining.

Leading the mourners from Shagari was Muhammadu's son, Muhammadu Iggi, whom the Shaikh had already "turbanned" so that he could take his father's place as "successor", or Magaji, in the village (the modern term Village Head was not then in use). He led the people back to Shagari. His brother Usuman, who followed him as leader, was father of President Shehu Shagari's grandfather.

The settlement was soon moved about a mile to the south, the present site of Shagari, and was rebuilt more durably to accommodate some of the Shaikh's lieutenants and scholars. The Shaikh himself died in 1817 and is buried in Sokoto, where his tomb is visited by pilgrims from as far away as Senegal. Near the tree under which the Shaikh and Shagari first prayed, and which still stands, was built a small mosque which today serves the people of Gurawa hamlet, one of those which come under the Shagari Village Head.

A Village Head in the Emirates, in spite of the democratisation and politicisation of local government in the northern states, as in the rest of Nigeria (Shehu Shagari himself, before standing down to participate in the presidential election, was an elected councillor for the Shagari area) still has important functions and considerable local standing. In the past his great job was local tax collection, a job now obsolete because of the abolition of "community" and cattle taxes. He was also responsible for law and order, and had his own court. This is now restricted to matrimonial cases, but he is still looked to for informal adjudication in personal disputes, and for dealing with disturbances. He is Registrar of Births and Deaths (he knows everybody and everything) and collects some tolls.

A man who is himself a District Head, Alhaji Shehu Malami, Sarkin Sudan of Wurno, in Sokoto, described the still continuing role of ward, Village and District Heads in the Nigerian emirates in a lecture to the Army Command and Staff College at Jaji in August, 1978. Village and ward heads, Alhaji Shehu explained,

> are the encyclopaedia of the administration. They know every single individual in their locality and have detailed knowledge of their movements. They know the location of all the farms and grazing grounds and to whom they belong; and have even detailed knowledge of how many wives a particular man has, how many children, and their various ages. The ward head even knows how many head of cattle or how many donkeys a particular person possesses. You may be surprised to know this. I never believed it myself until I became District Head in 1974.
>
> With this detailed knowledge of the area, security of the place is guaranteed. Indeed one of the cardinal duties of the ward head is to report movements of strangers with a view to preventing the villagers from harbouring thieves and other criminals. They must report immediately the occur-

rence of violent deaths and any outbreak of human or animal diseases ... as well as any unusual movements of livestock, game, and news of the appearance of locusts. They are even expected regularly to report the sighting of the new moon!! In addition to all these duties, with other ward heads supervised by the Village Head, they must play an active role in organising and implementing village social and economic activities such as adult education, community developments, etc., etc., etc.

The District Head, the Village Head's superior, is

both the Emir's on-the-spot agent and official head of his district. He performs not only the task of co-ordination but he also ensures that all the activities of the Government are carried out according to policies laid down ...

His regular touring reports covering all aspects of life in the district, from the condition of crops on the farms to self-help efforts, from availability or scarcity of water or food to the conditions of various roads are sent to the Emir, with copies to the Local Government and the State Government officials concerned.

This, said the Sarkin Sudan, was "the system that the British had found working in this country, a system that has now served us for nearly two hundred years."

The Village Head, in short, is rather like an Elizabethan Justice of the Peace. But he depends for the greater part of his living, like most of his people, on farming, as does the President's elder brother.

It was in 1930 that Alhaji Muhammadu, who is fourteen years older than the President, succeeded to the office now known as "Village Head" of Shagari at the age of nineteen, in place of his and the President's father. He completed fifty years in office in 1980. No manuscript sources for Shagari history have yet come to light; but the Magaji, a very traditional figure, tall and slim, always in traditional white robes with a turban, can confidently list his predecessors, of whom there have been a dozen. There is no rule of primogeniture about such appointments, but the Shagari Village Heads have

9

always, with short intervals, been descendants of the village's founder.

One break occurred during the reign of Sultan Abubakr (1873-7). Sule, grandson of Muhammadu Iggi, took over the Shagari leadership, which was still directly under Sokoto and whose holder needed the Sultan's confirmation. But so little was Sule respected that few men of the village, long famous as builders of walls, obeyed the summons of his drums to go to Sokoto to work on the fortifications there. The Sultan, thus made aware of Sule's ineffectiveness, finally sent two young nephews to act as Village Head, with the President's grand-father, Ahmadu Rufa'i, as "regent". The grandfather, Ahmadu, in due course succeeded.

Shagari was spared the sporadic warfare which for most of the nineteenth century affected much of the Caliphate; its life was uneventful. The original settlement expanded, more land was cleared for farming. Hausa people came to live in the village; the descendants of Shagari's Berebere slaves were integrated into the community. Shagari people went to trade as far away as Kano.

For many years Shagari men have also gone to the Gold Coast, later Ghana, to work, most as butchers, in which trade Hausa people have long held something of a monopoly there. They suffered with other Nigerians when Dr Kofi Busia, then Prime Minister, expelled the "aliens" from Ghana in 1969; and there are today men in Shagari who had spent fifty years in Ghana before being so harshly deported. A few Shagari men still go to Ghana, but permanent and temporary migration from the village now tends to be inside Nigeria.

Somehow Shagari people always return home. The town is still, too, in spite of the great new highway bypassing it, a place where migrant workers spend the night. There has never been a shortage of land at Shagari; but the soil was, and is, tired. Water was and remains the greatest problem – it rains in only three months each year and even then only about 25 inches fall.

Distinctions between the groups who made up the population became unimportant. But the nomadic Fulani, who were, and are, the cattle owners, constantly in search of grazing, have always been regular visitors. They had, as already noted, adhered strictly to their customs, religion and language. Their nomadic ways have damaged grazing in Nigeria's northern states because of the ceaseless movement of their stock; but conflict between them and the settled farmers, although always latent, and sometimes in some parts of Nigeria producing bloodshed, has troubled Shagari little.

Today, on the President's own farm, which consists of four hundred acres of ancestral land, there is a pool formed behind a dam, where the stock of villagers and nomads alike can drink. Like other "settled" farmers, Alhaji Shehu arranges with nomadic Fulani to tend his own cattle, some fifty in number. But in his case the Fulani concerned are actually related to him; his mother's mother came from a nomadic Fulani family who have their base, which he sometimes visits, near Shagari. The cattle are often herded over long distances and the President recalls an occasion when, as Federal Commissioner of Finance after 1971, in Borgu, some 150 miles south of Shagari, he saw some cattle under the care of Fulani. He commented on their good condition and was told there was nothing to be surprised at in this; they were his own.

Shehu Shagari keeps sheep, but has banned from his farm the red goats whose skins, sent across the desert from Sokoto, became famous as Morocco leather; for they destroy vegetation and erode the soil. The farm's crops are those of the village – food crops, particularly guinea corn and millet. The President criticises himself as an insufficiently dedicated farmer. He still treasures, however, the small farmhouse he has built on the farm, away from his Shagari residence. And away even from the farm paths is a small circular resthouse where he can meditate in solitude.

The village once contributed to what was Nigeria's major foreign currency earner, groundnuts, and has also grown cotton. To buy both crops traders established posts in Shagari; but the farmers, in common with tens of thousands throughout Nigeria's northern states, have gone over to food-growing, their surplus from which can find a market in Sokoto city itself. Some rice is grown, but it has suffered from competition with the more profitable tobacco. Sugar cane is grown, but to chew rather than for processing. Chickens provide some meat and their eggs are prized.

Only the smallest of wild animals have survived in the area. There is little for hunters to hunt and the once universal bows and arrows are now virtually museum pieces. Although the President and the Magaji have been accomplished horsemen since their boyhood, there are now few horses in Shagari. Camels still appear, carrying trade loads or sacks of grain. Donkeys are still used for local transport of thatch, firewood, etc.; but otherwise the car and lorry have taken over.

There was, however, one occasion in the last century when Shagari's peace was shattered. About 1890, just before the time when the President's grandfather, Ahmadu Rufa'i, became Village Head, Shagari was attacked for the first time in its history. The town was then fortified. The remains of the walls have now sunk into the red earth from which they were made, but they could still be seen when the President was a boy. The raid was made at night on livestock outside the walls. The stock were watched by children, among whom were Alhaji Shehu's father and his father's youngest sister. The raiders came from the neighbouring Emirate of Argungu, then under the great Sama, who carried on the tradition of previous Kebbawa rulers of that Emirate, which had successfully resisted Sokoto and the Caliphate. Sama was reputed to have burned down ninety walled towns under Fulani rule.

The raiders took the children with the stock, and demanded ransom for them. The boy was soon ransomed, but the girl was sold into slavery in Timbuktu. The President's father, Aliyu, who was later to succeed his own father as Village Head, became a trader in horses, which were sold in Bida in the south. As soon as he had saved enough money from this trade he went on foot to Timbuktu to ransom his sister. He found her now married to a Tuareg, and induced her, with her children, to visit Shagari. She returned to Timbuktu, and later married a man of Hausa origin, and finally died in Timbuktu. Many years later, when the President was Federal Commissioner of Finance in the early 1970s, one of her daughters got in touch with him and he arranged for her to visit Shagari. This daughter was then living in Ghana, and had a Ghanaian husband.

It was, no doubt, popular recollection of this Argungu raid which was responsible for an otherwise inexplicable episode in the 1979 general election. Alhaji Shehu Shagari's candidature for the Presidency naturally raised great excitement in the village, where the people were interested in only one party, the President's own, the new National Party of Nigeria (NPN). Early on in 1979, however, in Sokoto State the political running had been made by the Great Nigerian People's Party, the GNPP, of Alhaji Waziri Ibrahim. After the NPN's formation it was announced that the GNPP would be sending to Shagari an election team, led by a speaker who hailed from Argungu. The people warned the Village Head, the future President's brother, that an attempt by any Argungu man, of any party, to speak in Shagari might lead to violence. On Alhaji Shehu Shagari's advice the Village Head, much concerned at the bad publicity for his younger brother's cause if violence was shown to the representative of one of his opponents, told the people that they had to allow the Argungu man to move freely; but when he came they should shut themselves in their houses, and even shut up all their livestock so that nothing moved on the streets.

The police, whose nearest post is seven miles away, seldom appear in Shagari; but a criminal stranger, as we have seen, has no chance of taking up residence or even staying there. Everybody knows everybody, everybody is his brother's keeper, and traditional and religious sanctions still have force. This time, however, the police were warned that there might be trouble. The women brought enough water to the houses to resist a siege, and attempts were made to close the roads into the town. The Argungu man came; and found himself speaking to and abusing the empty air, listened to only by bored policemen.

In March, 1903, when Alhaji Shehu's grandfather was still Village Head, news came to Shagari that a British-led force

13

of some 1,000 men was on its way to the village from the great city of Kano, to the east, which a month before had capitulated to the British without a fight, to besiege Sokoto. This force was to join one from Argungu at Shagari itself, in preparation for the attack. The Village Head swore that he would never set eyes on these invaders; and at noon that day rode away from the village to join in the defence of Sokoto by Attahiru, the Sultan, and to tell him what he knew of the invaders. He was never heard of again. He may have been killed in the fierce but short resistance to the British outside Sokoto city on March 15 (the date chosen, in 1959, for self-government for Nigeria's Northern Region); or he may have joined the scholars and gentry who accompanied the Sultan in his slow flight to the East, and have been killed with him at the battle with the British at Burmi. He may even have found his way to the Sudan.

On the same day, March 15, was born in Sokoto Abubakar, son of Shehu and grandson of Mu'azu, eighth Sultan. Abubakar was removed, still on that same day, to a place of safety, carried in a calabash. Thirty five years later he was himself to become Sultan; and his was one of the influences which were to shape Shehu Shagari's life. His own life spanned the whole period of British rule in Northern Nigeria, and during the celebrations of Nigeria's independence in 1960 he was to entertain in his Sokoto palace, as the Queen's representative, Princess Alexandra.

In the reorganisation which followed the British conquest Shagari was made formally subordinate to Yabo, which, as noted earlier, lies some ten kilometres to the north, and is seat of Sarkin Kebbi, the District Head. Yabo was to have a major part in Alhaji Shehu Shagari's life. Not only was his mother, Mairamu, a daughter of the District Head there; it was to Yabo school that the future President was sent, since it was the nearest to Shagari. This was in 1931, at a time when not one in a hundred Sokoto children had any hope of modern education. His elder brother had been the first boy to go to school from Shagari, attending that same small Yabo school just after it had opened in 1927.

The Shaikh himself conferred the title of Sarkin Kanta on the then Sarkin Kebbi, Mohammadu Moijo, in 1804, the year in which the great leader took refuge in nearby Magaboshi, in Sarkin Kebbi's domain. Moijo proved himself to be one of the leading Fulani generals in the Jihad. So on both sides of his family the President has connections with the Shaikh. He belongs to the second rank of Sokoto families, those who in an earlier Britain would have been called the "country gentry".

After the British reorganisation the Sarkin Kebbi at first sent his own son to take over as Village Head at Shagari. When this son died the appointment returned to the Shagari family, first to the President's father's elder brother, Basharu, then to his father, Aliyu, himself.

The British administration was now fully established. It seems to have had little effect on Shagari. The administration ensured law and order and embarked on minor public works; but to Shagari people for many years the British appeared simply as strange people – District Officers, Public Works Department men, veterinary officers, an occasional doctor, agricultural officers. They would spend a night in the village's "bush resthouse" and demand the services – unpaid – of large numbers of porters to carry their inexplicably numerous "loads" – camp and cooking equipment, lamps, food and drink, clothing, books and the rest.

Communal effort has produced dispensary buildings in Shagari and the local authority now provides a dispenser and drugs. There is, however, no local electricity or telephone and the main local service is a water borehole. Tractors have appeared briefly on the farms and Shagari now has its own elementary school, with some 200 pupils.

For the people, however, the government has remained the Village Head and the District Head; while over them has towered the majestic figure of the Sultan of Sokoto, direct descendant of the Shaikh, and "Sarkin Musulmi".

2

PUPIL AND TEACHER

If their administration had little effect on the villages of Northern Nigeria, the British introduced to them, however hesitantly and slowly, a revolutionary agent – western education. Koranic schools are found throughout the Muslim areas of Northern Nigeria – Lugard estimated that there were at least 25,000 in 1914. Pupils in these, usually in the open air, are taught to recite, and sometimes to write, passages from the Koran by a "Mallam", who might himself have only a smattering of Arabic, and who teaches his pupils to use an Arabic script, but little Arabic. Shehu Shagari himself was attending such a school in his village at the age of four, using a wooden slate, a reed pen, and "home-made" ink. Real literacy in Arabic, and in Hausa, a language with a literary tradition centuries old, was confined to a small class of learned men.

Elsewhere in West Africa the British left the development of education in their colonies in the first decades of this century to Christian missions. But the administration in what came to be called the "Northern Provinces" of Nigeria was anxious to exclude Christian missionary activities from the Muslim areas, in which, Lugard had promised at the time of the British occupation, there would be no interference with the dominant religion; so the administration itself finally accepted responsibility for introducing western education into these areas. It was not until 1909, however, that a start was made, and even in 1931 there were only some 4,000 pupils in government schools.

By 1914 there was an elementary school at Sokoto. In 1927 a school was opened at Yabo, the town of Shehu Shagari's mother's brother, some ten kilometres from Shagari. It was a small clay building with a thatched roof, and it lacked even a football field. This obscure edifice was to be highly important in the life of the future President, and so in Nigeria's history.

Orthodox Muslim parents were then hostile to the new schools, which some feared – as a few still do – would expose boys to European, Christian and even atheistic influences. Parents were also reluctant to send their sons long distances away from home. The British administration, however, while sympathetic to such fears and anxious to avoid creation of a race of "clerks", wanted to train a small class of northern Nigerians to staff both the colonial and traditional administrations, and the new schools, and to be able to deal with traders and others from the south on equal terms.

Girls' education was not yet on the agenda, although several of the Shaikh's female relatives had been scholars. As late as 1930 the learned Madaki of Kano declared that if there was to be female education no girl should stay at school after she became twelve, the then age of marriage.

At a time when in the south of Nigeria there was keen competition for school places, which were multiplying at a far greater rate than in the north, traditional rulers and emirate officials in the most northerly parts of the Northern Provinces were in effect obliged by the British to send children to school. The first boy to go from Shagari was the President's elder brother. His father, then Village Head, may have been reconciled to the idea of sending the young Muhammadu to the Yabo school, the nearest, as we have said, to Shagari, in the late 1920s because he could lodge with the District Head there, the boy's uncle. But when the boy was chosen, with two others, to go on to the more developed Sokoto school, his father was unenthusiastic.

The only boy who actually went on from Yabo to Sokoto was the son of a man at odds with the District Head, who in this way was imposing a kind of "punishment". So Muhammadu returned to Shagari to become a "scribe" to his father – he was now literate in Hausa, though not in English. His father died a year later, in 1930, and Muhammadu, young as he was, became Village Head.

Soon the new Village Head, like the other twenty four Village Heads in the Yabo district, received orders from Yabo to send another Shagari boy to the school there. Shehu was now six years old; but the Village Head had not been persuaded by his own experience that schooling was desirable, and only reluctantly decided that his young brother was the obvious candidate.

The Village Head in 1934, however, was again ordered to find a pupil for Yabo; again he could find no candidate but Shehu, who was sent back to Yabo with a scribe. This time the District Head was away, so the scribe took his small charge straight to the school. There they found the junior of the two young Hausa teachers (there was also an Arabic teacher, Mallam Sabo, who was still teaching at the school when its most distinguished pupil became President) conducting numeracy tests and caning the failures who could not count up to ten. Shehu, however, could not help passing this test and was then made to slap his neighbours who failed, among an intake of some forty boys.

The President's mother was not worried because, as in his elder brother's case, young Shehu, if sent to school, would be able to live with her brother, the District Head in Yabo. A frightened and miserable Shehu was finally sent to Yabo – but with firm orders from his brother that he was to fail the numeracy test that the District Head would give him before he could be enrolled in the school. He dutifully failed the test and at once returned to Shagari, amidst family jubilation.

Discipline was harsh in those days; but today the Shagari Village Head recalls that the young Shehu never ran away from school – a common habit – never complained to him about his treatment by the teachers, and never fought other boys. The future President seems, indeed, already to have shown that studious disposition, and to have developed, at a very early age, that attachment to education, which were to be main features of his life.

18

A Visiting Teacher related how, now aged ten, together with one other boy, Bello Bodinga, Shehu competed for a Native Administration boarding scholarship at Sokoto Middle School (Yabo had then two classes only), being examined in reading, mathematics, geography and Hausa (in which all tuition at Yabo was given) and Arabic, already a great interest of his. While any Sokoto boy who went to school in those days could be counted lucky, whatever he or his family thought, only Alhaji Shehu Shagari, among the Yabo boys of his time, has achieved prominence, the others going to dignified, but sometimes obscure, service with the "Native Administrations".

This time there seems to have been little family objection to his new school at Sokoto. In his third year there he was introduced to a subject which was to engage his attention increasingly, science; but the subject's teacher, whom Shehu was ultimately to succeed at the school, encouraged him, too, with out-of-school tuition in Arabic, still a chief interest of his. Now English, a language of which he is a master, particularly of its Shakespearean mode, also became increasingly important.

Alhaji Shehu Shagari never pretends that among his family, or in his village, in contrast, no doubt, to many parts of southern Nigeria, there was that "thirst for education" (of a non-Koranic kind) which sentimental Europeans suppose to have been thwarted everywhere by the British imperial rulers. On the other hand, Alhaji Shehu cannot now resist the impression that the apparent reluctance of the British administration to develop modern education in the emirates was intended to perpetuate the division between "North" and "South" in Nigeria. And although British rule in northern Nigeria – indirect as it was – may have had little direct effect on the mass of the people, young Shehu Shagari, now in Sokoto Middle School, as it then was, felt sufficient resentment about it to produce, in 1938, an essay declaring that "the sooner the Europeans leave Nigeria the better". Even the senior British administrative officer for the Province, the Resident, was told of Shehu Shagari's great impertinence.

At Sokoto school the official Arabic teacher was the present

Wazirin Sokoto, Alhaji Junaidu, now the Sultan's chief functionary, who ranks in precedence above all emirs and chiefs in Nigeria's northern states, except for the Sultan himself, the Shehu of Borno, and the Emir of Gwandu. To the Waziri's scholarship all, of all races, who have written about Sokoto, have paid tribute, and in 1981 the Waziri received from his old pupil the Nigerian National Merit Award, a mark of Presidential respect for his learning.

The Waziri's own son, in 1980, was one of the first graduates of the new University of Sokoto to get a first-class degree, in education. One of this University's aims was to restore, after a long interval, Sokoto's reputation for scholarship, but now in a wider field than that of the religious scholars of old.

The President himself, who in March 1980 laid the foundation stone at the University's permanent site, had earlier said that he hoped that it might play its part in preserving Fulfulde, the Fulani language, as Latin had been preserved – his own father was the last member of his family to speak the language. But he also said that agriculture should be prominent in the curriculum – which meant that there could be no vacation in the conventional British "summer", the period of the rains, June to September, when planting takes place in Sokoto (the change at Sokoto to an academic year running from November to March, and from June until October, has now been made).

At Sokoto school the ambition of most of Shehu's schoolmates was to be an Islamic court functionary. Many succeeded; some like the present holder of the office in Sokoto, Halimu Binji, becoming Grand Khadi, or head of the Islamic court system in each state. One, however, Ali Akilu, was to become the highly effective head of the Northern Region public service under Sir Ahmadu Bello – and to die prematurely in a car accident in 1972. And just before Shehu arrived as a pupil, a teacher who had also been one of Sokoto's first pupils had left to become District Head in his own area; Sir Ahmadu Bello himself, Sardauna of Sokoto, who was later to be the first Premier of Northern Nigeria.

The President never claims to have enjoyed his schooldays. Although he, like his contemporaries, worked hard in school he did not see in his education the means to influence or power, or even to worldly success; and he was never a keen sportsman. But he has always seen in his education, and in the rigid, even harsh, discipline of those days and in the austere conditions in schools, valuable "character training" and experience of discipline which are now seldom found in Nigeria's educational institutions.

He once described Sokoto Middle School, which he attended from 1935 to 1940, and whose motto was "Nagarta" or "Diligence", as a "concentration camp". He was writing, in 1974, to Captain Bowler, a British education officer who had retired in Nigeria and who had, the letter recalled, done something to temper the school's rigid discipline. But the future President later commended the character training imparted to pupils by "a life which may appear hard and sometimes unpleasant".

At the school itself, now promoted to "Government College, Sokoto", he described life there in the 1930s to the 1976 Speech Day gathering, at which he was the chief guest. The school day, he said, began about five in the morning to the call of the school Muezzin – one of the boys. Any boy who failed to hear the call would be chased by the house prefect from his mat (there were no beds or mattresses) in the little round hut he shared with two or three other boys, to a cold bath. At 5.30 the Imam, a prefect, would lead school prayers. Each boy then took a broom to join in cleaning the school "compound" and put his bedding out to air. He then went to fetch water in a pot to water the neem tree entrusted to his care – the neem is grown as a windbreak and for fuel in the Sokoto savannah. P.T. followed, then lessons at 7.30. Even a minute's lateness earned a beating, and in class teachers slapped pupils frequently.

The first meal was at 9 o'clock, and the main one, usually millet balls with sour milk, occasionally with fish or meat, at 2.30 p.m. Prayers at the mosque followed, and then a second bath. Boys whose classes were not taking their turn in workshops or doing punishment chores, were free for a couple of hours until organised games, after more prayers. Work in the school farm or garden sometimes replaced games. At 6.30 all joined in fetching water for the school's needs, there were more prayers, then dinner; and from 8 to 9, evening classes which might include sermons or lectures. Lights – makeshift or hurricane lamps, with an occasional Aladdin – were put out at 9.30 except for boys who had permission to attempt extra study. Visits outside the school were confined to Friday afternoon and Sunday morning.

For teachers, too, who lived in the "compound", discipline was harsh – Shehu Shagari recalled one being dismissed for not wearing his uniform. But the £60 a year pay made them then in some ways privileged people, who might even own a bicycle or a horse, wear shoes, or smoke – smoking is a luxury in which the President still indulges, as does his elder brother, more freely than some of his friends think wise.

All this meant, the President insists, that in those days teachers and students lived in much the same way as ordinary villagers. They reflected, too, the respect for authority normal in the world outside school. But a few days after the 1976 Sokoto Speech Day, he was explaining at the speech day of the boys' Secondary School which had been established at Yabo itself five years before (largely through his efforts) the lessons he had learned from his schooldays at the Yabo Primary School forty years ago, from the "ordinary, simple but indefatigable peasant".

He is

the teacher who teaches you never to complain, but always to endeavour to make the best of what you have and be self-reliant. The peasant you see around you doing his daily routine of carrying manure to the farm, working from dusk till dawn tilling the soil on his own patch of land, building his own hut with the grass and mud he has collected himself; carrying his own water and firewood from the bush to his home, he never complains to anyone about the shortage of anything, except that he prays to Allah over the shortage of rain. He is forever determined to exploit God's bounties to his use; he would fish, or hunt for meat, wear only the scanty clothes he can afford or do without; but at the same time he is conscious of his civil responsibilities; he pays his tax regularly and participates actively in the Community Development work without demanding wages. He is self-disciplined, and respects authority to a fault. From him we have a lot to learn if we want to be happy, for he is obviously a happier person than the greedy and selfish pedant who lays more stress on his rights and privileges than on his obligations and responsibilities.

The peasant, however, was not to be envied; it was the schoolboy audience who were privileged.

We have been very fortunate indeed to be among those few in this country who have been given the benefit of free education at the expense of the poor peasants who form the bulk of the population of this Nation. This education has given every one of you tremendous opportunities to rise to the highest echelons of the society if only you can work half as hard as the peasant. The peasant, however, can never reach that position even if he works still harder, for he lacks the opportunities that you are enjoying due to no fault of his.

This was the theme to which he returned in a speech he called "The Dilemma of the Privileged African", given at Ahmadu Bello University at Zaria later in 1976, when he was thanking the University on behalf of all, including himself, who had just received honorary degrees. In the "so-called less-privileged countries", he said, "the educated Africans obviously enjoyed a privileged position. This fortunate group which I have been honoured to join formally today is the proud holder of the destiny of millions of poverty-stricken, ignorant and disease-ridden peasantry who form the bulk of the population". The fortunate elite who enjoyed "positions, status and high standards of living comparable with that of the élitists in the advanced countries" had indeed far greater responsibilities than their counterparts in "privileged" countries. "They have a duty and a formidable task of raising the standards of living of their numerous brothers and sisters everywhere around them to at least certain agreeable levels" to give meaning to life. This was a "debt of honour".

Later, on the same day, he told a gathering of Old Boys of Barewa College, the Secondary School he attended for three years and of whose Association he was now President, that the cult of the "Good Old Days" was understandable. In their school from 1922 until recently (there had just been violent disturbances there) "practically nothing was known about student disturbances and strikes". The standard of discipline was so splendid that the words of a house prefect in those days had more force of law and were more effective "than the decrees and edicts of the military regime".

Teachers, too, "were so devoted and so involved in their jobs that one can only compare the degree of their involvement with that of the present-day soldier in the trenches". The standard of learning in the old Barewa (Katsina) College, to which he was ultimately to be sent, was so high that it could be compared only with that of some universities these days. In contrast, he told the Advanced Teachers' College in Sokoto the following year, one of Nigeria's great problems had become the "dearth of good teachers"; he did not mean qualified teachers only "but also teachers who are truly dedicated to the task of bringing up our young men and women to grow into useful citizens of their country".

Yet they were also evil days, he said. There was complete subjugation of body and soul to foreign colonial domination. Corporal punishment, fatigue and even torture were "the order of the day" in schools. Hunger and poverty were so rampant that a square meal a day was regarded as a privilege. Students walked long distances, sometimes for days, to their schools. School equipment, books, teaching aids and other amenities were either unknown or very scarce, and were all imported. The number of students in the whole school in any year was fewer than that in one class in the present Barewa College.

When, he asked, would they appreciate the present and aspire to a better future instead of only looking back with

24

exhausted admiration to the past with all its faults? Progress, Alhaji Shehu concluded, "runs in a spiral and moves upwards and at each turn you appear to be returning to where you began; but in fact you are still going up and up until you reach the top – or you fall".

Shehu Shagari shared his Sokoto schoolmates' ambition which, we have seen, was to become Islamic court function-aries, and wanted to go on to the Kano School of Arabic Studies, which trained these officials. The Sokoto school authorities, however, had marked out the Shagari boy for another legendary institution of strict discipline, Kaduna College. This had been founded in 1922 in another ancient city of learning, Katsina, near Nigeria's northern frontier. It was financed as a boarding school by the government of the "Northern Provinces", not the "Native Administrations", and was then the only secondary school in the Northern Provinces.

It was intended to educate for the public service, includ-ing teaching, "young men of birth and standing" from the "Muhammadan emirates". But while Katsina College and its later manifestations have been likened to Eton, because of the family origins of the pupils and the high political offices so many eventually attained, the main object was to produce teachers of high quality. At a time when the colonial system seemed virtually permanent, no Nigerian boy, however well-connected, could have been trained for the exercise of real power. And this explains why, when the time came to com-pete for power, almost every leading northern politician was or had been a teacher. But a roll-call of old boys of the college also includes a number of emirs, senior emirate officials, politicians, senior federal civil servants and even senior armed forces officers.

In particular, as most "Barewa" teachers were British – and of high quality – the standard of English, in which all lessons at Katsina were conducted, was remarkable and stamped old boys of the institution. In 1938 the College, still maintaining its character, was moved from Katsina to Kaduna, then colonial administrative capital of the Northern Provinces; and it was when the College was at Kaduna that Shehu was a pupil, from

25

1941 to 1944. In 1949 it was moved again from the atmosphere of a new and artificial government headquarters to the outskirts of the ancient walled city of Zaria, some fifty miles away, when it became Zaria Secondary School, and finally in 1956, Government College, Zaria. Later the term Barewa ("Gazelle") College was applied to the institution in all its manifestations.

This was the school for which Shehu was destined in 1941. He purposely did badly in the examination for it, in the hope of being turned down; but he was still one of the only two Sokoto boys who passed the examination. He was then summoned to the august presence of the Sultan (the present Sir Abubakar) who may have been told of the reluctance of the younger brother of the Shagari Village Head to go to Kaduna to help fill what was in effect the Sokoto provincial "quota" for the College. His Highness, it seemed, was about to travel to a meeting at Kaduna; this boy must go with him. The College was on holiday when they arrived at Kaduna, but the Sultan summoned a Katsina man, Mallam Yazidu, who was a teacher there, to look after the Shagari boy. This teacher took him to the then Principal of the College, the late Tom Baldwin, a British official, who told him that he was indeed to become a pupil in 1941. The future President was as reluctant to take this further step in his education as he had been to take earlier ones.

For Nigeria's independence celebrations in 1960 each Minister was allowed to invite two "internal" and two "external" guests. Alhaji Shehu Shagari, then Minister of Economic Development, chose for his external guests Captain Bowler, the education officer who had modified the regime of the Sokoto "concentration camp", and Mr Anthony Shillingford, who had taught Shehu Yabo, Shehu Shagari's science teacher at Sokoto, and, as Provincial Education Officer in Sokoto, had taught English, used in the school's upper classes, to Shehu Shagari himself. Among the British it was the teachers, even if hard taskmasters, whom the older Nigerians, however much they disliked their schools, now recall with special affection from the days before indepen-

dence. The colonial administrators they recall sometimes with
respect, sometimes with animosity; but seldom with affection.

Of Kaduna College, although later as Commissioner for
Finance he was to be President of its Old Boys' Association,
Alhaji Shehu has no particularly affectionate memories. He
was, however, happy enough there and enjoyed the varied
curriculum, which included carpentry and gardening as well
as the conventional English, history, geography and other
subjects.

The future President's interest in farming was shown by his
essay in his first year on "What I would like to be". He wanted,
it seems, to be a farmer; but with an emphasis on poultry
and dairy farming, the "modern" attribute of the ancient
vocation.

The school's normal austerity was sharpened by war-time
shortages and import restrictions. Yet although the Northern
Provinces alone raised almost a hundred thousand volunteers
for the allied forces, Nigerians distinguished themselves in
Ethiopia and Burma, and during it 18,000 labourers were con-
scripted for Nigeria's own tin mines, the war seemed very
remote during Shehu Shagari's years at Barewa. Even the
presence of Vichy forces in Northern Nigeria's northern
neighbour, the French colony of Niger, caused no alarm.

At Barewa, too, he developed his knowledge of "rural
science", to which as a teacher he attached particular importance. It was a subject to be included in his *Wakar Nijeriya*,
"Song of Nigeria", the remarkable composition in Hausa verse
published in 1973 for schoolchildren, in which he dealt with
geography, economics, history and rural science (this small
book may have made him more famous throughout much of
Hausa-speaking Nigeria than did any of his numerous political appointments). He was disgusted when, in 1947, the
Northern Region government ended the teaching of science in
"middle" schools, as the government decided it was largely a
waste of time to teach the subject at this level.

Although its library was modest, Barewa allowed the young
Shehu Shagari to indulge his delight in reading, and he was
appointed the College's librarian. Anthony Shillingford found

unconvincing his claim to have read all the library's books right through; but the other boys strongly supported it. His "day and night" reading, he admits, was indiscriminate; but it did include much Shakespeare – he learned *Julius Caesar* by heart – and retains his delight in the poet's language.

Later his love of reading brought the young Shehu Shagari to the attention of the late H. A. S. Johnston, then District Officer (DO) in Sokoto in the colonial administration. One day soon after he had returned to Sokoto as a teacher in 1945, Shehu Shagari was in the Sokoto "Reading Room", hoping to find any book which he had not read. Johnston entered the building on a routine inspection and the young teacher complained to the DO that he had read all the books in the small library; he was able to prove his point by answering questions about each of them.

Johnston, whose own book *The Fulani Empire of Sokoto*, published in 1967, was to become a standard work, and who earlier compiled and translated *A Selection of Hausa Stories*, then invited Shehu to use the books in his own house. From time to time he discussed them with Shehu, particularly books on history. The Johnston library – and Johnston himself – was, however, quite unable to satisfy the young teacher's new thirst for books on economics. The DO could only suggest that careful reading of the *Financial Times* might help – a Utopian idea then, although today all London newspapers, brought by air, are easily available in Sokoto.

So regular were his visits to the DO's home that his uncle, Sarkin Kebbi of Yabo, warned him that he was too friendly with the white man; thereafter the two continued to meet, but only in Shehu Shagari's school. The acquaintance, however, as we shall see, had an important effect on the future President's political life.

When Shehu Shagari was in his last year at Kaduna, Shehu Yabo, the Sokoto Middle School science teacher, died. The Sokoto NA decided that there was only one possible successor – Shehu himself. So, although retaining his attachment for literature and languages, he was given a special science training at Barewa and did practice teaching at Zaria Middle School

– one pupil was his present Adviser on Petroleum and Energy Affairs, Alhaji Yahaya Dikko.

Shehu gained his Higher Elementary Teaching Certificate at Zaria Teachers Training College before returning to Sokoto as a teacher in 1945, to the school where so recently he had been a pupil and where, with one short interval, he was to stay until in 1953 he became Senior Visiting Teacher for Sokoto Province. This post he retained for some time even after he entered national politics in 1954.

In 1951 it was announced that Sokoto was to have its first broadcasting station. Shehu Shagari, in his village on leave from teaching, went to Sokoto to tell the Sardauna of Sokoto, then still Councillor for Education in the Emirate Council, that he would like to join the new service. His excellent Hausa, his Arabic, and even his poetic talents, he thought, might be put to good use in the station.

The Sardauna promised to look into the possibilities. Around this time, however, the headmaster of the Senior Primary School at Argungu, the city from which Sama had mounted his raid on Shagari in the 1890s, failed to gain the appropriate certificate and so had to leave the job. An appeal for a substitute was made to the Sardauna, since Argungu was in Sokoto Province. Once more Shehu Shagari was seen as the only man to fill the gap. With many apologies the Sardauna told him that he was going to Argungu, not to broadcasting.

The traditional hostility between his own village and Argungu did not concern Shehu Shagari. He told himself that he must be patient, and be grateful for what was in effect promotion.

At his new school the boys were aged from eleven to fourteen. There was an assistant teacher – now the Emir of Argungu, Muhammadu Mera – and an Arabic teacher. The young Shagari man was a considerable figure in the static society of this small but ancient emirate. Although it was only fifty miles away, Sokoto seemed very distant and he was sad to have left the new interests he was developing there. But he composed a poem, "Song of Patience", to express his philosophy about his situation.

Above all in Argungu he had to abandon the political activities in which he had become engaged. These he had resumed when he returned to Sokoto in 1952. He was still intent on a career in education, and was soon on a refresher course at Bauchi Training Centre, before his appointment as Senior Visiting Teacher for Sokoto Province. Within two years, however, at the age of 29, he was to become one of the Sokoto members in the Federal House of Representatives in Lagos; and to begin a national political career which in twenty five years took him through a wide range of political appointments and which culminated in the Presidency.

3

CALL TO POLITICS

Shehu Shagari's first real political experience was in the
national discussions which began in 1949, on reform of the
"Richards" constitution. That constitution, introduced in 1947
and named after the then Governor, Sir Arthur Richards (later
Lord Milverton), was the first which, however tentatively,
treated Nigeria as a single political entity, and brought the
"north" and the "south" into an (incomplete) administrative
and, for the first time, legislative union. The constitution was
criticised by nationalists, as much because no Nigerian had
been consulted about it as because of its provisions, which
were considered to give too little political responsibility to
Nigerians. Even Britain's House of Commons gave it only
29 minutes of debate, in a deserted Chamber.

In 1949 however, the Governor of Nigeria, Sir John Mac-
pherson – who had succeeded Sir Arthur Richards – and his
Chief Secretary, Sir Hugh Foot, elder brother of the Labour
Party leader and later to be Lord Caradon, were determined
that the entire country should be brought into discussion on a
new constitution. So there were village, district, provincial
and regional conferences to consider questions, framed by Sir
Hugh, such as whether Nigeria should now have a genuine
federal system with autonomy for its Regions, and how these
were to be represented in a new central legislature.

All manner of organisations submitted memoranda, and
discussions at lower levels culminated in a national conference
held at Ibadan in 1950. This was the first forum in which
politicians from northern and southern Nigeria had really met
each other. Since it contained seven important traditional

31

rulers, while the politicians were drawn entirely from the educated elite of the three Regions, and were, even when enthusiastic about self-government, gradualist in approach, the conference was in no sense a radical body. But, as is now clear, it set in train a process which would inevitably lead to independence.

Sir John and Sir Hugh, however, were concerned that Nigeria should not experience the same violent disturbances as the Gold Coast – hitherto regarded as Britain's "model" African colony – had faced because political change there had fallen behind expectations. They knew what they were doing. But his experience in Ibadan persuaded the late Sardauna of Sokoto, who was to become the Northern Region's first Premier, and leader of the Northern People's Congress, that, in his own words "we in the North would have to take politics seriously before very long".

Although the conference was able in the end to produce a set of proposals to put before Nigeria's Legislative Council, still nominally the colony's legislature, and then before the Colonial Office (in fact the authority which ultimately mattered) at times agreement seemed impossible.

The Northern Region contained well over half the total population of Nigeria, which the census of 1952-3 gave as 31,168,000 – certainly an under-count – with the Region's population as almost 17 million. The Region alone thus had a bigger population than any Black African state. It also comprised two thirds of Nigeria's area, or some 300,000 square miles, three times the area of the UK; and it stretched over 700 miles from east to west and over 400 miles from north to south.

So, although at the Ibadan conference there were only eighteen northern delegates against 32 from the south – the sole British official present was the Attorney-General – the northerners made it a condition of their support for any other proposals that their Region should be given as many seats in the proposed new central legislature as the Eastern and Western Regions together. They were unhappy about the proposal to appoint Nigerians as Ministers both in the centre and in the Regions; but in return for having their way over representation, they accepted this proposal.

Representatives from all Regions supported a federal form of government; and although a true federation is impossible under a colonial – as it is under a military – regime, or when, as in Nigeria's case then, one unit is greater than the others put together, under the new constitution which resulted from these discussions, and which came into force in 1951, Nigeria embarked on the road to her present true and democratic federalism.

Shehu Shagari's participation in these constitutional discussions went no higher than the Sokoto provincial conference. He was, however, still only twenty-five, and as the Sokoto conference included the Sultan, the Emirs of the Province, and other notables, his presence was questioned. He had in fact been nominated to the conference by the Sokoto DO, H.A.S. Johnston, whose library had played a part in Shehu Shagari's education; and he, no doubt, hoped that in this way one at least of the small group in Sokoto with Western education would have a chance of offering a view on the constitution. Johnston, indeed, seemed to have decided that Shehu Shagari was now the one man in Sokoto who could confidently be regarded as representative of the "educated", and to have chosen him more than once in that capacity.

Shehu Shagari's uncle, the District Head of Yabo, who had already warned him about his relations with the DO, told him that not only he himself, but the Sultan too, objected to the young man's assertiveness at the constitutional conference. Thirty years later Alhaji Shehu was to play a leading part in the national Constituent Assembly which approved the constitution under which he became President. But now, because he had been nominated by the DO, his elders regarded him as a tool of the British administration, and as being, in any case, too young to participate in these affairs.

Earlier, when "development areas" were established in the emirates Johnson had asked Shehu Shagari for his ideas about possible developments in the Yabo district. The development areas were in charge of British "development officers", usually

33

ex-servicemen whom Shehu Shagari regarded as "second-rate DOs", with little imagination or local knowledge. The young teacher produced what the DO called a "beautiful essay", implying that it was merely an academic exercise; but the author himself considered it to be a realistic plan. He envisaged schools in all villages, dispensaries, a cottage hospital for the District, feeder roads for the hamlets, an experimental farm, and extension officers to help the farmers. The river could be dammed for irrigation and a water supply could be guaranteed for everybody.

Was this really, Johnston asked, what the people wanted? To answer the question he toured the District for a week with the Yabo District Head – who was displeased at these questions being raised in this manner because of his young relative's "plans". These, in the end, had little effect on the District's development.

Although political parties, most confined to the coastal cities, had existed in southern Nigeria since the early 1920s, the politics of parties came late to northern Nigeria. There were, in fact, no parties in northern Nigeria before Nigeria's first general election, in 1951-2, in which the Region participated. Shehu Shagari, although still only 54 when he became Nigeria's President in 1979, was thus a pioneer in the north's party politics.

It was not until 1914 that the then Protectorate of Northern Nigeria, which Lord Lugard had established, was formally amalgamated with Southern Nigeria, British rule over which had been imposed piecemeal since the annexation of Lagos in 1861. Even then the "Northern Provinces" were not represented in the colonial Legislative Council in Lagos, except by British officials. A report of the 1942 Conference of Northern Chiefs and Emirs recorded that the Conference was satisfied that the Governor of Nigeria was "fully able to deal with all matters concerning Northern Nigeria".

Unofficial northerners first came to the Lagos Legislative Council in 1947, through indirect elections under the cautious provisions of the new Richards Constitution. That constitution also established an advisory legislature in each of the three regions, with limited powers but with unofficial majorities. The central Legislative Council, as the Sardauna of Sokoto was to say in his *Autobiography* was, so far as the north was concerned, at last "purged of its solid phalanx of mute officers". But the new central legislature, in which all three regions were represented equally, although it was a useful seminary for parliamentary pressure, was scarcely democratic in its northern representation. The new northern House of Chiefs and House of Assembly, the latter elected by the largely traditional Native Authority Councils of each province, elected the Region's members in the Legislative Council. In 1951, as we have seen, the Richards constitution was amended after very full consultation to provide for Nigerian Ministers both at the centre and in the Regions, and for direct elections to the new central House of Representatives, which replaced the Legislative Council. So now, while independence was still amost a decade away, Nigerian politics assumed some of the characteristics which were to lead to the breakdown of civilian government in 1966. In particular, the parties which dominated the new central legislature were regionally-based, while even the prospect of independence sharpened rivalries for place and power.

The constitutional separation of the northern and southern provinces had reflected to a large extent, but certainly not completely, a social separation. Although perhaps a third of the people of the Northern Region were outside the classic emirate system, being under non-Muslim chiefs with a variety of jurisdictions, the core of the Region was still the emirates. In these the rulers, in spite of British restraint on their autocracy, were still paramount, controlling local police and prisons, appointing local judicial officers and the senior local government officials, and hearing cases in their own courts.

Their position was reinforced in two ways. There was a religious sanction for Muslim rulers; and the British administration in northern Nigeria, while attempting to control the rulers and reform their NAs, always saw the survival of the emirate system, which they regarded as one peculiarly suited to the Africans, as their main task.

35

Exclusion of the "undesirable" activities of southern lawyers and politicians was seen by these officers as essential for the survival of this system. Its virtues, however, were little valued either by British officials in Lagos and in southern Nigeria, or in the Colonial Office. This bred a certain exclusiveness among British officials, particularly the administrators, in northern Nigeria. Indeed, reversing the hackneyed defence of colonial rule, it was said that so cool did relations seem between the two sets of officials that if the Nigerians were to leave Nigeria there would be serious bloodshed between the British in the north and in the south.

Shehu Shagari's first acquaintance with what, in the conditions of the Northern Region at the time, could be called politics, had come in 1945 when he had returned to Sokoto as a teacher. There was discontent among NA employees, including teachers, because the government did not extend to them the increase in the war-time cost of living granted to regional civil servants. The discontent led to the formation of an NA staff union, although southern Nigerians, of whom there were many in NA employment, working as clerks or artisans, were the main influence in this. Shehu Shagari found himself sympathetic to the malcontents; but, still only twenty and a scion of a ruling family, he could not afford publicly to show any support.

More important was the formation, also in 1945, of the Youth Social Circle in Sokoto, of which he was a founder and of which he became secretary. At that time such bodies, even when, like this one, it was designated as primarily cultural, were the only means in the Northern Region for the growing number of educated young men to give vent to their, usually very restrained, political feelings.

These concerned less the continuation of colonial rule itself than the absence of any change in the nature of the emirate government, whose more authoritarian features they found incompatible with what they were learning of the world outside, and which they believed might have been removed in the natural course of events but for the protection the British gave the rulers. Some, such as Shehu Shagari himself, saw reform in the system as essential for its survival, which they considered necessary if the northern provinces were to have their rightful place in the developing political system of Nigeria. Although it collapsed after a couple of years an early version of the Katsina ("Barewa") Old Boys' Association had, as early as 1939, ventured to express political views, which included the "oozing-out" of imperialism and a degree of democratisation of the NAs. Later its members helped to establish bodies similar to the Sokoto Youth Social Circle elsewhere – in Kaduna, Zaria, Kano, Bauchi and other emirate centres.

They were led by men such as Dr R. A. B. Dikko, a Fulani convert to Christianity and the north's first medical doctor, and Alhaji Maitama Sule of Kano, who, like Shehu Shagari, was to become a Federal Minister. There were, too, more radical politicians such as Malam Sa'ad Zungur, a pharmacist from a notable Bauchi family, who had been educated in Lagos and was to become for a time secretary of the eastern Nigeria-based NCNC. There was Abubakar Zukogi, a "patrician radical" from Bida, a founder of the Kano-based Northern Elements Progressive Association (NEPA), who was to become a founder and secretary of the Northern Elements Progressive Union (NEPU), also Kano-based, which emerged as a party in time for the general election in 1951-2.

The most important political influence in Nigeria's Northern Region in the late forties, however, was probably the Northern Teachers Association (NTA), formed originally in 1947, when he was on a course at the London University Institute of Education, by Malam Aminu Kano. He was a young man of impeccably aristocratic Fulani background; but he developed the most comprehensive assault on the NA system of any of its critics, maintaining that the Fulani rulers had betrayed the progressive precepts of Shehu Uthman Dan Fodio. He was to become leader of NEPU, the radical opponent of the Northern People's Congress (NPC) which dominated Northern Nigeria, and so the Federal Government, from 1952 to 1966.

NEPU, then reborn as the People's Redemption Party, was to present Shehu Shagari's National Party of Nigeria (NPN) with its greatest shock in the 1979 presidential elections, by winning

Kano. Shehu Shagari and Aminu Kano were also to oppose each other personally in the 1979 presidential elections.

The Northern Regional government for a time refused to recognise NTA, which was ostensibly a trade union; but when it was recognised it became, in effect, the first region-wide body of political significance and included in its membership many non-teachers. The first Federal Prime Minister, Alhaji Sir Abubakar Tafawa Balewa, who was a teacher, later became "General President" of the NTA.

Shehu Shagari met Aminu Kano in 1948 when he was on a teachers' refresher course in Zaria. They became, and have since been, personal friends as well as political opponents. There was even a possibility of their allying themselves politically after the 1979 general election, and they can always still engage in amicable dispute.

Malam Aminu today agrees that Shehu Shagari was no less critical of the conservatism of the NAs than he was. At one point Malam Aminu, who then had a curious respect for Mussolini, for some reason also sent Shehu Shagari a copy of Hitler's *Mein Kampf*. But while Aminu demanded radical transformation, Shehu Shagari – perhaps because his rural Sokoto differed significantly from urban, cosmopolitan Kano – has always advised a cautious approach to reform. He would claim that this approach, which has been that of successive northern Nigerian governments, has in fact, as he forecast, transformed the emirates in ways unimaginable thirty years ago. For now the emirs have lost their police, their courts, and their prisons; and while each old emirate, whatever its size, constituted a separate local government authority, now a big emirate can be divided into a number of elected authorities.

It was military rule, however – although in the Northern Region and then in the northern states the soldiers were on the whole cautious – which ended the emirs' domination of their courts and police and introduced elective local government of the kind which both Alhaji Shehu and Malam Aminu approved.

Shehu Shagari joined the NTA. More important, he became Sokoto secretary of the new Northern People's Congress. At

The Council of Ministers, 24 December 1959.

The President as Minister of Economic Development.

the time this was – insofar as any non-official association in the Northern Region could be – non-political; but the leaders of the various discussion societies had tried to bring them to-gether into a regional organisation. Shehu Shagari took part in these negotiations; and, in the end, the imminence of con-stitutional changes which would at last bring the north fully into the Nigerian national scene through elected unofficial legislators, made a regional political organisation seem urgent.

The Jami'iyyar Mutanen Arewa (JMA), or the Northern People's Congress (NPC), was founded in October 1948. It was still then a "cultural organisation" which used its Hausa, not English, name, although clearly it could not avoid political significance. It raised almost £50,000 to establish schools in a region where, in the most northern provinces, school atten-dance was well under ten per cent of those of school age. Some Kano members, however, wanted it even then to become an overt political organisation – an idea many less radical members would have accepted had they not feared this would alienate traditional authority and attract the suspicion of the British administration. The Sultan of Sokoto, for example, withdrew his support when he heard of the political demands made by the JMA.

In the meantime NEPU had come into the open as a political party. Its success in the Northern Region in the "primaries" of the 1951-2 elections – which because of the many "stages" lasted for some weeks – alarmed the more conservative northern politicians, who decided that they, too, needed a special political organisation, in spite of their earlier assump-tion that a close association with the NAs would guarantee their success. But they did not succeed in organising a real political counterweight to NEPU before, or even during, the elections.

It was after the elections that candidates elected to the Northern Regional House of Assembly, largely NA officials who had in fact needed no party organisation to ensure their success, organised themselves into a new NPC. The organisa-tion's 1950 Jos convention had turned the JMA into a political body which henceforth used its English name and was known everywhere as NPC. So the civil servants, such as Dr Dikko, who had played so great a part in organising it, left, since they were forbidden to participate in politics.

Later, as a headmaster in far-away Argungu, Shehu Shagari was disappointed to learn that at the July 1952 convention in Zaria, people successful in the elections then took all the central party offices, leaving pioneers like himself with nothing. NEPU men were still elected to NPC offices after the Jos convention – Malam Aminu, for example became auditor. But Shehu Shagari had been mandated by the Sokoto NPC branch to oppose Aminu Kano and his supporters at the Jos convention as enemies of tradition. The NEPU men finally walked out.

These two streams in northern Nigerian politics (another very important one, the desire of the one third of the region who were neither Hausa, Fulani, nor Kanuri, to break away from it, was to become increasingly important) were now established. The NPC was pledged to reform, and thus, as it claimed, to preserve the NA system – with the expected support of its main representatives. NEPU simply wanted to abolish the system, although they were uncertain about the precise alternative, as revolutionaries tend to be.

Shehu Shagari never became deeply involved in this Northern Regional controversy, although it was always in the background of his political life. His political future lay in the Federal Government and in national issues. After the 1951-2 elections NEPU claimed that the NAs began to victimise its members in every possible way, and that the British administration supported this campaign. Although secretary of the Sokoto NPC branch – Alhaji Ibrahim Gusau had taken over during his absence in Argungu – Shehu Shagari had no influence on the administration's or on the NAs' policy in these matters. His stand since gaining supreme power as President shows that he always seeks reconciliation with opponents. But the arbitrary treatment of the NEPU by the NAs after the 1951 elections was a sorry chapter in Nigeria's political history; this the President today, one supposes, would not deny.

Shehu Shagari, however, had not waited for the formation

of the NPC before taking an active interest in politics. The young schoolmaster was the only man of Sokoto origin to attend a meeting held in the city in 1946 by the southern-based National Council of Nigeria and the Cameroons (NCNC). The NCNC was touring the whole of Nigeria to raise funds to send a delegation to London to ask the Colonial Office to abrogate the Richards Constitution as undemocratic. The speakers at Sokoto were the veteran Herbert Macaulay, a Lagos man and doyen of Nigerian nationalists, and the rising star, Dr Nnamdi Azikiwe, the Ibo, under whom, as Governor-General and President, Shehu Shagari was later to serve as Minister from 1960 to 1966. An informer told the British Provincial Education Officer that Shehu Shagari had attended this meeting; as a punishment his teacher's salary increment was postponed that year.

Dr Azikiwe owed much of his influence in Nigeria to the newspapers he controlled, notably the Lagos-based *West African Pilot*. Small though their circulation was, they spread the nationalist doctrine far beyond Lagos, where otherwise it was confined. There was then no private or political newspaper for the whole of the Northern Region, although for a time Dr Azikiwe published in Kano the *Daily Comet*, a lively but very local broadsheet. People in the region with political interests were starved of anything to read.

Shehu Shagari was a keen reader of the *West African Pilot* and an admirer of Dr Azikiwe. The newspaper was banned in Northern Region schools, but in 1948 Shehu Shagari wrote for it an article pleading for a revival of the "Dual Mandate" – using the term in a very different sense from that used by its originator, Lord Lugard, who was advocating the reconciliation of the world's needs for African raw materials with the colonial powers' duties towards their subjects. Alhaji Shehu, on the other hand, was advocating consideration of the special position of the Northern Region in the event of Nigerian independence – such a distant dream, then, particularly in northern Nigeria, that it was remarkable that he wanted to discuss it. Because of the great differences in the social and political systems between the two parts of the country, he suggested, they could be united only in a loose federation, an idea which, in various forms, was to reappear in Nigerian politics down the years.

Mazi Mbonu Ojike, a famous columnist in the *Pilot*, attacked this thesis in an article headed "Fallacious Shehu Shagari", which denied that such a division existed – or should ever be allowed to exist.

Shehu Shagari had even produced, for private circulation, Hausa verse which could be called "anti-colonialist". There is no doubt that at this time he already realised fully that political advance in Nigeria had two aspects. There was the "phasing-out" of the British – in Sokoto no more vehement expression was then thinkable. But there was also the reconciliation of the attitudes to traditional authority and institutions of the leaders of the north and of the south. So a young man who, by the criteria then ruling in the Northern Region, and particularly in Sokoto, was a radical, found himself assailed as a reactionary by a southern politician. This was to be a continual source of unnecessary division between northern and southern politicians in Nigeria, arising from the long administrative and social division between the two areas and the consequent misunderstandings.

Shehu Shagari's final entry to the national scene was, however, melodramatic. In 1953 the Marafa of Sokoto, son-in-law of the Sardauna and a friend of the future President, one evening invited him to join him in his car. The Marafa drove to one of the plantations established on the outskirts of the city to provide firewood, and stopped at a point on the road where there were already a number of big cars. The Marafa, but not Shehu Shagari, alighted and entered the plantation for discussions with some of the gathering there. He then drove Shehu Shagari back to the city. On the way he told Shehu that his name was one of those being considered for the NPC nominations for the Federal elections, due in 1954. In these voting would, for the first time in Nigeria, be direct everywhere, although in the Northern Region women still would not vote, a right finally conceded to them in general elections only in 1979.

Shehu Shagari, who was believed to enjoy the patronage of the Sardauna himself, was in fact "drafted" by the "big men" in 1954 and was not even consulted about his candidature for the Federal elections, although he could claim to have been a member of the NPC before the Sardauna of Sokoto, then leader of the Northern Region government, or Abubakar Tafawa Balewa, then the senior NPC Minister in the Federal Government (who became Prime Minister in 1957) and was in no way to be considered their protégé. It was assumed, no doubt rightly, however, that he would readily accept the honour of the Federal nomination. But he resented the patronising attitude of the "big men" and has always since fought against behind-the-scenes leadership in a political party.

In the middle of 1953 Shehu Shagari, still regarded by "authority" as an educationist rather than as a politician who was about to make his national debut, went, with a small group of northern educationists, on a four-month British Council course in Britain, his first visit abroad. This followed the usual routine; study of teaching in different schools, some practice in teaching, study of British life. He stayed for a while in Scotland at Kirkcudbright (he is still very proud that he can pronounce it) at the house of a former officer of the Royal West African Frontier force.

There were a dozen teachers from the Northern Region on the course, led by Shehu Shagari's friend, the late Aminu Tafida of Sokoto. All their names and places of origin were to appear in a Hausa poem, 216 lines long, *Wakar Ingila*, or "Song of England" which he composed at the end of the visit.

The poem describes the flight, his first, from Kano to Heathrow, the feeling that "you are nowhere", the magical first glimpse of the snow-capped Alps "below you but touching the skies". The London crowds and buildings excited the young Sokoto man; road traffic like this he had never seen (in later life he would find Lagos, and now Kano, traffic as crowded). In Liverpool the Mersey Tunnel and the passenger liners which then served West Africa; in Blackpool the circus ("the horse and the leopard together; you won't believe that"), police walkie-talkies in Dumfries, tractors being manufactured in

43

Kelso ... they were all described. He visited Balmoral where
the young Queen who was soon to visit Nigeria waved to the
young men in robes. He "Hausaised" Kirkcudbright in the
poem to a musical "Kakubri"; but failed to do anything with
Birkenhead. Back in London there were the usual visits to
the Lords and Commons, Buckingham Palace and the Mint,
Madame Tussauds and the rest. So brightly lit was London
that there was "no night, no day". This was one British
Council scholar so observant that he – and his party – got full
value from his visit.

On his return to Sokoto Shehu Shagari was appointed
Senior Visiting Teacher (inspector) for all NA schools in the
Province. He toured the province extensively, and retained
the job after being elected in 1954 (the House of Representatives sat only for a couple of months each year).

His 1954 constituency for the elections to the Federal House
of Representatives was Sokoto West, which included Yabo
and Shagari. He had an opponent, standing, unexpectedly,
for the southern-based NCNC. This was Alhaji Umaru Altine,
mayor of Enugu, whose claim to be descended from a family at
Sifawa, the town in the constituency where Shaikh Uthman
dan Fodio had resided, did not convince many voters. Alhaji
Umaru lost his deposit.

The 1954 election campaign in Sokoto concerned purely
local matters – most voters cared nothing about national or
even regional affairs. To have talked of independence or
even local government changes would have scared them; and
perhaps, Shehu Shagari maintains, it would have brought
down the wrath of the District Head, Yabo, still the dominant
political influence in his life. Such a constituency, however,
demonstrated the truth of the adage that the NPC, conservative as it was, saw the wisdom of calling on the people of the
north to defeat the potential radicals.

As his first national task Shehu Shagari was nominated by
the Federal House as a member of the Federal Scholarship
Board. He had only once been to his capital, Lagos, before his
election; then, in 1949, he had himself unsuccessfully applied
for a Federal university scholarship to the UK. Now he could

see from the inside how woefully few were the northerners qualified to win such scholarships. He described the situation in a memo to the Prime Minister, as Abubakar Tafawa Balewa was to become – a memo which played a part in the decision to appoint him Minister of Establishments and Training in 1960.

He advocated a drive in the Northern Region to persuade NA staff and school-leavers to join the Federal Service, which then, to most people in the north, seemed impossibly distant. Alhaji Abubakar sent him on a tour of the Northern Region; he visited all parts, spoke to NA Councils, to pupils about to leave secondary schools, and to leaders of opinion. Many years later, as a Minister, he was gratified when the pilot of a Nigeria Airways aircraft in which he was flying joined him in the passenger cabin and confessed that it was because the then MP had assured him, a boy at the Christian Gindiri School near Jos, that he could become a pilot, that he had joined Nigeria Airways.

In 1958 Shehu Shagari was chosen to attend in London a course organised by the Commonwealth Parliamentary Association, a body he was to serve well in later years. In London he met many other Commonwealth MPs and studied parliamentary procedure. He was delighted to find that Nigeria's printed records of Parliamentary debates ("Hansards") which in Lagos and Kaduna were always available on the day following the debates in the Houses, compared favourably in their speed of production with those of many other Commonwealth countries and, although much slimmer, stood comparison with those of Westminster. But the big difference, he found, between MPs in Nigeria and in Britain lay in their relations with their constituents.

For where the British MP was constantly visiting his constituency and dealing with a host of problems presented by his constituents or by organisations there, few such demands were made on Nigerian MPs, many of whom might absent themselves from their constituencies for long periods without anybody noticing or caring. He might then have recalled a judgement he had formed in Sokoto when the DO, Johnston, and the District Head were assessing the value of his plan for

45

the district, that Christian missionaries, though they worked only in non-Islamic areas, seemed to be closer to the people than administrators – or perhaps politicians.

Later, in 1958, he became Parliamentary Secretary to the Prime Minister.* He had scarcely known Alhaji Abubakar, a man as temperate and balanced in outlook as himself, before being elected to the House of Representatives. But his name was brought to the Prime Minister's attention during a dinner party at the Lagos house of Alhaji Muhammadu Ribadu, the Federal Minister of Lands, Mines and Power, a powerful NPC politician generally regarded as being closer to the party leader, the Sardauna of Sokoto, than was the Prime Minister himself. The Sardauna was present to hear the chief guest, the genial and avuncular Sir Frederick Metcalfe, who had been invited to act as a neutral Speaker of the House of Representatives (he was an experienced Clerk of the House of Commons) speak warmly of the young Sokoto MP's parliamentary Secretary. The great man must have been surprised at the lukewarm response to an invitation which opened up the path to power. But Shehu Shagari, who many people later saw as the Sardauna's political son, still had his eyes on the lonely schools of Sokoto. It was with reluctance that he fell in with his political master's wishes.

A Nigerian Member of Parliament in those days had few duties when Parliament was not sitting – which meant for ten months in the year. For even the most conscientious there was relatively little to do even during the sessions. That was equally true of the Prime Minister's new Parliamentary Secretary, who, as we have seen, retained the post of Visiting Teacher in Sokoto after the election in 1954. Although he had to give the post up when he became Parliamentary Secretary he continued to do voluntary teaching during the long recesses. Indeed he maintained that the Prime Minister scarcely noticed his presence or absence; and he finally told Sir

---

*Alhaji Abubakar Tafawa Balewa was appointed to the newly created office of Prime Minister of the Federation in 1957. He was knighted in 1960.

Abubakar that he objected to being idle and would return to teaching if he had nothing to do. So the Prime Minister asked his Chief Secretary, Peter Stallard, a former administrative officer in the Northern Region, who was later to be Governor of the Isle of Man, to find some worthwhile task for the impatient young man, who had a room and a desk but no work.

Stallard loaded Shehu Shagari's desk with a mass of material concerning citizenship in various Commonwealth countries, from which he was to produce a memorandum as a basis for law on Nigerian citizenship. Shehu saw this as a challenge for a non-lawyer and his final draft was admired by Sir Abubakar. But he warned Stallard that he would do no such job again; he had shown that he could do it, but this was civil servants' work and he was in no sense an assistant to a civil servant, even one as senior as Stallard.

Shehu Shagari took no part in the succession of constitutional conferences between the Nigerians and the British in London and in Lagos which, beginning in 1953, paved the way, first for self-government in each of the Regions – for which the Northern Region chose a date, 15 March 1959, later than the others – and for the independence of the Federation, on 1 October 1960.

The absence at the constitutional conference in London late in 1958 of the Minister, his friend Zanna Bukar Dipcharima, a former NCNC man from Borno who had come over to the NPC, gave Shehu Shagari an opportunity to act as Minister for Trade and Industry. This was the first of a succession of ministerial offices he occupied, which was to last until the overthrow of the civilian government in 1966.

In 1959 came another Federal election, to an enlarged House of Representatives. In this the Northern Region was allocated 174 of the 320 seats, a majority, on the basis of population, although alone among the Regions – to which the Southern Cameroons, as a Region, and Lagos, now as Federal territory, were added after the 1953 and 1954 constitutional conferences – it still did not give the vote to women. Offsetting this northern preponderance in the House of Representatives, the

Regions had equal representation in the indirectly elected, but largely powerless, Senate.

This time Shehu Shagari was opposed in his constituency both by a candidate representing the NCNC and its northern partner, NEPU, and by a candidate from Chief Awolowo's Action Group, whose base was among the Yoruba people of the Western Region. Some 30,000 had registered as voters in the constituency, almost a quarter of the total population. This was not an unimpressive figure in face of the acute shortage of literate people, which in some areas of northern Nigeria led to the use of senior schoolboys as assistant registration officers. Moreover, since in parts of the Region tax rolls were used to assist the registration officials, there was some suspicion about the object of the unfamiliar operation. But in an election when the great majority of the electors were still unfamiliar with voting, the turn-out of voters was over 90 per cent of the men registered.

Shehu Shagari secured 85 per cent of the votes cast in his constituency, against some 10 per cent for the NEPU-NCNC, and just over 4 per cent for the Action Group candidate. No doubt many voters supposed that the NA and the British expected them to support the NPC. But in voting which was unquestionably secret, Shehu Shagari received the same degree of support as he had in his first, open, election.

From the election the NPC emerged with the biggest number of seats in the Lagos legislature, although these were all from the Northern Region and did not constitute a clear majority. Alhaji Abubakar Tafawa Balewa formed a coalition with Dr Azikiwe's NCNC. Dr Azikiwe, however, did not serve in it. He became President of the Senate, as the first step towards his later formal withdrawal from politics to become Governor-General of independent Nigeria the following year. Chief Awolowo became Leader of the Opposition in the House of Representatives.

4

IN SIR ABUBAKAR'S
GOVERNMENT

In the new Cabinet Alhaji Abubakar Tafawa Balewa, the Prime
Minister, gave Shehu Shagari his first Ministry, the Ministry of
Economic Development. At the time this, a new Ministry, was
not nearly so important as it has become in the era of multi-
billion naira development plans. Public investment under the
1962-68 development plan, for example, was estimated to cost
only £800m., compared with over ₦70bn. under President
Shehu Shagari's own 1981-85 plan. The Federal Government's
only responsibility for agriculture, in particular, then lay
in research; but even this was mostly shared with other
Commonwealth West African countries, for example for
cocoa. There was little machinery and there were few staff
for development planning, although there were and had
been national and regional development plans, and the new
Ministry was to produce the 1962-68 plan. The Ministry's
Economic Planning Unit had only nine Nigerian economists,
who had little experience in this field, supported by three
expatriates. The Ministry was also overshadowed by the
powerful Federal Ministry of Finance, and to some degree
by the Central Bank; and even by the Economic Adviser
to the Prime Minister, then a distinguished Indian economist,
Dr Narayan Prasad.

There was, however, no shortage of work for the new
Minister (similar ministries were established in the Western
and Eastern Regions). He was responsible for co-ordinating
central planning and external economic relations; and he

dealt with the then significant matter of external "aid" to Nigeria. He was responsible, too, for the new Niger Delta Development Board, established to answer the complaint that both the Western and the Eastern Regions neglected the huge delta area, which spread into both regions, and whose swampy terrain and innumerable waterways made any economic development very difficult. The interest he then developed in the area, where he made long journeys by launch, Shehu Shagari has retained.

Examination of the possible use of the great River Niger to produce hydro-electricity was another responsibility of the new Ministry, which, at a time when Nigeria's vast reserves of oil and natural gas had not been finally proved, seemed particularly important. The Prime Minister had been to the United States, where he had visited the Tennessee Valley Authority (TVA). This US project attracted world-wide attention at the time, not only because of the scale of its hydro-electricity generation, but particularly because of the social and economic development TVA promoted in the areas affected by its operations.

There was already available in Lagos a detailed study, prepared by the Dutch consultants NEDECO, of the hydro-electric possibilities of the Niger River's course, particularly of a major dam at Kainji on the borders of what are now Nigeria's Kwara, Niger and Sokoto states. This was ultimately built at a cost of over $200m. to which many foreign countries and international bodies subscribed, and was commissioned in 1969, during the civil war. The dam, the first of many of various sizes which were to put Nigeria's rivers to work in the following decades, was intended not only to make hydro-electricity generation possible, but to control the seasonal flow of the river, to develop fisheries, to promote irrigation, and to improve navigation (this last aim has so far conspicuously failed). The Ministry was given responsibility for furthering this huge project, which would mean the resettlement of 100,000 people.

The River Niger, however, flows through two other francophone states after its rise in the Futa Jallon mountains of

Guinea, where a Fulani state had been established in about the tenth century. For these two countries, Niger and Mali, the river is a major highway, and for Niger a major source for irrigation. Any possible interference with its flow, even if to control it would benefit them, would require their consent.

So the new Minister for Economic Development, complete with his, still British, Permanent Secretary (Mr C. P. Thompson) and Ministry experts set off in February 1960 on a mission to reassure these two governments that the proposed dam would in no way injure their interests.

Nigeria was still a colony, although independence had been fixed for October 1 that year. Mali was still part of a collapsing federation with Senegal; but both Mali, as a separate country, and Niger were due to celebrate independence some weeks ahead of Nigeria. In Niger the young Minister found that he and the Niger Ministers needed no interpreters, as they could converse in Hausa, which few of their respective officials – on the one hand British and on the other French – understood. But at an official function he also discovered to his surprise that he was ranked below the local French army commander.

This last experience was instructive for Shehu Shagari, showing him how much less seriously the French took the near-independence of their colonies than did the British, who would have given precedence to a Minister. The visits were, however, successful, even though since the Kainji dam was commissioned there have been complaints from Niger that it affected the passage of fish and, less justifiably, from some people in Nigeria that Niger must have been responsible for the fall in the river's level which affected power generation at Kainji in the drought years of the early 70s.

Such as it was, federal Nigerian planning was governed at the time when the Ministry was established, by the 1955-1960 Development Programme, based on the 1955 report of the World Bank Mission to Nigeria. The programme has since been dismissed as a "random collection of projects", while the development programmes of the four governments of the Federation, none of which was fully executed, have been described as "competitive in character". The American

51

economist, Wolfgang Stolper, who was sent by the Ford Foundation to head the Economic Development Ministry's Economic Planning Unit in 1960-2, drew on his experience for his book *Planning without Facts.**

The 1955-60 plan period was, in fact, extended to 1962, to allow the new Ministry time to formulate, in consultation with the Regional Governments, what was the first National Development Plan for independent Nigeria, covering 1962-68. Under this, although it was still criticised by economists – and the 1966 military take-over and the subsequent secession of the Eastern Region prevented its completion – there were significant achievements, apart from the commissioning of the Kainji Dam and power station. The bridge over the Niger between Onitsha and Asaba was, for example, completed on the eve of the overthrow of civil rule, and the Port Harcourt oil refinery was opened.

These and many other projects were under discussion in other Ministries before the new Development Ministry took responsibility for them. Alhaji Shehu, however, was not left at the Ministry long enough to influence their planning. On Independence Day, October 1, 1960, the Prime Minister transferred him to the then Ministry of Pensions, whose functions were to be extended far beyond those it discharged before independence and which its name suggested, to make it virtually a Ministry for Nigerianisation. When told the name of his new Ministry Shehu Shagari remarked that it seemed to have an unsuitable title for a young man to take, nor did it reflect the task which the Prime Minister set him. So he was allowed to change the name to Ministry of Establishments and Training.

Ten years later he was to return to take charge of the Ministry of Economic Development, as a civilian Commissioner under the military regime of General Gowon. Then renamed Ministry of Economic Development, Rehabilitation and Reconstruction, it had been enormously expanded; but it was still suffering from shortage of experienced staff, although

*Harvard University Press, 1966.

supported by a bewildering variety of advisory bodies. For a second time he was left in that Ministry for too short a time before being transferred; this time, in 1971, to the Ministry of Finance – still in uneasy partnership with his former Ministry – for the four years which were to be the most important of his ministerial career.

Before independence, early in 1960, Shehu Shagari, still Minister of Economic Development, was a member of Nigeria's delegation to the Tangiers conference of the UN Economic Commission for Africa (ECA). He was left to lead the delegation because the flamboyant Minister of Finance, the late Chief Festus Okotie-Eboh, had to return to Nigeria. Day-to-day relations with ECA, whose headquarters were in Addis Ababa, were the responsibility of the Ministry of Economic Development. ECA, one of four such world-wide "area" commissions intended to assist the New York-based UN Economic and Social Council, had been dominated since its establishment in 1958 by the colonial powers. But although it has always remained a UN agency, receiving its funds from the UN and not the African governments, 1960 saw its membership transformed because of the independence of Nigeria and other colonies.

The Commission was already promoting a study of an "African Common Market" – a study which ultimately, after many set-backs, in 1975 played a part in establishment of the Economic Community of West African States, ECOWAS, in whose formation Nigeria played a leading role. Shehu Shagari saw such a body, even in 1960, as an instrument for furthering that economic co-operation among West African states which he has always considered essential if the weaker ones were to be freed from dependence on countries outside the continent, the stronger ones were to assist the weaker, and the artificial barriers to trade in the region raised by the colonial frontiers were to be overcome.

From this time on Alhaji Shehu was to lead or to be a member of countless Nigerian missions abroad. For example, at the end of 1961 he led the delegation to the tenth anniversary of Libya's independence. The King still ruled in Tripoli and nobody could have forecast that twenty years later Shehu Shagari, as President, would authorise the expulsion from Lagos of Colonel Gaddafi's men who had come to establish a "People's Bureau". Earlier he was at the GATT ministerial conference in Geneva, where he raised the issue of EEC discrimination against African countries like Nigeria which were not then, as the former French and Belgian colonies and Somalia were, "associated" with the EEC.

In 1962, as acting Minister of Economic Development in place of the substantive Minister, he was again to attend the ECA, leading Nigeria's delegation to the Commission's third meeting at Addis Ababa, the first which Nigeria attended as a full member. There he strongly urged price stabilisation arrangements for tropical products, contrasting the problems of tree crop producers who could not escape from their dependence on their crops, with those of industrial producers, who could change their products overnight. He was an early champion of the now fashionable, but still ineffective, "Commodity Agreements".

Then, too, he had his real initiation into international politics. For in Addis Ababa, apart from calling on the Emperor, he was approached by diplomats from the USSR, Poland and Czechoslovakia who wanted to open embassies in Lagos, where the government was then absurdly cautious, as it seems now, about opening diplomatic relations with communist countries. On the other hand, he found that French influence, which he had encountered in Niger, was now changing the earlier stand of nominally independent Niger and of Dahomey over the question of excluding the former colonial powers from ECA, an issue on which he felt strongly, since nearly all African countries were now independent.

An echo of Shehu Shagari's attitude on this issue was to be heard as far ahead as 1981. Then, as Nigeria's President, he virtually vetoed the association of non-African countries with the African Development Bank (ADB), which ECA had sponsored. Several of these countries were ready to contribute to ADB's capital; but their subscriptions would have given them a vote in the bank's proceedings. These subscriptions would have been very attractive to an institution whose African members were themselves seriously in default; but the President, whose own country had contributed far more to the ADB than her formal subscription, felt that this was a matter of serious principle. Africa must begin to rely on herself and not call on non-African money for what should be her own bank.

Shehu Shagari led the Nigerian delegation to the first session of the Economic and Social Commission of the newly-established Organisation of African Unity (OAU), held in Niamey at the end of 1963. But this was a disastrous, ill-prepared meeting which he prefers to forget.

As Minister of Establishments and Training, he led the Nigerian delegation to the 1961 London conference of the Commonwealth Parliamentary Association (CPA), an organisation to which he has given much service. Britain was at the time already negotiating her entry into the European Economic Community, the EEC. He strongly emphasised to the conference that if Britain was in the EEC she would be obliged, under the then "Yaoundé Convention" arrangements, to discriminate in tariff policy against products from Commonwealth African countries, notably cocoa, in favour of the former French, Belgian and Italian colonies which were already "associated" with the EEC. He proposed that Commonwealth countries should themselves establish regional "Common Markets".

The London *Daily Express*, devoted to what Lord Beaverbrook still insisted should be called the "Empire", particularly extolled his stand against the EEC, as did its sister *Evening Standard*, which carried a big photograph of Shehu Shagari – "an impressive figure" in his robes. Praise from such a quarter, and reference to an "Empire common market" may not have been entirely welcome to the young nationalist. He might, however, have agreed with the *Express* description of his view of the Commonwealth as "a family of nations linked more closely for the benefit of all members . . . with foreigners strictly on the outside". And, declared the *Express*, with a swipe at Sir Alec Douglas-Home, then Foreign Secretary, "many people will know whom they would prefer to speak for them at UNO.

"Mr. Shagari."

In fact, Nigeria herself soon began negotiations for a special arrangement with the EEC, which, but for the secession of the Eastern Region in 1967, might have come into force long before Britain's entry into the Community in 1973. France used the secession as a pretext for deferring her ratification of the agreement.

On his return to Nigeria from the CPA conference Shehu Shagari emphasised that the Commonwealth had important economic aspects. There were still Commonwealth preferences, and the sterling area remained significant (a significance which did not, in fact, long survive). He also declared, however, that Africa should be neutral in a future world war and should allow no foreign bases on her soil.

At a later CPA meeting Shehu Shagari ridiculed the idea that to prevent war you must be fully prepared for it. He asked the big powers to surrender their Security Council veto and to admit more non-aligned countries to the Council. "Blocs", he said, were the main obstacle to the success of the UN: a view he still strongly holds.

He was chairman of the next CPA conference, held in Lagos in October–November 1962. Previously he had attended a CPA General Council meeting at the House of Commons, and at the Lords. At this Lagos meeting the Minister of Justice of Ceylon insisted on "reading his palm" after congratulating him on his opening speech, and prophesied: "you will be Prime Minister one day". To ensure that his own Prime Minister, who had planned to be elsewhere, was present to open the Lagos meeting, Shehu Shagari arranged with the then Minister of Defence, Alhaji Muhammadu Ribadu, that there should be a "technical" delay to the Prime Minister's Nigerian Air Force flight, which enabled him to attend.

Dr Pius Okigbo, the distinguished Ibo economist who was Nigeria's envoy to the EEC, kept Shehu Shagari, now Minister of Internal Affairs, in touch with the Brussels negotiations between Britain and the EEC in November 1963. Dr. Okigbo always explained that Nigeria was in a different position from other Commonwealth African countries and was thus obliged herself to try to reach an accord with the EEC if Britain reached one. Shehu Shagari and Dr Okigbo both emphasised that "association", the relationship established between former French, Belgian and Italian colonies with the EEC under the "Yaoundé Convention", was unacceptable. A "free trade" area "outside Yaoundé" was the best arrangement for Nigeria, even if it had to be based on the agreement signed at Yaoundé, the Cameroon capital, between the EEC and the African "associates".

At his new Ministry of Establishments and Training, in spite of its apparently technical nature, Alhaji Shehu Shagari was faced with matters of the highest political significance. "Nigerianisation" of the public services was an issue which before 1960 often raised more political heat than the issue of independence itself. And independence, so far from settling it, served to emphasise the number of senior posts which the British (now called "expatriates", since in many non-administrative branches of the public services citizens from other countries, largely Asian, were serving and still serve) held in the services of the Federation and of the Northern Region, and to a lesser extent of the Western and Eastern Regions. For the Northern Region there was the additional problem that good people from there had to be persuaded to join the Federal services, the problem to which Shehu Shagari himself as a member, elected by the House of Representatives, of the Federal Scholarship Board, had drawn the Prime Minister's attention in the memorandum he addressed to him in 1957.

It was, however, the "administrative service" which attracted political attention – few Nigerians would claim that their country then, or even now, needs no expatriate staff for the medical and some other professional services, or for the education service. The administrative services, however, represented the "scaffolding" of colonial rule. And although this theory was abandoned as independence drew near, it was earlier widely held that the colonial system of "field administration" by Residents and various grades of District Officers (DO's), jacks-of-all-trades who supervised and tried to inspire government services of all kinds in their areas, and had responsibility for "law and order", would not be necessary after colonial rule ended. Their functions would be largely taken over by elected local authorities, and the authorities' leaders and officials – as now at last they have been in Nigeria. For many years after independence, however, the British system, which after all had close affinities with France's domestic "prefect" system, survived, over most of the country, but with Nigerian officers.

The "scaffolding" theory, the assumed antipathy of traditional rulers to the appointment of Nigerians as their "supervisors", and the likely reaction of politicians to the influence of senior administrators if they were Nigerians, reinforced the British reluctance to hasten the recruitment of Nigerians to the administrative services, and to supersede conventional methods of recruitment, promotion and training for this purpose.

Establishment of ministries with Nigerian ministers as political heads in 1952 both strengthened the administrative services, although still almost entirely British, and altered their nature. For although some administrative officers had always been needed in the purely colonial "secretariats", few stayed long away from "the field". The new ministries, however, had an insatiable appetite for administrators, and those in federal ministries, in particular, might now have no opportunity of field experience. It was the manning of the top jobs in the ministries by the British, above all the Permanent Secretaries – the civil service heads – which aroused the ire of politicians who might have seen the Residents and DOs in the field only as a colonial institution due to disappear. There was a special campaign against the Prime Minister's secretary, Peter Stallard, although nobody questioned his complete loyalty to Sir Abubakar.

Britain's failure to prepare for independence by ensuring that Nigerians, through timely recruitment to the administrative services, were available to man a high proportion of the senior jobs in the Ministries, had significant political consequences.

In 1958, in response to newspaper and Parliamentary pressure, the Nigerian House of Representatives appointed a backbench committee to consider Nigerianisation of the public services. In 1959, on the eve of independence, the committee reported. It may have been ill-informed, but it was scarcely revolutionary, led as it was by the Rev. T. T. Solaru, who was to become head of the Nigerian branch of Oxford University Press.

The Committee was concerned that when Nigeria became independent in the following year there would be 58 "super-scale" expatriates in the Federal Administrative Service, in the 73 posts, but only eight Nigerians – the other posts were vacant. They wanted the 58 expatriates replaced as a matter of urgency. In view of the introduction of generous "lump-sum" compensation, in addition to their pensions, for such expatriates if they retired early, the Committee could see no reason why they should not be quickly superseded by Nigerians. The Committee paid a handsome tribute to the British officials, but said that "so long as non-nationals control and direct the affairs of this country the people of Nigeria would not even be aware of the nature of the problems confronting them". The number of Nigerians in the civil service was not the point, since in total they obviously outnumbered expatriates heavily. It was the number in "control posts"; in these there were virtually no Nigerians. Nigerianisation should begin from the top down, said the Committee. In any case the British officials would soon take their compensation and their pensions and go, even if they were asked to stay and at present intended to stay.

The government – which meant the Nigerian ministers, including Alhaji Shehu Shagari himself – could see no practical way of Nigerianising these 58 super-scale posts at once; and conscious of the always loyal and usually efficient service they received from their British administrative staff, they may have been slower than the backbenchers to see the political importance of the issue. In answer to the Committee the ministers

listed all the government's careful plans for Nigerianisation –
granting of scholarships, in-service training, etc. But neither
then nor after independence were the Federal ministers prepared to lower qualifications for the administrative service to
accommodate Nigerians. Nigeria became independent in 1960
with almost all the top jobs in the federal administration still in
British hands.

In the offices of the Regional ministries matters were little
better. In the East, only the Chief Secretary, Chief Jerome
Udoji, and two Permanent Secretaries were Nigerian. In the
West, only the Head of the Treasury, Chief Simeon Adebo, the
Secretary to the Premier, and one Permanent Secretary were
Nigerians. In the North, although there the most zealous
efforts had been made since 1955 to Nigerianise the administrative service, which had depended most heavily on the
British, at independence only two Nigerians were among the
28 most senior administrative officers – and they were near the
bottom of the list.

Certainly the Colonial Office, and some senior British
administrators in Nigeria, always attached more importance to
"safeguarding" the interests of British administrative officers
than to building-up administrative services for an independent Nigeria. Perhaps it was thought that the British would
play indefinitely the role of the Brahmin Ministers of the old
Aryan kings; and a few British administrators did, indeed,
carry on in Nigeria's service after independence for a surprisingly long time. In the Northern Region there were still
over 30 British administrative officers in 1965, although some
had been seconded to Ahmadu Bello University and a number
had been recruited on short-term contract after independence.
It was, too, British officers who played a major role under the
direction of the then military rulers in setting up the six
new states into which the Region was divided in 1967. But, as
Mr Solaru's Committee had expected, the great majority of the
British in the administrative services stayed only a short time,
in spite of invitations to remain.

By the end of 1960 there were 41 "super-scale" expatriate
officers in the federal administrative service against 19

Nigerians. Fourteen British Permanent Secretaries left that service between independence and the end of March 1962, to be replaced by Nigerians. Five were left, of whom two were expected to leave soon. Relief at the voluntary departure of these officers was tempered by concern on the part of ministers at the lack of experience and training of their successors. And while gaps left by the departing British in technical branches of the service could in emergency be filled by overseas recruitment, politically that was out of the question for the administration.

The Nigerian successors in the administrative services, however, at once showed, and continued to show, remarkable competence and devotion. To them, more than to any other group of Nigerians – and particularly to those who had been brought in to the administrative services from outside government service or from other branches of government – was due the survival and relatively smooth operation of the government machines in face of political violence and insecurity, military coups, military indiscipline, civil war, and enormously increased government activities.

If Nigerianisation of the administration was the urgent political problem – solved more by force of events than by the government's careful planning – a special problem in Nigerianisation was presented by the police. Even as late as February 1, 1963, British officers still dominated the higher ranks. A pensionable European was acting Inspector-General, although a Nigerian, the late Louis Edet, was about to be given the substantive appointment. Four of the six Commissioners – the next rank – four of the six Deputy-Commissioners, and twelve of the seventeen Assistant-Commissioners, were British. Just over half the Senior Superintendents were expatriates and even seventeen of the forty Superintendents, although some of these were specialist officers on contracts.

Here again the departure of the British in the following years, however slow, left gaps which it was difficult to fill with local men, particularly as service in the police appealed to few highly-educated Nigerians. To meet this problem there had been entirely inadequate preparation before independence.

Even in the middle of 1966, however, there were still seven British Superintendents. It says much for the tolerance of Nigerians and for the officers themselves, that these officers found little difficulty in working either with the public or with their Nigerian colleagues. But their politically anomalous position was emphasised when, following the 1966 military take-over, the police for many months were at times the only force standing between Nigeria and anarchy; while in the 1962 Awolowo treason trial expatriate police officers had been key witnesses.

In an effort to speed up change a "Nigerianisation Office" was established in the Cabinet Office, with which Shehu Shagari's Ministry worked closely. Its first head was Francis Nwokedi, a former Labour Officer, who was to become prominent in Biafran affairs. He was succeeded by Michael Ani, who in turn was succeeded by Muhammed Bello. This latter official Shehu Shagari had early appointed as "Careers Officer" in his Ministry – an appointment intended, in part at least, to encourage northerners to enlist in the federal services.

Government jobs are at the centre of Nigerian politics. The apparent reluctance of the Northern Regional Government after independence to recruit from southern Nigeria, for example, and its preference for recruits from overseas over southern Nigerians, led to much rancour in the south. Defenders of the northern policy claimed that while foreigners on contract could always be displaced to make way for newly-qualified northerners, southern Nigerians would be difficult to remove for this purpose. They also pointed out to the continuing difficulty northerners found in claiming a fair share of places in the federal service.

The reluctance of many northerners to live in Lagos, however, as well as the relative educational backwardness of the Region, were also to blame. Shehu Shagari was much criticised in the southern region when he decided that, to attract suitable northerners to the federal service, some government houses in Lagos previously reserved for "expatriate" officials should be made available to northern Nigerians. Headlines in a

Lagos newspaper announced that "The Mallams are coming". Another claimed "Northerners invade the Federal Service".

There were only 750 people of Northern Region origin in federal service at the end of 1960 out of a total of some 40,000. Almost 800 northerners, however, transferred to the federal service in 1961, ten to the administrative grade.

The problem of speedily increasing the numbers of northerners in the federal service was shown, for example, by figures for the Geological Division of the Ministry of Mines and Power, which then operated mainly in the Northern Region. Twenty-one northerners were reading geology in universities in 1961; but none would be fully qualified for some years. And it was clear that Nigerian geologists in any case did not find the Ministry's terms attractive, and might prefer private employment.

It was not only relations between "North" and "South", however, which were affected by animosity over the filling of government jobs. In the tense period leading up to the 1964 federal election, for example, after Shehu Shagari had left the Ministry of Establishments and Training, Yoruba politicians, as a central element of their case against the NCNC, alleged that that party, being based in the Eastern Region, neglected no opportunity anywhere in the country of insinuating Ibos into government jobs. In each Region, too, there were complaints from "minorities" that the majority groups tried to exclude them from government employment. These complaints greatly strengthened the demand for the three big Regions to be divided into smaller "states". Yet as soon as these were established – twelve in 1967, increased to nineteen in 1976 – the same complaint was made in many states against those who now constituted new majority groups, by those who remained minorities.

In his speech to the House of Representatives during the 1961 budget session Shehu Shagari, while explaining the division of responsibilities between his Ministry and the Federal Public Service Commission, explained that 96% of the "General Executive class", then the most numerous class of senior officers, were now Nigerians. He emphasised, how-

63

ever, how great was Nigeria's need for outside assistance. He also explained why Nigeria could not accept the proposal that the UK Government should meet a significant part of the pay of British officials recruited for sovereign Nigeria. He explained, too, that his Ministry was producing "General Orders" appropriate for a truly indigenous service.

In May, 1962, Shehu Shagari went with a party of civil servants to study civil service training in India and in Pakistan. Earlier he had gone to Freetown with his permanent secretary, Chief Michael Ani, who was to become Federal Electoral Commissioner in 1978 and who had just taken over from an expatriate, to take a message from Sir Abubakar inviting Sierra Leone, soon to become independent, to take the same line as Nigeria on the British offer to find part of the pay of officials recruited in Britain for the independent governments. In return Nigeria would assist Sierra Leone to finance Fourah Bay College, West Africa's oldest institution of higher education, which had long attracted many Nigerian students. Shehu Shagari stayed with the ageless, remarkable and upright Sir Milton Margai, Sierra Leone's Prime Minister. A physician, he brought a dispassionate, clinical eye to all government activities. Sir Milton did not tell his anxious civil servants of the nature of the Nigerian Minister's mission, but he did bring two of his Ministers, Alhaji M. S. Mustapha and Dr John Karefa-Smart, into the discussion. Sierra Leone, however, accepted the British proposals; but Nigeria financed at Fourah Bay as an "independence gift" the Nigeria Hall of Residence.

With India and Pakistan arrangements were made for sending Nigerian administrative officers on courses. It was only to the Indian Staff College, however, that it was decided to send Nigerian army officers. Pakistan's President, Ayub Khan, protested; but Nigeria's tough Minister of Defence, Muhammadu Ribadu, replied that there had been no military coup in India.

Once more Shehu Shagari was not to be left in a Ministry long enough to see the results he had hoped for. The departure in 1962 of a senior NPC Minister, Alhaji Usman Sarki, who was at Internal Affairs, to succeed his father as Etsu Nupe, Emir of Bida, created a vacancy which the Prime Minister decided must be filled by Shehu Shagari. He was unenthusiastic about the move, particularly as Internal Affairs had acquired a reputation for corruption in its handling of certain matters, notably the immigration of Lebanese and other businessmen. But the Prime Minister insisted on the change.

The new Ministry's responsibilities were diffuse. They included, for example, regulation of money-lenders, immigration and citizenship matters, ex-servicemen's and Boy Scouts' affairs, fire services, prisons, film censorship, and the registration of marriages. The police, however, were the Prime Minister's affair, although there were still local police forces under local control in the Northern and Western Regions which the federal government tried to persuade those regional governments should come under federal control.

Politically the most significant responsibility of the Ministry of Internal Affairs was the conduct, through the Federal Electoral Commission, of federal elections (the first to be held in independent Nigeria was due not later than January 1965). The Ministry's decisions about the exclusion of certain British defence counsel, including Sir Dingle Foot, in the Awolowo and Enahoro "treason trials" in 1962 and 1963 became a major political issue (ironically, as Nigeria was still a "monarchy", the accused were charged with an intention to levy war "against our sovereign lady, the Queen").

During his three years at Internal Affairs, and later as Minister of Works, Alhaji Shehu was also to lead a number of Nigerian delegations abroad; he represented Nigeria at Sir Winston Churchill's funeral. In 1963, too, the Sultan honoured him by making him Turakin Sokoto, an honorary title, like Tafida and other such titles, indicating that the holder is regarded as a man of rank, coming from an eligible family, and a member of the Sultan's Council.

An opportunity to study another country's "Ministry of the Interior" – but an establishment very different from his own Ministry – came in 1962. President Nasser had offered Nigeria's Prime Minister the opportunity of inspecting Egypt's security arrangements. Sir Abubakar sent his Minister of Internal Affairs and a Senior Assistant Secretary, Malam

Mohammed, a Northern Christian, for a preliminary inspection. It is doubtful if the young Minister learned much about security, although Egypt's Ministry of the Interior was actually situated in the National Security Headquarters. But, as he always has on official visits abroad, he did some sightseeing, going to Alexandria and the Aswan Dam.

On this occasion, however, the sightseeing was not of his choosing. His hosts suddenly and surprisingly became reluctant to interest him in their security arrangements, and were anxious that he should, instead, study tourist attractions. Egypt's then Ambassador in Lagos, a former security adviser, was on leave in Egypt and appeared not to have known about the invitation to the Nigerians to study security in Cairo. When he learned of Shehu Shagari's mission he at once told his government that it was imprudent to reveal any secrets to a Nigerian, even a devout Muslim; for Nigeria enjoyed diplomatic relations with Israel and the Minister of Internal Affairs was a member of the Cabinet which had agreed to establish relations with Israel.

It was, incidentally, the Federal Government's recognition of Israel which caused one of the many rifts between the NPC Ministers in Lagos and their party leader, the Sardauna of Sokoto. It was one of those matters which led the Northern Premier and his lieutenants to refer to their NPC colleagues in the Federal Government as "Dan Carter Bridge" – people who had passed over the bridge into Lagos and might then forget the Northern Region's supposed interests.

Shehu Shagari also visited the Aswan military airport. There he saw an aircraft crash. He later expressed his sympathy to the appropriate Minister; but when no word of the crash appeared in Egyptian newspapers he realised, for the first time, the nature of a controlled press.

In 1963 Shehu Shagari was Nigeria's delegate to the CPA conference in Kuala Lumpur. Then, in December, 1965, less than three weeks after Ian Smith's "Unilateral Declaration of Independence" (UDI), came the CPA conference in Wellington, New Zealand. There, on December 1, Shehu Shagari opened the conference discussions. Previously international matters had been discussed at the closing session. This time it was agreed that the conference should grapple with the subject of Rhodesia at the start, and that an African should lead the discussion.

Shehu Shagari's denunciation of the Wilson Government's craven inertia in face of the Smith rebellion was probably the most caustic speech ever heard at any CPA conference since they were first held in 1911. It asserted the case Nigeria was to urge right up to the Zimbabwe settlement, and foreshadowed the dissension which for years was to undermine relations between Nigeria and Britain. It was a fortunate chance that by the time Shehu Shagari became President, in 1979, the Zimbabwe settlement was in sight.

The central point of his Wellington speech was that in her long colonial history Britain had never renounced the use of force, either to uphold the principles of democracy and the rule of law, or to suppress treason. The British once "executed their own king in defence of democracy". Now in "striking contrast to their mistake in handling the Suez crisis, when the British used force in an attempt to keep what was not their own, they have dramatically swerved and refused to use force in order to keep what is legally their own". Did this mean that Britain would now hesitate to fight for the ideals for which Nigeria had fought beside the British in two world wars? Rebellion under British law was treason "punishable not by sanctions, Mr. Chairman, but by death". Yet Britain now promised four million Rhodesian Africans only that "economic sanctions will be used effectively to starve them, after which the rebels will be forced to come to terms". What an extraordinary way to deal with a rebellion!

Of course, Alhaji Shehu continued, he understood the "kith and kin" argument, which maintained that British soldiers could not be expected to fight their brothers by blood. But Britain had never hesitated to use African troops to fight Africans – or to fight Europeans or Japanese. Those Africans fought "because they believed in the cause for which they fought".

Unrelieved denunciation is not Shehu Shagari's way. He

spoke of the admiration Britain had earned by her timely acceptance of the claims for independence elsewhere. In a reference to the white settlers he spoke of admiration for those "with a spirit of adventure" – so long as they did not deny their rights to a country's original inhabitants. He acknowledged that the British had made genuine efforts to "dissuade Smith from his mad venture". But the rebels "defied the Crown with impunity". "What else can anyone expect from armed bandits who are determined to rob and suppress others by force when they are armed, that their armed rebellion would not be met with force but only with verbiage?" He ended the speech with a Shakespearian quotation:

> There is a tide in the affairs of men,
> which, taken at the flood leads on to fortune ...

Shehu Shagari was deeply interested to find that New Zealand, an agricultural country, was very prosperous. After the Wellington conference he went on his own to Australia, where he spent three days in Sydney incognito, his first "unchaperoned" visit abroad. He returned home, paying his own fares, via the Philippines, Hong Kong (where he spent three days), Tokyo, where he spent a very short time, Seattle and New York.

CPA conferences are intended for discussions not decisions. Did the British representatives at Wellington report Shehu Shagari's expression of Nigeria's views to Harold Wilson? Certainly Nigeria made it so plain to Britain's Prime Minister that she was concerned about his handling of the Rhodesia affair that he agreed that a Commonwealth Prime Minister's Conference should be held in Lagos in 1966. Rhodesia was to be the real subject; and for the conference Shehu Shagari was in Sir Abubakar's delegation.

Unhappily Harold Wilson had scarcely left Lagos after the conference to go to Lusaka for further discussion with President Kaunda, before Nigeria's civilian government was overthrown. Sir Harold, it was said, was furious that he had nearly been caught up in this event. The news, however, that Sir Abubakar had been murdered caused Wilson to forget his own

indignation and to mourn for a great Commonwealth statesman.

An issue in which Shehu Shagari found himself at odds
with his party leader in Kaduna arose when he was at Internal Affairs. Regulation of "pools" betting was one of the
Ministry's responsibilities. Nigerians have long been devotees
of this type of betting, based on English and Australian soccer
results (they are very keen on their own soccer, too). But at this
time the Northern Regional Government alone banned the
operation of pools firms in its Region, on religious grounds,
supported by Islamic leaders such as the Grand Khadi of
Northern Nigeria. Shehu Shagari was no less devout a Muslim
than any northern minister, and has never bet in his life. But
the Federal Government had a stake in the firm Nigerpools,
and he could not agree that in this matter there could be
different laws in different Regions. Apart from anything else,
he argued, the Northern Regional Government could not prevent people in the Region from clandestine pools betting; and
in a country with as long an Islamic tradition as Egypt not only
pools betting but casinos, he knew, were permitted. This was a
battle he won by quiet persistence; northerners were allowed
to lay their bets on far-away soccer teams.

It was the 1964 federal election which provided the greatest
test Sir Abubakar Tafawa Balewa's government had faced
since independence. The campaign for the election, held
on December 30, was long, bitter and sometimes violent.
It was a contest between the Nigerian National Alliance
(NNA) and the United Progressive Grand Alliance (UPGA).
The first alliance was dominated by the Northern People's
Congress (NPC), which now had a majority in the House of
Representatives because of by-elections and creation of new
constituencies. But NNA included the party which then
held precarious power in the Western Region, the Nigerian
National Democratic Party (NNDP), led by Chief S.L. Akin-
tola, as well as minor southern groups heavily dependent
on NPC funds. Although NCNC Ministers still served in Sir
Abubakar's Cabinet, as they had since 1959, their party, under
Dr Michael Okpara, Premier of the Eastern Region, now led

the fight in the country against the NPC and its allies, and was the main force in UPGA.

Prominent in the UGPA alliance, however, was that section of the Action Group which remained loyal to Chief Awolowo, who had been sentenced to ten years' imprisonment in 1963 for alleged treasonable felony (the Action Group had split in 1962, Chief Akintola taking one faction, which was to become NNDP, out of the party). UPGA included, too, the Northern Progressive Front (NPF), which brought together the NEPU of Malam Aminu Kano (who had been a member of the House of Representatives since 1959 and was already a vice-president of the NCNC), and the United Middle Belt Congress (UMBC), led by the late J. S. Tarka, which wanted to create a new "state" out of the non-Muslim areas of the Northern Region.

The two alliances issued detailed election manifestoes. In these NNA stressed the importance of stability and national unity, while UPGA claimed that, in ways unspecified, it would reform Nigerian society. The real issue in the election, however, the first federal election to be held without British supervision, was whether the NPC was to continue, with or without partners, to be Nigeria's ruling party. This was the time when the NCNC, in spite of the presence in the Federal Cabinet of Ministers belonging to the party, was speaking vociferously of the menace of "feudalism" in the emirates and of "northern domination" of the Federation. For his part the NPC leader, the Sardauna of Sokoto, felt obliged to declare that "the Ibos have never been true friends of the North and never will be ..." An official Eastern Region newspaper spoke of "cattle-rearing legislators" from the North; the government-owned *Nigerian Citizen* in the Northern Region spoke of "half-naked fellows in the East" – these are among the less insulting gibes made at the time.

Dr Okpara's genuine antipathy towards the NPC was strengthened by his belief that in the November 1963 census, on which voters' rolls and constituencies were based, the population of the Northern Region had been deliberately "inflated" to ensure that well over half Nigeria's population was attributed to the Region. Thus, so long as the NPC, by

Sir James Robertson, Governor-General, with Sir Abubakar Tafawa Balewa, photographed at Government House, Lagos with Princess Alexandra, who represented the Queen at the Independence celebrations in October 1960. Alhaji Shehu is second from the right in the back row.

Shehu Shagari as Federal Minister of Establishments with the Nigerian Prime Minister Tafawa Balewa, in the Capitol, Washington D.C., with Vice President Lyndon B. Johnson in July 1961.

whatever means, continued to dominate the Region politically, it could dominate the Federation too, through control of the House of Representatives.

In fact, if there was inflation of the census figures in the Northern Region, inflation was even more prominent in the Western Region, and was also marked in parts of the Eastern Region. But for Dr Okpara and those who felt like him it was the prospect, which the census figures gave, of permanent hegemony over Nigeria by the NPC which seemed intolerable.

In the end UPGA decided to boycott the elections, a decision implemented almost completely in the Eastern Region, where little voting took place; but elsewhere it meant only strengthening the position of UPGA's opponents.

Although Minister of Internal Affairs, Shehu Shagari was not directly concerned with the problems of law and order during the election campaign. His chief worry was the inability of the Government Printer to print preliminary voters lists, and then final lists after errors had been rectified, in time; for this he took personal responsibility, although the Federal Electoral Commission was in charge of voting arrangements. The election date was for this reason postponed five times; finally printing machines, and printers, had to be flown from Britain.

Immersed in the problems of electoral administration, Shehu Shagari did little campaigning in his own constituency, and at times was the only Federal NPC Minister in Lagos. In the case of his constituency that scarcely mattered, as this time he was unopposed – one of the 64 NPC MPs to be thus elected in the Northern Region's 167 seats. There were UPGA allegations that some unopposed returns – in other Regions as well as in the North – were secured through malpractices and intimidation. Yet the late Professor John D. Mackintosh, in his authoritative *Nigerian Government and Politics,** wrote that the final results in these Northern Regional seats would not "have been significantly affected" by the intimidation. For, he explained, opposition to the NPC in the Region had been

---

*Allen and Unwin, 1966

weakening since 1959, as had already been shown in the 1961 election to the Region's House of Assembly, when the opposition contracted from 33 to 10. In the end only four seats, two in Tiv constituencies, were won in the Region by the NPC's opponents.

The UPGA leaders in the early stages of the election campaign were genuinely convinced that the northern "masses" were awaiting "liberation" from "feudalism" and would see southern politicians as their liberators. But, as Professor Mackintosh put it, this illustrated "the simple failure of Southern leaders to study or understand the North". This failure was exemplified most strongly by the apparent belief of some southern leaders that the mere appearance of non-Hausa-speaking southern Ministers in large cars could, in Sokoto for example, influence the voting. The voters, instead, were just puzzled; "who", they asked after the cars had gone, "were they?"

Genuine and strong opposition to the NPC in the Northern Region, however, was still evident in some NEPU "pockets" and in Kano; and particularly among the Tiv people of the south-east of the Region. Ironically in the election fifteen years later which was to win him the Presidency, the Tiv and their leader, the late J. S. Tarka, who was arrested for "incitement" just before the 1964 election, were to be among Shehu Shagari's keenest supporters; while NEPU, on the other hand, was to beat him in two northern states.

As a result of the UPGA boycott only 253 of the 312 seats in the House of Representatives were declared filled. Of these the NPC had 162, its NNDP ally – profiting from the boycott in the Western Region – 36, and UPGA supporters and independents, 55. The NPC thus had a majority on its own of the "declared" seats and with the NNDP a majority of all seats in the House. Sir Abubakar and the NPC naturally expected that Dr Azikiwe (who in 1963 had automatically been transformed from Governor-General to "ceremonial" President when Nigeria became a Republic), in spite of the misgivings he had expressed about the conduct of the election, would re-appoint the Prime Minister and invite him to form a government. There followed, however, an episode which, according to one's point of view, was either a victory for constitutionalism and the Nigerian elite's talent for political conciliation, or a demonstration of the frailty of constitutional conventions in Nigeria.

Apart from his own natural inclination, President Azikiwe was convinced by UPGA leaders and lawyers both that, as Head of State and Commander-in-Chief, he could issue operational orders to the police and armed forces, and that because the election had been incomplete, and, in his view, unreliable, he could appoint anybody he chose as interim Prime Minister. His appointee could then hold a fresh election and perhaps arrange a new census.

Senior lawyers, including the Chief Justice of the Eastern Region, supported the Prime Minister's argument that he had never vacated his office, that the remedy for any irregularities in the election's conduct lay in the courts, and that operational control of the police and the armed forces was vested in the Prime Minister by the constitution. In the end, resisting the political pressure placed on him, Dr Azikiwe agreed to a peace formula suggested by the Federal Chief Justice and the Chief Justice of the Eastern Region – although the Prime Minister was unable to accept all its points.

In these complicated negotiations Shehu Shagari played an important role "in the middle", informing the absent Prime Minister of the President's apparent intentions, and keeping in touch with the Chief Justice. With the Sardauna he communicated in code, and also in Nupe, the language of the people of Bida emirate.

Because a statement by his doctor, asserting that the President was in excellent health, was issued to newspapers at 1 a.m. on the morning of January 4, 1965, it was widely believed at the time that Dr Azikiwe had got wind of a rumour that the NPC Ministers intended to remove him from State House to a Nigerian naval vessel, which would take him outside the three-mile limit. This would allow the Government to declare that the President was unable to carry out his functions, which could then be performed by the Chief Justice.

Whatever the truth of this melodramatic suggestion, it seems certain that the NNA leaders, including the Sardauna and Chief Akintola, had decided that the deadlock could not be allowed to continue, particularly as militant trade unionists and the mass of Lagos people would back the President. Dr Azikiwe too, was inevitably showing signs of strain.

The peace formula, as finally agreed, pledged all concerned to respect the constitution and the Federation's unity. It promised that new elections would be held in constituencies where the courts decided that conduct of the election had been seriously irregular; and that voting could take place in those constituencies in the Eastern Region where there had been a complete boycott. It also promised a "broad-based national government" based on "the results of the last election". The President duly re-appointed Sir Abubakar as Prime Minister.

UPGA leaders had expected to gain more than this. In the end, however, the "broad-based" government consisted of all NPC members of the former Cabinet, including Shehu Shagari, some pro-NPC independents, and NCNC members of the previous Cabinet (who indicated that they saw no reason to abandon their agreeable appointments because of what they saw as a temporary disagreement between their party and the NPC). There were also two NNDP men, of whom one was Chief Adisa Akinloye, who was to become chairman of President Shehu Shagari's party, the NPN.

Dr Okpara, now denying that he had ever threatened to secede, was left in unchallenged control of his own Eastern Region Government; and the NCNC also remained in charge of the government of the new Mid-West Region, which had been created out of the Western Region in 1963. Dr Azikiwe remained in State House.

Thus ended, without any actual infringement of the constitution, and with apparent civility, a crisis which, in view of later events, now seems like a mere politicians' squabble. But it was to be followed within ten months by elections in the Western Region. In these violence and malpractices were prevalent; and after them the Region experienced widespread disorder. A diarist in the weekly *West Africa*, commenting on the news conference given by Alhaji Adegbenro, acting leader of the defeated Action Group, held in the imprisoned Chief Awolowo's house during a power cut, wrote; "I had an uneasy and perhaps unwarranted premonition that here, among all Chief Awolowo's legal books, by flickering candle-light, was being enacted the funeral rites of the Westminster model as a practical proposition in African politics".

Within two months the army was to end civilian rule, which would not be restored for thirteen and a half years, and then with Alhaji Shehu as President.

Because of the NCNC's election boycott there was a temporary vacancy at the Federal Ministry of Communications, which was, for three months, added to Shehu Shagari's responsibilities. He found a curious problem waiting at the Ministry. It seemed that Hamani Diori, President of Nigeria's northern neighbour, Niger, had made an informal agreement with the Sardauna of Sokoto that Niamey, his capital, should be linked by telephone with Sokoto. The Sardauna, as a Regional Premier, had no authority to enter into such an agreement. The former NCNC Minister of Communications had been embarrassed by it and had been ordered by his party leader to suspend work on the project. The Prime Minister also told Shehu Shagari that the Northern Premier had in this exceeded his authority. Hamani Diori had complained that he had kept his side of the bargain. During his brief tenancy of the Ministry Shehu Shagari tried to complete the Nigerian side of the agreement, but without success.

Even now Shehu Shagari had not completed his federal ministerial experience. (He had acted briefly as Minister of Health, in the absence of the Minister, Dr Ade Majekodunmi.) In May 1965 he took over the Ministry of Works from Alhaji Inuwa Wada, another NPC Minister, who went to Defence to succeed Alhaji Muhammadu Ribadu, the Minister who was said to be closer to the Sardauna than the Prime Minister himself, and who had died. Works was the biggest spender among Federal Ministries; but, as is still the case, it was short of experienced engineers to prepare and supervise contracts. Inevitably it was a prime target for accusations of corruption.

This was a Ministry, however, which enabled, and obliged, the Minister to travel widely throughout the Federation, particularly to inspect work on federal trunk roads. So his time at the Ministry, short as it was, allowed Shehu Shagari to see more of Nigeria by road travel than he was to see until his 1979 Presidential campaign. His own party, however, insisted that too much was being spent in Lagos, not enough in the regions.

The two biggest jobs exercising the senior officials of the Ministry at the time were the Eko bridge, a new link, desperately needed, for Lagos Island to the mainland, for which Shehu Shagari signed the contract with the German firm Julius Berger, and the Niger bridge, linking the west and the east of Nigeria from Onitsha to Asaba, the first road bridge across the great river. It fell to the Prime Minister to open this bridge on January 4, 1966, his last public appointment outside Lagos.

Symbolically, less than two weeks before the military take-over which was later to lead to the secession of his Eastern Region and to civil war, Dr Okpara, the Eastern Premier, refused to attend the ceremony, which was intended to signify the closer links now made possible between his Region and the rest of Nigeria. The great bridge itself was one of the first casualties of the civil war.

5

RETURN TO SOKOTO

On the morning of January 15, 1966, Shehu Shagari rose at 4 a.m. It was Ramadan, the time when Muslims fast in daylight hours. He was in his detached ministerial house, 19 Kingsway, near the hotel and the golf-course in spacious Ikoyi, which the British had laid out as a pleasant, green residential suburb across the water from crowded Lagos Island, and which was now a favoured place of residence for Nigeria's public men. As he took his breakfast before dawn Shehu Shagari heard what sounded like shots. He thought nothing of it; whatever might be happening in the sprawling slums on the way to Lagos airport, or in the Western Region beyond, open violence was still unthinkable in decorous Ikoyi. He returned briefly to bed.

Later he was to learn that Brigadier Maimalari, a Borno man, who in 1950 was one of the first two Nigerians to pass out of Sandhurst, and was now, after rapid promotion, one of the most senior army officers, had left his house on the other side of Kingsway after receiving a telephone warning in the early morning that mutinous soldiers were on their way to abduct him. The Brigadier was hurrying on foot across the Ikoyi golf-course, beside the road leading to his objective, the army's Dodan Barracks, when he recognised moving on the road the car of Major Ifeajuna, another Sandhurst man, who was his own Brigade Major at the Lagos-based 2 Brigade which he commanded. The car stopped and the Major, who had been allotted the task of abducting Maimalari by the seven officers who had planned a military coup, left the vehicle, with

another officer, and then calmly shot and killed his Brigadier –
the shots which Shehu Shagari heard. Ifeajuna, who was one
of the principal plot leaders (he was, incidentally, the first
Commonwealth athlete to clear 6 ft. 9 inches in the high jump)
went on to the Ikoyi Hotel. There he killed another Borno
officer, Lt-Col. Largema, who was staying in Lagos during
a visit from his Ibadan-based battalion – he had come down
from Kaduna where he was said to have attended a meeting
with the Northern and Western Premiers to discuss the
restoration of order in the Western Region by the army. He
was shot, wearing his pyjamas, at the door of his hotel bed-
room. Later Ifeajuna was to murder the Prime Minister, whose
kidnapping, together with that of the Minister of Finance,
Chief Festus Okotie-Eboh, he had led before his encounter
with his Brigadier – the Prime Minister may even have been in
his car.

Before dawn Alhaji Ahmed Kurfi, then deputy Permanent
Secretary in the Ministry of Defence, came to Shehu Shagari's
house with the news that the Prime Minister, with the Finance
Minister, who came from coastal Warri, had been abducted.
Army lorries could now be heard moving around Ikoyi; and as
dawn came the young Minister could see them and their
armed occupants – but since the coup had already failed
in Lagos these could have been troops loyal to the Federal
Government. Shehu Shagari's telephone was not working –
then, as now, there was nothing unusual about that. So
he walked to the neighbouring house of Chief Adeniran
Ogunsanya, a Lagos Yoruba lawyer, member of the NCNC
and Minister for Housing and Surveys in Sir Abubakar's
Cabinet. Ogunsanya was asleep; awakened, he was stunned
by the news of the military plot, which startled him no less
than it had his NPC colleague.

Shehu Shagari then went to the house of his old friend, Sir
Abubakar's Minister of Transport, Zanna Bukar Dipcharima,
in nearby Bourdillon Road, to awaken him with the warning
that the soldiers had mutinied. The next visitor to Dipcharima's house, Shehu Shagari recalls, was Dorothy Schwarz,
wife of the British journalist Walter Schwarz. The Schwarzs'

were then stationed in Lagos (his standard book on Nigeria, which included an account of these events, was published in 1968) and Dorothy used to ride one of Zanna Bukar's horses each morning – the Borno people remain the most enthusiastic horsemen in Nigeria. Like most people in the middle-class areas of Lagos she had heard nothing of the night's grim events. Zanna Bukar, still perhaps not realising how fateful these events were for all those then in power in Nigeria, told a servant to bring Mrs Schwarz a horse as usual.

At 9 a.m. that day news came to Lagos of the murder in the early hours of the morning in his house in Kaduna of the Northern Premier, the Sardauna of Sokoto, who had returned only a few days earlier from Mecca. With him were killed the two most senior army officers stationed in Kaduna, both Yorubas. The murders were the work of Kaduna-based troops commanded by Major Chukwuma Nzeogwu, another Sandhurst-trained Ibo officer, who was the leader of the seven majors. News came, too, of the murder in Ibadan by soldiers led by Captain Nwobosi of Chief Akintola, Premier of the Western Region.

For a couple of days Nzeogwu exercised control over most of the Northern Region, but elsewhere General Aguiyi-Ironsi, the first Nigerian to become General-Officer Commanding the army, and who was reported to be one of the mutineers' intended victims, regained control. Nzeogwu was finally persuaded to surrender on January 17, on terms which were not honoured.

January 15 and 16 saw a confused series of ministerial meetings. All Federal Ministers were in Lagos, but Dr Azikiwe, the President, was abroad on holiday, staying in the Burford Bridge Hotel in Sussex, and was entirely out of the picture. Acting for him was another veteran Ibo former NCNC politician, Dr Nwafor Orizu, whose indecisiveness was an important factor in the final breakdown of civilian rule. Some Ministers lived on Victoria Island, the expensive new residential area then being developed across the lagoon from Ikoyi. In party groups or all together the Ministers met in various houses in Ikoyi or on Victoria Island, sometimes that of

Dr Orizu. Leaderless because of the disappearance of the Prime Minister and the reluctance of Dr Orizu to appoint anybody to act in his place. NPC Ministers wanted Zanna Bukar Dipcharima to be appointed. He was a very senior politician, some seven years older than Shehu Shagari, and he was now the senior Cabinet Minister. The final fates of Sir Abubakar and of Chief Festus remained unknown.

The US Ambassador, Mr Joseph Palmer, had asked Zanna Bukar if there was anything the Americans could do to help. The British, however, without whose co-operation the Nigerians felt no US help could be accepted, said that they could act only in response to a written request from the Prime Minister or from a properly appointed deputy – NPC Ministers urged Zanna Bukar to tell the British that he *was* de facto such a deputy. The police had also, in the early morning of January 15, appealed to the British High Commission to transmit a request for help to London; but nothing came of this. Dr Orizu, it was said, invited the NCNC Federal Ministers to a meeting at his house in Inner Crescent, Ikoyi; but Gen. Aguiyi-Ironsi also came to the meeting with a heavily armed escort, who sat silently in the sitting room where the meeting took place. There was some communication with the NPC Ministers, but Orizu, it was claimed, hoped to be able to appoint an NCNC Minister as acting Prime Minister. On that Saturday too, Parliament – 33 members out of 312 attending, with one Minister, who had been appointed only the previous day – adjourned itself.

In the end Ministers were summoned on the evening of March 16 to the Cabinet Office, the GOC later promising escorts to absentees who wanted them. The General told them that he needed authority to suppress what was in fact a widespread mutiny, not an attempted "coup". The Ministers, including Shehu Shagari, agreed that he should be given this authority. But Aguiyi-Ironsi said that although he himself was unwilling to take over the government completely, there were those in the armed forces who insisted that he should, and that civilian authority should be suspended completely.

It is by no means clear that the powers the General

demanded were essential for the task in front of him. It was clear to the Ministers, however, that drastic measures were essential, since it was only in Lagos that the Federal Government now seemed to retain clear control.

One Minister at the meeting, said to be Alhaji Waziri Ibrahim, moved that the government should be temporarily handed over to the General – but only for the suppression of the mutiny. It transpired, however, that at this hastily-summoned meeting there was no stationery to record any decision; one of the Ministers, Alhaji Abdul Razaq, found a suitable piece of waste paper on which to write the minutes (the "sense of the meeting"), which the Ministers signed. The communiqué issued later meant the end of their offices, although nothing in the constitution authorised such a hand-over of power to military authorities.

The General then advised all the now "ex-Ministers" to stay in their houses, and promised them protection. The rest of the story has been narrated so often that here we recount only the events which directly affected Shehu Shagari. Nor is it now possible, or fruitful, to examine the question whether the General, whose mother was Ibo but whose father was Sierra-Leonean, played a double game. It has been alleged that he was privy to the plot, but took over in place of the plotters. Those who knew the jovial General, including this writer, find this impossible to believe, and the plotters themselves have given no credence to the idea.

On March 16, the President recalls, he met the late Dan Ibekwe, then a Minister in the Ministry of External Affairs, a young and talented Ibo lawyer, who expressed his sympathy over the death of the Sardauna and the presumed fate of Sir Abubakar since he knew Shehu Shagari had had close relations with both leaders. Showing great prescience, how-ever, since he feared that there might be northern "revenge", Mr Ibekwe, always a Federal man (he had, as Solicitor-General in the Eastern Region, advised Dr Azikiwe during the 1964 elections that the Prime Minister's case was a sound one), emphasised to Shehu Shagari that the attempted coup, from which they were now escaping, was the work of irresponsible

young men and was in no way an "Ibo plot". Even Major
Nzeogwu, its leader, had been born in the north and was
unknown in the Eastern Region. In fact, among the fourteen
officers later accused by the Federal Government of leading
the mutiny, all were, except for two Yorubas, Ibos. But in view
of the composition of the officer corps at this time and the
general political situation, this did not necessarily mean that
the attempted coup was an Ibo plot.*

Shehu Shagari assured Ibekwe that people like himself
believed in fate rather than in blaming individuals. But he
also told him that the Inspector-General of Police had now
privately confirmed that the Prime Minister was dead – the
official announcement was not made until January 22. At this
news Ibekwe wept, as had Dr Kingsley Mbadiwe, an Ibo
Cabinet Minister, when told of the tragedy.

Fearful, as all politicians were then, for the safety of his
family, Shehu Shagari arranged with the chairman of Nigerpools – we have recorded his responsibility for the pools
business as a Minister – to send his senior wife and three of his
children in the company's own aircraft to Sokoto. During the
four troubled days in Lagos he learned that Zanna Bukar was
planning to go back to Borno for Sallah, the coming end of
Ramadan, in an aircraft belonging to the Customs and Excise
Department, with another senior northerner, Alhaji Sule
Katagum, Chairman of the Public Service Commission. Shehu
Shagari tried to dissuade his friend from leaving Lagos, telling
him that, even if now relieved of their duties, ex-Ministers
must not appear to be running away. The best course would be
to ask Gen. Aguiyi-Ironsi, now Head of State, for leave for all
northern Muslim ex-Ministers to return home for Sallah.

This leave was not at first readily given by Gen. Aguiyi-
Ironsi; Shehu Shagari, however, telephoned the General's
secretary on the matter, only to be told that they could all go.

The President recalls today that at the Cabinet meeting
when the General told the Ministers that he must have complete power if he was to restore order, he had wept when

---

*The Nigerian Army, by N. J. Miners (Methuen, 1971).

speaking of the murders of his brother-officers. Shehu Shagari
does not support the view that the attempted take-over of
power by the young majors – and it must be emphasised that
they themselves failed to win power and were later detained,
even if their attempt led to military rule – was an "Ibo plot". He
is, however, highly critical of the measures later taken by
Aguiyi-Ironsi. These were intended to centralise administration and authority in Lagos, which antagonised those vast
areas of the Northern Region scarred by the murder of Sir
Abubakar, the Sardauna, and those northern army officers
whose high rank, for many northerners, including their own
soldiers, represented a great northern achievement.

Shehu Shagari drove to Ikeja Airport from Lagos to join
Zanna Bukar's aircraft, in a Customs Department Landrover,
with a uniformed Customs man. This was the first time he had
left central Lagos since January 15. The little Customs aircraft –
the same one in which Zanna Bukar was later to meet his death
in an accident – flew his passengers over Kaduna, the Nigerian
air force's main base. There the pilot was ordered to leave the
airspace, so he flew on to Kano. This city was still in effect
under the control of the commander of the local battalion,
the 5th, commanded by the then Lt.-Col. Ojukwu, who had
already been named as Military Governor of the Eastern
Region by Gen. Aguiyi-Ironsi. He had confined all troops
to barracks, and Kano International Airport was ghostly.
Shehu Shagari was able to telephone his friend Alhaji Aminu
Dantatta, the wealthy Kano merchant, and to ask him to send
two cars to the airport – one to go to Sokoto, the other to Borno.

Before the cars arrived at the airport Zanna Bukar took
Shehu Shagari aside to tell him that he found himself short
of money, and to ask whether it might be possible to borrow
from NPC party funds, thought to be held by Alhaji Aliyu,
Makaman Bida, Minister of Education in the Northern Region,
since the soldiers, in Zanna Bukar's view, would ultimately
confiscate all party funds – the military authorities had, in fact,
started to do this. Shehu Shagari rejected this course and himself advanced some money to the embarrassed ex-Minister.

His 350-mile journey to his house in Sokoto was uninter-

rupted, although the Dantatta car had, after leaving the airport, to go through the Kano army barracks while Shehu
Shagari hid himself behind a newspaper. In Sokoto there were
no troops, so the city was saved the uncertainties – and often
the harrassment – suffered then by citizens in a few centres
where the small Nigerian army was quartered. But it was a sad
and shocked city, whose great son, the Sardauna, had been
murdered with little prospect that his murderers – although
now they were in army custody – would pay the full penalty
for their crime. Shehu Shagari was embarrassed to find that he
was expected by everybody, including the Sultan, to have
more up-to-date information about national events than he
was in a position to give. In Shagari itself he found only
bewilderment.

In due course he and other NPC leaders were summoned to
Kaduna, capital of the Northern Region, by the new Military
Governor, Major Hassan Katsina, son of the Emir of Katsina,
to discuss the funds of the NPC since, as Zanna Bukar had
foreseen, the military rulers were intent on "freezing" all party
funds. But the NPC leaders satisfied the Governor that there
were no party funds, as such, that they could transfer to his
government.

Shehu Shagari now returned to his main interest, education
in Sokoto. He wanted nothing to do with either the new
military Federal or Regional Governments. But in Sokoto it
was not possible to live in isolation and to swim against
national currents. In May came the riots in many northern
centres against the Aguiyi-Ironsi government, in which a large
number of Ibos, identified by northerners with that government, were killed and injured, and much Ibo property was
plundered. Muslim northerners had been affronted by what
they saw as the arrogance of Ibos – and there were large Ibo
communities in all northern centres, including Sokoto – an
arrogance based on the belief of Ibos, loudly expressed for
example in markets, that the Federal Government was now
theirs. Very serious in its effect in the north, too, was a perhaps
unintentionally insulting article about the late Sardauna in a
Lagos magazine.

The immediate cause of the May anti-Ibo riots, however, was Gen. Aguiyi-Ironsi's ill-considered, arbitrary and poorly-presented plan to replace the federal form of government with a unitary one. In Muslim northern areas this could mean only one thing; an intention that they should be run by Ibo civil servants. After the riots the General adopted a more conciliatory attitude, but the damage had been done and Nigeria was set on a tragic course.

In Sokoto, however, partly because of the conciliatory influence of the Sultan – which earned him temporary unpopularity among some of his people – the riots were less serious than in other main northern cities, although much Ibo property was destroyed. Again in the July disturbances, when the renewed northern-Ibo hostilities were largely confined to the army, there was little trouble in Sokoto. In September-October, however, the city, in common with centres throughout the Northern Region, saw more violent riots – this time against southerners of all kinds – and the flight to the Eastern Region of virtually all Ibos.

Before the July disturbances Shehu Shagari was "invited" by the Force CID in Lagos to come from Sokoto for an interview in the capital. Such was the atmosphere in Nigeria that the Sultan summoned him to say "we pray for you". In Lagos most of his former friends shunned him, but he stayed in the house of the private secretary who had served him when he was Minister of Works.

The CID wanted to know about his relations with the Sardauna of Sokoto and the late Prime Minister – an extraordinary example of the leanings of the new military government. He even had to answer written questions. He was then asked about his bank account. It says more for the CID's thoroughness than for the accuracy of their information that he was particularly questioned about a sum of £17,000 which went through his bank when he was Minister of Internal Affairs. The sum had in fact been paid into his account before the 1964 Federal elections by the NPC. He was the only NPC leader who could be certain of being in Lagos at that time, so that the money could be distributed among the party's impecunious and importunate southern allies – the Dynamic Party and the rest – for their election expenses. He could show that he had in fact passed on to these parties rather more than he had received. But after three days of questioning he could tell the CID nothing about the origin of this money, paid into his account by Alhaji Muhammadu Ribadu, who had died.

He was the only NPC leader thus to be investigated. Indeed, the contrast in the treatment by the military regime of NPC politicians, none of whom it detained, and those of other parties, some of whom were detained for months, was astonishing; and to some extent answered the accusation that this was an Ibo "take-over".

When he was allowed to leave Lagos Shehu Shagari went to see Alhaji Hamzat Ahmadu, a senior civil servant who was the Head of State's then secretary, who asked him if he could stay in Lagos to see General Aguiyi-Ironsi. The General was then in Ibadan for a meeting of traditional rulers but would see him at a later date. Shehu Shagari, however, seeing little purpose in such a meeting, returned to Sokoto.

The General never came back to Lagos. On July 28-29, his first night away from the capital since he took office, he was murdered, together with his brave host, Lt-Col. Fajuyi, Military Governor of the West, by northern army officers. The murders were part of a general move by northern officers in an operation which many saw as "delayed" retaliation for what had come to be regarded as the Ibo murders of the northerners' respected and popular senior colleague on January 14-15.

Although in 1968 during the civil war Shehu Shagari was to undertake a mission abroad for the Federal Military Government, it would be four years before he again played any part in the administration of the Federation.

In his speech on October 1, 1981, marking the 21st anniversary of Nigeria's independence, President Shehu Shagari declared that the years from 1960 to 1966, as well as the years before independence after he entered national politics in 1954, were "characterised by ignorance and unfamiliarity, and therefore fear and mistrust, among the various ethnic groups – or to be more accurate, the nationalities – of Nigeria". Pre-independence "apprehension and suspicion" were carried over into the post-independence "parliamentary democratic era". It was fear and mistrust which brought to an end "with varying degrees of bloodshed", the federal government of which he was a member, and the then regional governments. It was not the constitutional system itself, said the President, whatever its defects, which was to blame; "our failures stemmed from inordinate ambition, ethnic suspicion and chauvinism".

This caustic condemnation of the pre-1966 politicians, extending to his own former party, the NPC, and to himself, and embracing his presidential adversaries, accurately defines the nature of pre-1966 politics in Nigeria. Before independence politics were concerned less with the "struggle" for independence – which called for no sacrifice from the senior politicians but was a process of negotiation with Whitehall – than with the division of power and spoils when it would be achieved. After independence politics were concerned with the same objectives.

That is not to say that both before and after independence the Nigerian ministers and parties could claim no achievements. There had been, for example, significant advances in education everywhere; Nigeria also now had five universities, with two faculties of medicine. Roads had been greatly improved. Efforts, later to prove disappointing, had been made to establish, even in the emirates, representatives and effective local government. Nigerianisation of the administrative services had gone smoothly. The Niger Bridge and the Borno railway extension were completed; work had begun on the Kainji dam. There were many, if not very successful, efforts to modernise agriculture. The economy was expanding and per caput income, though deplorably low, was increasing. Mineral oil offered the prospect of greatly increased external earnings.

Sir Abubakar Tafawa Balewa was recognised internationally, if not by Ghana's Dr Nkrumah, as a statesman whose standing was such that Harold Wilson, for example, believed his support to be essential over the Zimbabwe issue; while Sir Alec Douglas-Home, as Prime Minister, flew to Lagos just to consult him (over what I could never – nor I think did Sir Abubakar – discover). The Prime Minister had also played a leading part in establishing OAU. But it was still Kwame Nkrumah, Sekou Touré, Julius Nyerere and Kenneth Kaunda who, among black Africans, claimed the international publicity; and politically-conscious Nigerians felt that their country did not play in African "liberation politics" the role which her size required.

All the time corruption was, and was known to be, widespread, particularly in the award of official contracts and in the disposal of the funds of statutory marketing boards. Sir Abubakar, when taxed with this, maintained that he would deal severely with any instance which came to him authenticated on a file; instances did not come.

More important was the tendency for all regional governments to become "one-party" regimes, using the repressive and discriminatory measures against their opponents which such regimes employ. The multi-party democracy which functioned at the centre was not practised in the regions.

Nigeria was facing, however, more fundamental political problems than these; the problems emphasised by Shehu Shagari in his October 1 speech. There were many other examples of the "ignorance and unfamiliarity" and hence of the "ethnic suspicion and chauvinism" of which the President spoke. But the great division in Nigeria remained that between "the north" and "the south"; a division which had persisted in spite of the "amalgamation" of the two parts of the country to arrange which Lugard was brought back from the Governorship of Hong Kong to Nigeria in 1912.

An important recent book, *Central Administration in Nigeria** by Jeremy White, argues that the "amalgamation" in fact changed very little. Those who decided on it had no vision of a great new country; it was a matter of administrative con-

---

* Irish Academic Press and Frank Cass, 1981.

venience and economy. In practice, under Lugard, few government departments were "centralised" and there was only a skeleton central government. The only real centralisation was that of "power and authority in himself".

Lugard's ambitions, however, included the standardisation of laws, a countrywide network of communications, the extension to all areas of the northern system of "indirect rule" and, most significantly, a "unified approach" to education. In fact, in Mr White's words, "there grew up in northern and southern Nigeria two different and even rival administrative traditions which were to exercise a profound influence on Nigeria's political future".

In the north "indirect rule", particularly under the scholarly Richmond Palmer, became a "dogma". Some British administrative officers saw the northern "Native Administrations", such as Sokoto, as at least semi-independent states, and considered maintenance of their status more important than reform of their deficiencies. Instead of modernising ideas developing in the south spreading to the north, the opposite, for various reasons, happened.

The tragedy was the insistence on the part of the dominant British in the northern provinces, and then the Northern Region, that their domain was and must remain "different" from the rest of Nigeria. This difference, they maintained, extended for the most part even to those non-Muslim areas of the northern provinces whose social system had affinities with the south and which, until the advent of the British, shared no kind of political unity with the emirates, although these areas had enjoyed far more contacts with the states of Hausaland and Borno than was recognised until recently. The idea of northern "separateness" was taken over from the British by leading northern politicians, to emerge, under the Sardauna of Sokoto, virtually as the concept of a "nation" constituted by the Northern Region.

The notion of a "Regional Nation" may not have been so highly developed in the Western and Eastern Regions; but in these the notion that on the one hand the Yorubas and, on the other, the Ibos, constituted "nations" – however justified that notion was, and is, from a cultural viewpoint – had much the same political consequences as did the Regional Nation idea.

Because the "amalgamation" was never really consummated, even a strong and far-seeing Governor in Lagos like Cameron could make relatively little headway against the entrenched and closed northern system. Colonial Office officials, although questioning, for example, the idea that the Northern Provinces were a natural and permanent unity, and emphasising the goal of a united Nigeria, in practice left things to "the men on the spot".

Personalities played an important part as did the real physical problems of administration in such a vast area. But, as Mr White says, in dealing with, for example, the conflict between the British heads of centralised departments and the British northern administrative hierarchy, there were "neither team-spirit nor clear ideas, nor authority".

All this does not mean that there were not profound differences between the emirates and most of the rest of the country; and those who blame the civil war on the survival of the "two Nigerias" should remember that among the strongest supporters of the federal cause were Nigerians whose forbears had been among the first to come under British rule in the south, as well as the emirates and the non-Muslim areas of the former Northern Region. But the insistence that the totally arbitrary north-south boundary should remain intact was unreasonable. Even a man so devoted to the principles of "indirect rule" as Temple saw the need to break up the northern provinces into smaller groups. A statesmanlike approach, too, would have sought to diminish, not emphasise, the differences.

In spite of Lugard's ambition considerable imbalance in western education between the Muslim north and the south was inevitable, at least for many years. Hostility to western education (which was seen, too, in the great Yoruba, and largely Muslim, southern city of Ibadan) ensured that. But this hostility was reinforced by the British Administration's policies. The concept of basing all education on local culture was admirable; but when this excluded teaching of the English language, essential both for employment in central government service and for international links, it made the "Northern Provinces" into a "reservation". The tragedy of the north, as Mr White puts it, was that "long after it was really necessary the British Administration continued to remain so preoccupied with short-term political issues that it completely failed to realise that, in the long run, there could be no more vital political issue than that of western education".

Here was the central failure of "amalgamation" and the most disastrous consequence of the "extreme" school of indirect rule. In 1919 Lugard lamented that "the Northern Protectorate does not at present supply a single clerk or artisan from its intelligent population". This lament was repeated in the following year by his successor, Sir Hugh Clifford, who found that no person in the northern provinces was "sufficiently educated to enable him to fill the most minor clerical post in the office of any government department". Clifford urged Muslims to "recognise the disadvantage of allowing all posts in the public service to be held by aliens of a different creed".

In fact the traditional leaders of the Muslim areas were not greatly interested in nation-wide Nigerian institutions, regarding their own "Native Administrations", together with the British officers on the spot, as "the government" – as did so many British officials. This view was shared by the vast majority of their subjects. And in these administrations, although they frequently employed southerners in technical jobs, northerners predominated.

A new book by two Nigerian educationalists, *Education in Northern Nigeria**, has emphasised the contradictions in British educational policy in the Northern Provinces as shown by the history of Shehu Shagari's own Barewa College. From its opening in 1921 much emphasis was given in it to the teaching of English and to inculcating the English public school ethos. Yet previously educational policy was concerned with

---

*Allen and Unwin, 1981, see Bibliography.

"insulating the Muslim north from outside influences and ... rooting education in local culture"; so in government schools in Muslim areas Hausa alone was used. Now there was a reversal, an attempt to produce "black Muslim English gentlemen". In the end the school "undramatically changed" to the conventional system operating in southern Nigeria.

It is unrealistic now to complain that men who exercised power, at a time when independence seemed infinitely remote and the unity of Nigeria was a mere vision, did not see much further ahead than did all but a tiny handful of those they ruled. Yet insofar as Nigeria's political instability in the post-independence years was the result of the imbalance in size – and in education – between the Regions, and of what President Shehu Shagari called "ignorance and unfamiliarity and therefore fear and mistrust" between Nigeria's nationalities", the dominant policies of the former British Administration in the north cannot escape much of the blame. If, however, Nigerians themselves, provided since 1979 through their own efforts with political institutions carefully calculated to minimise "fear and mistrust", still fail to achieve national unity, those responsible will rightly earn opprobrium far greater than have those foreigners whose fault was largely their arrogant conviction that they sincerely knew best what was good for Nigerians.

The fact that the Region which was able, because of its size, to call Nigeria's political tune, had so few educated people caused tensions. Northern leaders objected to their dependence on the south even for semi-skilled workers, and suspected southerners, because of their management positions, of trying to exclude such northerners as were available from jobs, even in the Northern Region, in favour of their own people, in private as well as public employment. The northern leaders succeeded, however, in establishing a 50-50 "quota" system for recruitment between "north" and "south" into the Nigerian Army.

Southerners suspected northern leaders, with little justification, of pushing unqualified northerners up the federal promotion ladder, and resented what they saw as their own exclusion from jobs in the Northern Region for which they were fitted but for which no northerners were available. They had no sympathy with the northern policy of "positive discrimination" on behalf of those left behind in education, although this now represents fashionable liberal thinking in Britain and the US. The "apprehension and suspicion", in Shehu Shagari's words, caused by these circumstances embittered Nigerian politics. Indeed, the imagined causes of resentment and "apprehension" between "north" and "south", were probably more bitter than any real ones.

Yet, whatever the deficiencies of the 1960-66 civilian regime and however popular its overthrow – and this was popular in all parts of the country – the right to remove an elected federal government which in due course would again submit itself to the electorate, even in an imperfect election, cannot be conceded to self-appointed military saviours. And in Nigeria the higher courts remained independent – although some politicians questioned even that – and in Lagos at least, there was a considerable degree of press freedom. But the sincere belief of many southern politicians that, for example, the 1963 census had been "rigged" in favour of the Northern Region caused them to question the legitimacy of the Federal Government. Such questioning was adopted by the would-be military revolutionaries. The Federal Government was not buttressed by supporting federal and regional institutions and traditions of the kind which are essential if those defeated in an election are to be content to await a later election in which their views might prevail.

Nor, in Nigeria (although the soldiers who exercised power were different from, and detained, those whose attempted coup resulted in the end of civilian rule) was the military regime to demonstrate either the freedom from corruption or the immunity to tribalism which the military revolutionaries had promised in January 1966 that they would ensure.

The Nigeria to which, almost fourteen years later, under President Shehu Shagari, the soldiers were to restore civilian rule, however, would be a very different country from the Nigeria from whose Federal Government he had been so abruptly removed; and the great and salutary differences were those which, perhaps, only military rule could have ensured.

6

GRASS ROOTS AGAIN

Believing that in all his ministerial appointments he had conscientiously laboured to serve all the people of Nigeria, Shehu Shagari resented both his peremptory dismissal from office by the self-appointed military despots and his own treatment by the military government. It says much for his own integrity, but less for his powers of observation, that he seems genuinely to have failed to appreciate how widespread was the resentment at the corruption of some of his colleagues in the Federal Government, and how miserably democracy had been eroded in all the regions – though certainly not nearly to the same extent in the centre.

He had still not developed any great political ambition, and seems to have decided that his role in national politics was now ended. He had his farm at Shagari, and his house in Sokoto City; and there was work enough to occupy him in Sokoto, particularly in education. After a brief period of re-cuperation he enthusiastically devoted himself to local affairs. Lagos, it must be remembered, still seemed very remote in Sokoto, where no troops were then stationed. There the end of civilian government seemed to make little difference. Even under the new military regime awareness that Nigeria was a single polity ruled from Lagos was still undeveloped.

Shehu Shagari would not, in fact, find it easy, even in the short run, to avoid national politics or government responsi-bility. Immediately, however, he was able to immerse himself anew in Sokoto education. He became, at a nominal salary, secretary of the Sokoto Province Education Development Fund. While he was secretary this financed the opening of over a hundred primary and three secondary schools. It had ambitious plans for more schools, for teacher training, and for technical education. Its 1967-72 development plan was estimated to cost over £½m, with ever-mounting recurrent costs. Funds came mostly from a levy on the salaries of NA employees, from fees, and from state government grants. Shehu Shagari and his colleagues were highly critical of their rich fellow-citizens, including senior civil servants, who contributed in 1966-7 only £100.

If Lagos seemed remote, Sokoto was not to be immune from national currents. There were the two major outbreaks of violence which led to the flight of Ibos from the Northern Region, and ultimately to the schism of the Eastern Region, which was followed, in 1967, by civil war. In May 1966, for several days the violence and destruction in Sokoto and some other centres of the province was as brutal as in other places in the Northern Region where substantial numbers of Ibos and other southerners lived and worked. The absence of a garrison spared Sokoto the violence inside the army itself, which broke out in July. The murdered General Aguiyi-Ironsi was then replaced by Lt-Col., later General, Yakubu Gowon. The second, and longer, round of violence against southern civilians, in September 1966, again shattered the calm of Sokoto.

One factor which, in addition to those noted in the last chapter, led to bitterness against the Ibos in northern towns was sheer resentment at their commercial success. Yet in Sokoto, as elsewhere in the Northern Region, many northerners took considerable risks to help their southern friends.

On both occasions Shehu Shagari was in the city, helpless to do anything to restrain the rioters. Hooligans and criminals, devoid of political motives, joined in the violence. Years later, but before the civil war was ended, as a Commissioner in the new North-Western State, Shehu Shagari was to write a memo to the "Interim Common Services Agency" (ICSA) which was still "winding-up" the former Northern Region, supporting the controlled return of Ibos to Sokoto "as fellow countrymen not vanquished foes". But he strongly urged the need to prevent the revival of any "segregated" Ibo schools, churches and clubs. "Northernisation", he wrote, was now dead; but each northern state had the right to reserve permanent posts in its public services for its own people. If it had to recruit outside the state, a state government could offer contracts of whatever length it felt to be appropriate.

The Ibos, however, eventually returned to the cities of the northern states, including Sokoto. The terrible days of 1966 looked like an evil memory and seemed to belong to a distant age. As in other parts of Nigeria – for the Ibos had fled from Lagos and the west as well as from the north – their surviving property was safeguarded in Sokoto. Rents payable on it were put into official bank accounts to await their return.

Political parties were outlawed by the military regime in January 1966. But after General Gowon took over there was talk of an early return to civilian rule – he released from gaol both Chief Awolowo and Chief Enaharo, as well as politicians detained by his predecessor. In September 1966, an *ad hoc* constitutional conference was held in Lagos, bringing together "Leaders of Thought" of all four Regions. The September outbreak of violence in the north against southerners soon wrecked this initiative; but the talks lasted long enough for two developments to become clear. Animosity between the majority Muslims and the minority non-Muslim areas of the Northern Region had disappeared; so had hostility between former NPC and former NEPU people. Representatives from all parts of the Region, including former NPC supporters, had abandoned the concept of a "Northern Nation" and were converted to the idea of breaking up the Federation, including the Northern Region itself, into a number of "states".

The Region's Military Governor, Major Hassan Katsina, was an important influence in bringing about this change of heart even before General Gowon had taken over. He summoned Makaman Bida, the senior surviving NPC leader, Malam Aminu Kano, leader of the former NEPU, and Chief J. S. Tarka, leader of the former United Middle Belt Congress and staunch adversary of the old NPC, to suggest to them that "politics" were no longer appropriate. They must together try to pursue the interests of the Region as a whole. The three leaders toured the Region together, visiting every Province and preaching regional unity and fellowship. They were assisted as their secretary by Alhaji Umaru Dikko, who in 1979 was to become Shehu Shagari's Minister of Transport.

After General Aguiyi-Ironsi's overthrow a consultative committee was established in the Northern Region to consider the constitution under which Nigeria might return to civilian rule. Later the Region was divided into six states, but it retained some of its identity and Kaduna was still a centre to which all six states looked. The Governor asked the leaders of the former NPC, NEPU, and the United Middle Belt Congress each to nominate five people to sit on a consultative body which would meet in Kaduna to advise ICSA – but also to be an informed political forum of a kind probably "illegal" from the point of view of the military rulers in Lagos.

Shehu Shagari, who did not attend the September "Leaders of Thought" meeting in Lagos, now took Makaman Bida's place in the Kaduna consultative body. It included the leaders of all three of the political bodies concerned, as well as trade unionists and university people; and once more Umaru Dikko was secretary.

Looking back, this body – although nobody then intended this – can be seen as the nucleus of the National Movement, from which the National Party of Nigeria, Shehu Shagari's party, was to emerge. For early on attempts were made to bring southern politicians into discussion with the Kaduna consultative body. Shehu Shagari himself toured the Northern Region on the committee's behalf and had private meetings in Kaduna with southern politicians. Even after he had returned to Federal Government service, in 1970, Shehu Shagari continued, during weekends in Kaduna, the political and constitutional discussions which had begun in 1966.

On May 30 1967, the then Colonel Ojukwu, Military Governor of the Eastern Region, announced the secession from the Federation of the Region, under the name Biafra, taken from the then name of the Atlantic "bight" which washed its shores. Immediately before this announcement the Federal Government had decreed the division of Nigeria into twelve "states", to replace the Regions and to assume individually for their areas the wide range of responsibilities the Regions had enjoyed. The object of the move was partly to strengthen the loyalty to the Federation of the non-Ibo areas of the Eastern Region, which were divided into two states and formally removed from Ojukwu's control. The Federal Government, however, was able to assert its authority over these states, Rivers and South-Eastern, only after months of fighting.

Gowon, however, is also himself from a "minority" group; and he and some of his closest advisers believed that the break-up of the big Regions – in fact, the Western and Mid-Western were little affected – would stimulate local development and strengthen the Federation's unity. The change of heart on the part of the northern "Leaders of Thought" was also an influence.

Sokoto Province now found itself allied with Niger Province, to the south, in the new North-Western State, with a senior policeman, Usman Faruk, as Military Governor, assisted by civilian "commissioners" in charge of ministries, and with Sokoto City as capital. The new state covered 167,000 square kilometres and was in area the second biggest among the twelve. It had a population of some six million; but only about a quarter belonged to Niger Province, whose area was just over half that of Sokoto Province. This disparity between the two provinces in size and population was reversed in the matter of education which, though still limited, had made much progress in Niger. One result was that of the Permanent Secretaries in the new state's ministries eleven came from Niger and only five from Sokoto, in spite of the latter's great preponderance in population.

This imbalance caused resentment in Sokoto. It reached the point where, in 1969, Shehu Shagari, now himself a civilian commissioner, was invited by the Governor to be chairman of a committee to examine allegations that officers from Niger –

and more precisely those of Nupe origin – were abusing their strong position in the civil service.

The committee found that the allegations were not proved. Niger people, for their part, claimed that the capital of the new state, Sokoto, was even further away from their own provincial capital, Minna, than had been Kaduna, capital of the former Region. There were other objections to the merger of the two provinces. In both, therefore, their transformation in 1976 into the separate states of Sokoto and Niger was to be highly popular.

Shehu Shagari was not among the North-Western State's first civilian commissioners. His experience in half-a-dozen federal ministries would have been of great value to the new administration, but his distaste for public office was still strong. So he carried on with his educational work and his farming. In 1967, however, he accepted nomination as the state's non-official representative on the highly important Northern States Marketing Board, which bought, among other crops, the groundnuts which were the chief foreign currency earner for the Federation during the civil war. He also briefly represented the state on the board of Kaduna Textiles. He was still determined, however, to devote himself to education in his state, whose needs were limitless. In spite of the modest progress which had been made in Niger Province, only some 8.5% of all children of school age in the North-Western State were at school.

It was not until October 1968 that Shehu Shagari was persuaded to take a Commissioner's portfolio, that of Establishments and Training. The appointment meant that he left the Marketing Board, as well as the service of the Sokoto NA.

Sokoto City had long been the headquarters of a major province; but the requirements of a province were modest compared with those of a state, however poor, consisting of two provinces. Accommodation had to be found for a Military Governor and his office, and for a range of ministries and other state bodies. For years, until a New Delhi-style secretariat was ultimately built outside Sokoto City, most state officials worked in makeshift offices scattered all over the city, some on top of shops. For every 6,000 people there was only one hospital bed in the state; there was no modern hotel in Sokoto City; the state's telecommunications were uncertain; its roads and bridges were inadequate; state transport was decrepit; Sokoto City had no water treatment plant until 1969.

Indeed the "Committee on Post-war Reconstruction" in the state, of which Shehu Shagari was a member, recorded that it "had little to reconstruct".

Above all the state lacked trained and experienced staff. The first problem of the state's Ministry of Establishments and Training, which was technically part of the Ministry of Finance, was that it lacked staff itself. It shared its civil service head with two other ministries. Shehu Shagari found this official "uncooperative" – so much so that he reported the fact to the Military Governor. Under the military regime civil service heads of ministries tended to see civilian commissioners, unless they obviously carried political weight, as figureheads, and would often themselves deal directly with the Head of State in Lagos or the governor of a state. Shehu Shagari, with the experience of Federal ministries behind him, expected different behaviour from a senior civil servant. The official apologised – and cooperated. Later, in the Constituent Assembly which preceded the return to civilian rule in 1979, Shehu Shagari was to observe that in a military regime civil servants formulated policy, and in the event of a dispute with them the commissioner nominally in charge of a ministry would be moved. In civilian rule parties had detailed programmes which the civil servants had to carry out – or be themselves moved.

To strengthen the state administration Shehu Shagari made some professional officers into administrators – a change never popular with administrative officers themselves. He urged officials from the state working for the Federation to return to Sokoto – and accelerated promotion. One returnee became Permanent Secretary at the state Ministry of Education. The ministry devised training schemes and sought a link with an American university for this purpose.

One obvious task for the ministry, since its plans for training

Nigerians would not show results for years, was the recruitment of expatriates, mostly Asian. In 1969 it recruited six doctors and three accountants out of a total expatriate recruitment of 54. In 1970 there were 112 graduate teachers in the North-Western State's schools and colleges – but 72 were expatriates. In the Ministry of Works there were 45 expatriates. Typical of the ministry's problems was how to balance the need to give serving Nigerian officers university training against the university claims of secondary school leavers.

In 1969 Shehu Shagari became state Commissioner for Education, the job originally promised him by the Governor if he would join his administration. In this post he toured continuously, inspecting institutions of all kinds in a state which ran for over 300 miles from north to south, and which had very poor roads. He exhorted staff, encouraged students, urged local dignitaries to support the schools. He introduced the provision of houses for village teachers, and the grant of loans for them to buy motor cycles so that they could visit the towns and their shops.

Such encouragement was indeed necessary. For while in 1967 119 out of 192 candidates in the state – a woefully small number – for the West African School Certificate were successful, in 1968 it was only 90 out of 230. Shehu Shagari had also to wrestle with problems such as the teaching of Hausa in primary schools in the absence of qualified teachers. To meet the shortage of staff he tried to recruit teachers, including Ibos, from the liberated areas of Biafra, where many schools were awaiting restoration.

It was the North-Western State Current Affairs Committee which, rather in the manner of the pre-1951 discussion bodies in the Northern Region, kept political discussion going in the state – the similarities between colonial and military rule were close. In this committee Shehu Shagari was an active member, constantly discussing the type of constitution civilian Nigeria would need, problems of local government (the term "Native Authority" in 1969 gave way, at the committee's suggestion, to "Local Authority"), and Nigeria's place in the world.

The committee was established by the Military Governor in

Shaking hands with Queen Elizabeth during one of Shehu Shagari's many visits for the Commonwealth Conferences.

Swearing-in ceremony of Alhaji Shehu Shagari as Federal Commissioner for Finance by Gen. Gowon.

1968 to advise him on local, national and – surprisingly, since technically they were no concern of the state government – international matters. It was scarcely a democratic body since at first it consisted only of commissioners, senior civil servants (among them the senior official whom Shehu Shagari had found to be uncooperative) and senior NA officials. It was, however, entirely civilian. Later it was broadened to include, for example, Alhaji Suleman Takuma, then a United Africa Company manager, who after the elections became national secretary of the National Party of Nigeria (NPN) under whose banner Shehu Shagari was to win the Presidency (the big British firms had long, if unintentionally, afforded a refuge to would-be politicians in the Northern Region, since they alone offered non-official salaries "without strings"). All members of the committee, moreover, were supposed to serve in a private capacity.

The committee was concerned mostly with technical administrative matters. It did, however, recommend changes in the structure of local government, as well as in the name. It could also at least discuss matters of political significance. For example, some members felt that the Sokoto-Niger antipathy mentioned earlier could be softened if a third province was created in the state out of the other two. The idea was at first accepted, but later rejected, by the committee as a whole.

The main purpose of the committee, however, was to keep alive during the period of military rule the conviction that the soldiers – and in the case of the North-Western State, a single policeman, the Governor – could not possess a monopoly of wisdom on all matters affecting the work of government. Shehu Shagari, among the most regular attenders at the committee's meetings, felt strongly that limited though its functions were, they should be stretched to the limit.

Sokoto, like Shehu Shagari himself, was not greatly affected directly by the civil war. It was at the end of the road for the distribution of goods and probably felt shortages more than most places, and its commerce and public services were, like those of other northern centres, affected by the flight of the southerners. In May 1968, however, before he had become a state commissioner, Shehu Shagari briefly dropped his educational work and at the Federal Military Government's request set off on a tour of three European countries and the Vatican.

He was to attempt, as a private Nigerian, in no way depending on Nigerian embassies, to combat the then powerful pro-Biafran propaganda and sentiment in those places, particularly among Roman Catholics. Other well-known former politicians, such as Alhaji Maitama Sule, were sent to other countries on similar missions. His own rather lonely tour lasted some three weeks, and Shehu Shagari will now make no claims for its success, except perhaps in Switzerland. Yet it is certain that this polite, modest, scholarly man was so unlike the federal ruffians of hostile propaganda that he must have impressed at least those whom he met during his mission.

France proved the most difficult country, although Shehu Shagari recalls that he was much helped by the late A.G. Leventis, an imposing figure in Nigeria's commercial life, who lived in Paris. He found that the Nigerian Embassy, where the Ambassador, Ralph Uwechue, had defected to the Biafran cause (he later adopted a neutral stance) had given up flying its flag. France herself had not moved to open support of the Biafran secession. Just before and during Shehu Shagari's mission, however, President Houphouet-Boigny of the Ivory Coast, who recognised Biafra, was actually in Paris (Gabon, Tanzania and Zambia were also to recognise Biafra, as was Haiti). The Ivorian President's standing with President de Gaulle was very high; and his advocacy did much to persuade the General, against the advice of his Foreign Office and those French firms with substantial investments or contracts in Federal Nigeria, to supply Biafra with arms channelled through Gabon, the Ivory Coast and the Portuguese island of Sao Tome.

The Paris visit was not helped by an outbreak of strikes. Shehu Shagari, however, was able to talk to a number of journalists, both friendly and hostile, and to businessmen associated with French oil and banking interests in Nigeria. With the businessmen his technique was straightforward. As a former senior minister he would ask for a meeting to discuss Nigeria's economic prospects. During the meeting he would emphasise the inevitability of a federal victory and invite his hosts to reflect on the consequences of this for their Nigerian interests. Whether the visit strengthened the hand of those in de Gaulle's administration who were anxious to stop him – and his adviser on African Affairs, the enigmatic Jacques Foccart – from openly recognising Biafra's sovereignty is not clear. In fact there was no formal French recognition. Yet, as John St Jorre put it in his standard book, *The Nigerian Civil War**: "French intervention decisively saved the Biafrans from defeat, decisively prolonged the war and – equally decisively – fell short of enabling them to win it".

To counter Biafran propaganda federal spokesmen had to concentrate on three points. The first was that the war had no religious significance. It was not a struggle, as was widely claimed, between Muslims and largely Catholic Christians. General Gowon was a devout Christian, as were Chief Awolowo and other members of his government. The majority of the federal army were also Christians or non-Muslims. The second point was that the starvation in Biafra was the fault of the Biafran leadership, who refused to allow food from abroad into the enclave by daylight flights or by the "land corridor" offered by General Gowon. The third point to emphasise was General Gowon's insistence that there must be "no victors and no vanquished" and that federal forces must respect strictly the "code of conduct" towards civilians he had laid down for them.

Shehu Shagari was able to argue this case with sincerity, for it reflected his own views. But whatever effect it might have in France, it was essential to get it over in Italy and to the Vatican. Pope Paul VI had gone beyond diplomatic bounds in expressing sympathy for the Ibos, and the Catholic relief organisations grouped in Caritas adopted an almost fanatical pro-Biafran stance. Indeed in many Catholic countries attitudes to the Nigerian civil war deeply affected domestic

---

*Hodder and Stoughton, 1972

politics. This writer remembers calling on the official in charge of West African affairs in the Austrian Foreign Office in the summer of 1968. "I'm glad you've called", she said; "there are now two of us to support the federal cause in Austria". It was not only among the Catholics, however, that the Biafran cause aroused strong emotion. During the Addis Ababa OAU Conference on the civil war in 1968 I was telephoned late at night at my hotel by the Finnish Ambassador to Ethiopia; so important were attitudes to the Nigerian struggle in Finnish domestic politics that he wanted my account of the day's proceedings so that his Minister in Helsinki would know first thing in the morning what had happened.

Shehu Shagari's arrival in Rome coincided with the Italian general election – and the news that federal forces had captured the key town of Port Harcourt, and that President Kaunda had recognised Biafra. At the Vatican he was received politely, but he could not tell with what effect. In Milan he felt that he had more success, particularly in his talks with businessmen, some of whom had Nigerian interests.

Then from May 25 to 31 he was in Geneva, centre of the external Biafran information services, and headquarters of the International Red Cross, whose cavalier attitude to Nigeria's national sovereignty the Federal Government was to criticise. In that city, Shehu Shagari says simply, the secessionists "had many friends".

The "friends" included, apart from the International Red Cross, Markpress, the American-owned public relations firm which engaged in highly inventive, but often very successful, propaganda on behalf of the Biafrans. This they did partly by the device of issuing, as though they were authentic news agency reports of the ordinary kind, accounts of imaginary events. I was present, for example, in the summer of 1968 on the southern front of the civil war when the federal forces were advancing slowly and with difficulty. At that time Markpress issued a report, which was prominently displayed in the London *Times*, that a precise and very large number of Ibo civilians had been massacred by the federal forces during this advance. In fact no civilians had remained in the area. I found no evidence at all of the alleged massacre; and the federal military authorities, after a thorough enquiry ordered by General Gowon, could find no evidence. The "report" was a fabrication.

To counter such inventions was difficult, since, as Dr Goebbels decided, the bigger the lie the bigger the task of refuting it. But in his book *Nigeria returns to civilian rule,*[*] Okion Ojigbo claims that after Shehu Shagari's visit to Geneva "the support which the relief agencies in Switzerland gave Biafra became more discriminating, restricted to relief supplies to the Biafran population ... Swiss officials began to cut off Biafra's major oxygen supply from Switzerland – international finance".

In spite of the resolution he made in 1966, this "private mission" for the Federal Government was later to be followed by a far more important role for Shehu Shagari in military government in Lagos. And this was to last for five years.

---

*Tokion (Nigeria) Company, Lagos, 1980.

7

BACK TO THE CENTRE

In June 1970, Alhaji Yahaya Gusau, the civilian Federal Commissioner in charge of the Ministry of Economic Development and Reconstruction, told Gen. Gowon of his intention to resign. A Sokoto man, he had been a colleague of Shehu Shagari in education there, and had later become a respected senior civil servant. He had been a federal commissioner throughout the civil war, which ended in January 1970. The second National Development Plan, covering 1970-74, which was the responsibility of his ministry, to whose name "Reconstruction" had been added to emphasise its special post-war responsibilities, was being prepared. Alhaji Yahaya, although still only 54, decided that he should now leave the stage to another actor.

Perhaps, as a former senior civil servant, he may have been influenced by the development under Gen. Gowon of a small "inner cabinet" of Permanent Secretaries, who appeared to have constant direct access to the Head of State, even if they went behind their commissioners' backs. One of the most influential of these three or four officials was the permanent secretary of Alhaji Yahaya's own ministry, the talented young Oxford economist, Mr Allison Ayida. The older man felt that his permanent secretary was bypassing him.

With Ayida Shehu Shagari was to have a close relationship over five years, first as Alhaji Yahaya Gusau's replacement at the Ministry of Economic Development and Reconstruction, and then at the Ministry of Finance, where they both served from 1971 to 1975, the longest ministerial term Alhaji Shehu Shagari ever served.

The future President, however, still thought Lagos and federal office distasteful. So how did he find himself once more in Lagos, after an interval of five years? In seeking a successor to Alhaji Yahaya Gusau to be in charge of the Federal Government's great post-war programme for reconstructing war-affected areas and developing the country as a whole, Gen. Gowon sought the advice, as he did in the case of all senior appointments, of Mr Abdul Aziz Atta, Secretary to the Federal Government and Head of the Federal Civil Service, a Balliol man. Since the outgoing commissioner had come from the then North-Western State, Gen. Gowon followed the convention of seeking a replacement commissioner from that state. The state's military governor was certain that his Commissioner for Education, Shehu Shagari, was the right man to be a federal commissioner. Gowon and the Secretary to the Federal Government agreed, although for some months Gowon himself took charge of the ministry.

The convention did not oblige the Head of State to give the new commissioner his predecessor's portfolio. Shehu Shagari's experience as first Federal Minister for Economic Development, however, as well as his reputation as an honest administrator, marked him as the man for the development ministry. Gen. Gowon brushed aside the objection apparently made to him that the Sokoto man had been a leading NPC politician; as he wanted all kinds of experience in his Executive Council such a background was no disqualification.

Perhaps Gowon and Atta did not realise that Shehu Shagari, content with his increasingly successful educational work in Sokoto and the North-Western State, where he had proved an inspiring, if very demanding, Commissioner for Education, was unenthusiastic about going to Lagos at all. If he had been offered some other ministry he might have refused. The Ministry of Economic Development and Reconstruction, however, offered him the right kind of challenge. He was influenced, too, by friends from NPC days who urged him to take this demanding job to help demonstrate the capacity of a former NPC minister.

If the 1970-74 Development Plan was the ministry's main

long-term undertaking, reconstruction called for all its immediate energy. A particular difficulty, for example, which at once became apparent, was the matter of "abandoned properties". These were the properties elsewhere in Nigeria of people who had fled back to Biafra. In Lagos and in some northern cities, especially Kano, they were considerable; and there was the particularly delicate problem of Ibo property in Port Harcourt, which had been part of the secessionist area but was now capital of Rivers State.

Nowhere had Gen. Gowon's reconciliation policy shown to better advantage than over this issue. As we have noted for Sokoto, state governments established machinery, hard-pressed though their new administrations were, both to safeguard the properties of Biafrans and, in appropriate cases, to collect rents from them to be accumulated for their refugee owners. After the war identification of these owners was exceedingly difficult, and there was a flood of bogus claims. In Rivers State, however, where inside the former Biafra conflict between Ibos and non-Ibos had been particularly bitter, the state government and its people were reluctant to return properties.

Everywhere, too, there were the serious problems arising from neglect of maintenance during the war. Above all, displaced people had to be resettled and their farms, homes, businesses and social services rehabilitated. This aspect of his new ministry's work had a particular appeal to Shehu Shagari since the beneficiaries would be the peoples of the former secessionist area. Now in a practical way he could take part in an enterprise which illustrated the sincerity of the Federal Government's professed policies towards these people, of which, with limited success, he had tried to persuade the peoples and governments of France, Italy and Switzerland during his missions to them during the war. At the same time he could see the force of the complaint which came to him from some of the poorer states in the north of Nigeria, that they did not qualify for "reconstruction" since they had nothing to reconstruct. The problem of reconciling the needs of war-affected areas and the poorest areas of the country which, though undamaged by the war, had been left behind in development, was always present.

The new commissioner, although anxious not to appear to "interfere" in the detailed administration of relief, the deficiencies in which were all too obvious, constantly visited the affected areas. Transport was the great problem for all relief and rehabilitation. Gen. Gowon had, symbolically, ordered destruction of the Uli runway which the Biafrans had improvised out of a trunk road and which, for a time, certainly at night, was one of Africa's busiest airports. From it Ojukwu had flown to the Ivory Coast as Biafra collapsed. Two of the three airports of the former Eastern Region, Port Harcourt and Enugu, were also out of action, as were the Port Harcourt berths and the railway running north from them. Supplies had to go from Lagos eastwards over poorly maintained roads – and then across the Niger by the damaged bridge which Sir Abubakar Tafawa Balewa had declared open in January, 1966. The bridge was made serviceable by German engineers and the Royal Engineers – because of strained relations with France, which, however, were rectified with remarkable speed, the French contractors for the bridge were not called on.

The British government provided over 100 Bedford lorries and some 40 Landrovers. In spite of the resentment of the Federal Government, and Shehu Shagari himself, against the activities in Biafra of some foreign relief organisations during the civil war, help for relief and rehabilitation was welcomed by the commissioner from a number of countries. Hungarians, Norwegians and the Swiss, for example, helped to rehabilitate the hospitals. The British helped to restore libraries. The Americans provided money for repairing roads, and helped to bring plantations back into production. The UN provided a "food-for-work" programme. CARE helped fishermen to resume their calling. Bulgaria, Canada and other countries all made contributions.

The main supports for relief and resettlement – objectives which Shehu Shagari's ministry replaced as soon as possible by "reconstruction and development" – were the federal

111

government and its agencies. Federal funds were provided as necessary. The Nigerian Red Cross supplied 50,000 tons of food for war-damaged areas in the first half of 1970.Farmers in particular were helped by the provision of implements; material was provided – including rope for scaffolding as well as block-making machines – to help people repair their own houses. There was even assistance for restoring village shrines. Millions of naira were provided to allow people to change reasonable amounts of Biafran or obsolete Nigerian currency into valid Nigerian currency. The activities in the war-affected areas for which the Ministry of Economic Development and Rehabilitation was responsible were bewildering in their variety and scope.

One of the great problems in administering relief was the strained relations between those Ibos who had supported and those who had criticised the Biafran cause. There were also serious administrative failures on the part of the authorities of the new Eastern states (the Federal Government for the most part could only work through them), and there was, inevitably, considerable corruption. There was the well-known case of some 250 generators supplied by the Americans which, nine months after they arrived in Enugu, were still not installed, because the state government would not ask the help of the federal electric power authority. Since a visit of US Congressmen was expected, Shehu Shagari's ministry itself moved in and saw to their installation in the places for which they were intended – hospitals, schools, water plants, etc.

To the disbelief of those outside Nigeria who had been persuaded that the federal army was maltreating Ibo civilians, the soldiers proved to be invaluable relief workers in the war-affected areas. In addition the personal and official spending by federal army units in these areas was so important for the local economy that local people threatened rebellion if, as was rumoured, the army was to be withdrawn.

The nature of the 1970-74 National Development Plan was also to some extent affected by the demands of post-war rehabilitation.

Nigeria's first National Development Plan, covering 1962-68, had been widely criticised as a mere list of projects, desirable in their eyes, which ministries had somehow contrived to have included in the Plan and which affected statistics of economic growth rather than individual welfare. In any case it had to a large extent been frustrated by the political crisis and the civil war, although, for example, the great Kainji hydro-electricity scheme was inaugurated during the war. Preparation of the new Plan, which should have followed the 1962-68 one, was also delayed by the war.

When it finally appeared, the 1970-74 Plan envisaged total net public investment by the federal and the state governments and public bodies of all kinds of just under £1,000m. Compared with the ₦70,000m. estimated as public capital investment under the 1981-85 Plan, which, as President, Shehu Shagari proposed in 1981, the sum seems modest.

It represented, however, almost twice the actual expenditure under the 1962-68 Plan, and the planners questioned Nigeria's capacity to spend such a sum.

They used ambitious language, however. They promised that the Plan would produce from "the scars of the civil war" a "viable national economy" in a country which, the outcome of the civil war had shown, was no longer a "mere geographical expression" but a united polity. The aim was not only to produce a dynamic economy, but a just, egalitarian, and free society, and a truly independent country which would be a new force in the world. To achieve these ends the Federal Government would itself have to control essential sectors of the economy. Planning would now become "a deliberate weapon of social change".

With such aspirations the new commissioner had complete sympathy. But the language was not Shehu Shagari's language nor could he share the young planners' confidence, based, perhaps, on the economy's war-time success, that economic planning had now become highly effective, almost scientific, in Nigeria, and could in a short five years produce the promised transformation. Then, too, as when he became President, he saw the only true economic revolution to be the

"Green Revolution" in agriculture. The new plan offered little prospect of that.

It did, however, to Shehu Shagari's satisfaction, emphasise the importance to Nigeria's economy of what it called "households" – the millions of individual proprietor-farmers, petty traders, self-employed craftsmen and artisans, and single-vehicle transport operators. Together, it was estimated, they provided the greater part of employment in Nigeria and still accounted for most of the Gross Domestic Product. About an eighth of the proposed public investment, or some £123m., would go to this sector, although this was to prove to be one of the most difficult parts of the programme to make effective.

Transport was allocated about a quarter of the proposed investment. The great trunk road programme then started, and continued under later plans, has transformed long-distance travel in Nigeria, and is one of the answers to those who ask what happened to the oil money. Education had the next biggest allocation, with the universities taking over half the £50m. allocated.

Major industrial development was proposed. A plant would be built to liquefy for export the natural gas produced in abundance in Nigeria either independently or in association with petroleum. Much of this latter gas was "flared" and wasted. Yet twelve years later this plant was still under negotiation with the foreign partners who are essential if the product is to have an assured market. Nigeria's negotiators may have failed to realise how plentiful are the world supplies of this source of fuel, and so stood out for unrealistic terms.

At the end of the plan period construction was also expected to start on an integrated iron and steel plant, in which the Soviet Union was to be the chief technical partner. Construction of this did not start, however, until 1980 and the delays – partly due, it was said, to the Russians sending plans with instructions only in their language – have led to some criticism of the Russians in Nigeria.

The Lagos ministry to which Shehu Shagari had returned was totally different from the new one to which he had gone in 1959. It was still understaffed for its responsibilities. But there were economists of all kinds, there was a conference of planners to bring together state and federal officials, an economic planning unit which was being expanded into a full-scale central planning office, an economic advisory committee, etc. Relations with the Ministry of Finance, however, had still not been satisfactorily defined – nor perhaps, ever will be.

The first "Progress Report" on the 1970-74 Plan was optimistic about what was being achieved in the first year and very optimistic about the recovery of the economy after the war, although admitting that inflation and unemployment gave cause for concern. It also sounded a warning, which has been constantly heard since. Agriculture was lagging behind while oil was a wasting asset – there was no sign of the "Green Revolution". Yet, said the planners, "steady growth of the economy will to a large extent depend on what is happening to the agricultural sector".

Once more, before he had had time to come to grips with the problems of a new ministry, Shehu Shagari was to move. In October, 1971, he succeeded Chief Obafemi Awolowo as Federal Commissioner of Finance, the post which, with External Affairs, and Petroleum Resources, was one of the three most important among the commissionerships allocated to civilians (Chief Awolowo was also Vice-Chairman of the Federal Executive Council, a position which now lapsed).

Chief Awolowo, even his enemies admit, is a competent and earnest administrator. He is above all, however, a politician and he had sensed that in the competition among civilians for power after the soldiers retired – a prospect which the end of the war had brought – it could be an advantage to be detached from the military regime. For this regime, in his view, was certain to become increasingly unpopular. His release in 1967 from Calabar jail, where he had been serving his sentence for alleged treasonable felony, had been intended by Gen. Gowon as a gesture towards the unity of the Federation. Many of the Chief's people, the Yoruba, doubted if there had been a conspiracy at all.

It was, in fact, to be eight years before Chief Awolowo was able to test his popularity with the Nigerian electors, in the

1979 presidential election. Gen. Gowon abandoned his plan
for a return to civilian rule in 1976, and it was partly because of
this that he was overthrown by his military colleagues on July
29, 1975. It was left to the military regime which then took over
to make immediate and meticulous plans to hand over to the
politicians in 1979. In the election that year Awolowo was to
be defeated by Shehu Shagari.

When Chief Awolowo announced his intention of resign-
ing, Gowon and the Secretary to the Military Government,
Abdul Atta, after surveying the field, once again came independently to the same conclusion. It was, some thought
surprisingly, supported by Allison Ayida, who had already
gone to Finance. The man to succeed Chief Awolowo was
Shehu Shagari. Once more, however, he was a reluctant
appointee. Important though the Ministry of Finance was, its
work seemed arid in comparison with the development and
reconstruction work undertaken by his existing ministry.
Moreover, although resumption of oil production and the
recovery of the economy were reviving revenue, and the
policy of pay-as-you-go followed during the civil war meant
that it had left no burden of debt, the Ministry of Finance was
still the ministry whose main job was to say "No". Yet it said
it with unconvincing authority, since its commissioner was not
a member of the Supreme Military Council, the country's
sovereign body, while the most strident demands for spending came from the soldiers themselves. Gen. Gowon was also
unnecessarily indulgent to the demands and the overspend-
ing of the state governments, which depended almost entirely
on federal funds; for he regarded the states as "my babies".

Gen. Gowon's choice of his commissioners was shrewd. His
method of announcing their appointments and of inducting
them into office, however, was unpredictable. The announcement of Shehu Shagari's appointment to the Ministry of
Economic Development and Reconstruction was so delayed
that he went home for the Sallah. In Sokoto he received
instructions to lead, in his new capacity, the Nigerian delegation to the UN Economic Commission for Africa meeting at
Tunis. There he went without a briefing. He was told of his

appointment to Finance long after Chief Awolowo had left, so there was no "hand-over" between the two men later to be presidential rivals.

To replace Awolowo as a commissioner and Executive Council member from the Western State, Gowon chose Dr Adebayo Adedeji, a highly qualified economist, with wide experience as a senior civil servant and later Professor of Public Administration at the University of Ife. Not surprisingly Dr Adedeji expected to go to the Ministry of Finance. Gen. Gowon told him that a replacement commissioner had no right to the portfolio of his predecessor, and that he would take Shehu Shagari's place at the Ministry of Economic Development and Reconstruction. He was later to become Executive Secretary of the UN Economic Commission for Africa, in which capacity he presided at the launching in Lagos of the collection of Shehu Shagari's speeches, *My Vision of Nigeria.*

In Nigeria the annual budget is the main instrument for regulating the economy, although the greatest influence on the economy is still the behaviour of external markets for oil. So important is this budget that when Shehu Shagari was Commissioner for Finance only Gen. Gowon himself and Allison Ayida knew its contents until a few hours before the early morning broadcast in which its outline was given by the Head of State. The Commissioner would later give a more detailed explanation at a news conference. Anybody who had advance information about budget prospects, particularly about import duties, could make a fortune. No allegations about this were made against these three, although they had been made about some in charge of the budgets under the 1960-66 civilian regime.

Management of Nigeria's swelling revenues was a problem for officials unused to such plenty. A country like Kuwait or Saudi Arabia looks abroad for profitable investment for its surpluses. Arab government investment in London property, for example, is vast. While a growing number of private Nigerians own flats or houses, sometimes very costly, in London, the Federal Government has been concerned to keep its surplus funds liquid and safe – available for spending fairly soon after being acquired. So under Shehu Shagari the ministry adopted a policy of placing surplus funds abroad, where they could earn short-term interest, not just in Britain, where traditionally such funds had been held, or in the US, but also in the currencies of other major suppliers. Nigeria never, as was alleged at the time, put "pressure" on sterling by withdrawing funds from London to indicate her dislike of Britain's southern African policies. Such a withdrawal, by weakening sterling, would have reduced the value of Nigeria's remaining sterling holdings.

Unlike some of the Arab governments Nigeria, to sustain her development plans, is now a major borrower in the international market. The Federal Government also backs state government loans abroad, particularly for water supplies. Since the Federal Government itself has to raise loans, for example for the steel industry, there is no question of funds being left unemployed.

African governments, particularly military ones, are even more reluctant than others to devalue their currencies. Devaluation suggests failure and, apart from its practical consequences, gives ammunition to critics. In February 1973, however, Shehu Shagari, who had a reputation among civil servants for being a very effective spokesman for his ministry, had to ask the Federal Executive Council for a speedy decision about devaluing the naira. The US dollar had just been devalued by 10%, following an 8.5% devaluation a year earlier. Sterling had also effectively been devalued by some 10%.

If the naira, which had been linked to these two devalued currencies, now kept its former value Nigeria would receive less in naira for her exports. Oil was obviously the main issue; yet scarcely less important were the overseas earnings of the producers of export crops, whose output was falling. Devaluation would make possible an increase in the naira price paid to them by the government marketing boards. The low naira price encouraged smuggling of produce into Nigeria's neighbours. Devaluation would mean that imports from countries which had not devalued, notably Germany and Japan, would cost more, including imports for Nigeria's industries. But industry would benefit because of the rise in the naira price of imported competitive products. Devaluation would also increase the local costs of the development plan projects. It would limit imports of consumer goods, at a time when more were needed to combat inflation.

In a lecture given in Lagos in 1974 Shehu Shagari explained that in fact, regardless of the devaluation of the currency with which it was associated, the naira should have been devalued anyway. Nigeria was

> losing its share of the world export market to her competitors. For example, export earnings from agricultural products which were of the order of ₦400m. before the war, fell to only ₦330m. by the end of 1972 – the lowest since 1958. In addition, smuggling of export produce was known to be on the increase, costing Nigeria heavily in foreign exchange and government revenue. Black marketing in Nigerian currency was also known to be carried on at a cheaper rate than the official rate.

In the end the Federal Executive Council agreed to a devaluation of 10%, the first devaluation of Nigeria's currency since 1958. Within a year, however, the naira had appreciated by more than 10%. In January 1982 it was, in fact, devalued as a result of the use of a new method of calculating its value against foreign countries. The naira remains strong, however, although this reflects oil earnings rather than any real strength in the economy.

Shehu Shagari was to criticise, in a paper on revenue allocation which he delivered at a symposium in Lagos in 1977, the arbitrary handling of funds by the military rulers. "In many instances development plans and accepted norms of financial management were recklessly disregarded with the result that many states became hopelessly short of funds." Eventually the Federal Government "itself came to realise that the much trumpeted oil boom can no longer be regarded as a panacea to all financial and development ills". The absence of parliamentary control over the disbursement of public funds meant that military authorities developed a

dangerous habit of ordering the creation of new projects out of the blue, or imposing new and outrageous dimensions to existing projects with little or no regard to the financial implications and to sound planning. States which became short of funds as a result of mismanagement of finances and/or plan distortions were awarded dish-outs from federal coffers in the form of loans which they had no intention of repaying or grants which had no relation to their performance or needs.

State governments committed the Federal Government to

huge foreign exchange expenses by entering into contracts with foreign firms without clearance with the Federal Ministry of Finance. Even some federal ministries, notably Defence, were in such nasty habits to the extent that in a number of cases the Head of State had to intervene and over-rule the Ministry of Finance in favour of the delinquents. On the other hand there were occasions when governors of oil producing states were summoned and ordered to surrender more than half of their states' shares of mining rents and royalties to the distributable pool account in order to help less fortunate states.

Although Gen. Gowon, to whom this criticism was particularly directed, had been overthrown, there was still a military government in Nigeria, and few in Shehu Shagari's audience supposed that his remarks did not, in part at least, apply to military rule in general.

Civilian commissioners in Nigeria's military regimes were in no doubt about where power lay. But their appointments, in spite of Chief Awolowo's decision to take no chance, were generally assumed to indicate not their approval of military rule but their desire to help in the administration of their country, or to emphasise that the soldiers could not manage without civilian help. Certainly Shehu Shagari never saw his terms of office as state or federal commissioner as an endorsement of military rule.

For example, an address he gave to the Nigerian Institute of Journalists in May 1973 he called "On political freedom as a pre-requisite for economic freedom". In this he condemned the view that "any kind of political arrangements can be combined with any kind of economic arrangements", a view which he feared was widely held in Nigeria, not least among intellectuals. He, however, maintained that freedom was man's ultimate goal, however much importance was attached to "welfare". He realised that under a military regime "however benevolent" the same standards could not be applied as to an elected government. Yet they had a military regime only because "the political parties in the first republic were so intent on getting into power that they were prepared to go to any extreme to achieve their goal". That was the lesson he was to emphasise after he had become President. That he could, in 1973, speak in this way without attracting any criticism from the soldiers, indicates the tolerance of the military regime. Yet he did not for a moment consider that question before deciding to say what he did.

A major problem suddenly raised for the Ministry of Finance was Gen. Gowon's unexpected announcement, made in Sokoto in 1974, that Nigeria was to have Universal Primary Education (UPE). The Head of State had, apparently, consulted nobody about the cost of this plan, which would be one of the world's greatest social experiments. It meant that, when it was fully implemented, some fifteen million children would be in primary schools. From 1966-7 (Gowon had announced an earlier year) all children reaching the age of six would be admitted to schools, so that by 1981 all children aged between six and eleven would be in school.

In Shehu Shagari's own North-Western State, the government noted that although only seven per cent of children of school age were at school in the state (most of the rest attended Koranic schools) the annual recurrent cost of education was £650,000. If UPE was introduced, the cost would be £9m., a sum which the Federal Government would have to find.

Another of the problems for the Commissioner for Finance was raised by the "Udoji Commission". This commission sub-

121

mitted a report in September 1974, after a long examination of the public services. The report recommended substantial increases in salaries for civil servants – but linked the increases to what is now called "productivity". The senior civil servants, supported, it was alleged, by Gen. Gowon who was seeking popularity at all levels in the civil service, were able to ensure implementation of the salary increase proposals, while ignoring the recommendations about productivity and the Central Bank's advice against backdating the awards. The Commissioner of Finance seems to have been scarcely consulted about these decisions, although, because all salary and wage levels were adjusted to reflect those of the civil servants, the consequences for the inflation rate were momentous, and were never rectified.

Years after he left the Ministry of Finance Shehu Shagari was to be asked by journalists, after politics had "returned", whether he accepted any responsibility for the serious financial malpractices which, after the overthrow of Gen. Gowon in 1975 – Shehu Shagari remained Commissioner of Finance until then – had been revealed by commissions of enquiry. He himself was, as always, completely cleared by these commissions. His reply was that the Ministry of Finance was concerned with the collection and allocation of revenue, not with the details of actual expenditure, which were the concern of other agencies such as the Auditor-General or, now, the legislature's committees. His ministry had no control over the making of contracts, provided these fell within the financial allocation given to those making them. Nor had it any control over the way in which states spent the federal revenues allocated to them as of right, although it was concerned with special allocations for specific purposes.

Obviously he was aware that some military governors, in particular, were believed to be enriching themselves. Yet, as he was to find as President, some of the allegations about corruption most confidently made in Nigeria prove to be baseless, or to be unsupported by evidence, while some of the most serious instances go unsuspected.

As he took office as Commissioner for Finance, Shehu

122

Shagari could expect national revenues to mount, though not as fast as demands on them. Total federally-collected revenues in 1970-71 amounted to some ₦1,170m. In 1971-2, his first year at Finance, they came to ₦1,404m. In 1972-3 they rose to almost ₦1,700m. – and Nigeria was not yet suffering from the inflation which was soon to make people ask whether oil was, after all, such a blessing.

Shehu Shagari, however, could never have foreseen the revenue explosion which followed. Because of the OPEC price rises, revenue in 1973-4 was, at ₦4,537m., almost three times that of the previous year, an experience which few ministries of finance can have known. The next year's rise alone was also some ₦1,000m., or a sum almost as great as the total 1970-1 revenue.

Nigeria had now become an international economic force, and the framers of the 1975-80 National Development Plan could say – wrongly as it proved – that finance was no longer a constraint on national development. Yet the financial danger of almost complete dependence for revenues on oil, and so on world market demand for it, was clear.

It was a danger constantly emphasised by the new Commissioner of Finance. His warnings, however, were given little attention by some of his colleagues or by those in charge of the finances of the states, although they depended almost totally for their funds on their share of federally-collected revenue, and so on the oil market. In 1973-4 over 82 per cent of federally-collected revenues derived from oil alone. The percentage was not to vary greatly in subsequent years, some of which, notably 1978, when federal revenues fell heavily, showed how vulnerable Nigeria's finances were. Again, after Shehu Shagari had become President, revenue estimates for 1982, at ₦11,63bn., showed a drop of over ₦3bn. over those for 1981.

The states' allocations from federally-collected revenues increased hugely – from ₦86.5m. in 1968-9 to well over ₦1,000m. in 1975-6. Such was their extravagance, however, and so little control could the Federal Ministry of Finance exercise over them, that nearly all ran deficits, in contrast to the Federal Government. Other African governments, however, looked enviously at Nigeria whose external reserves when Shehu Shagari left the Ministry of Finance in 1975 exceeded ₦5,000m.

So many were the international conferences which Nigeria's Commissioner for Finance was obliged to attend that he must now find his presidential travels, although their scope has been criticised, very restricted. There were the meetings in various capitals of Commonwealth Finance Ministers in preparation for the annual meetings of the World Bank and the International Monetary Fund (IMF), of both of which institutions he was a Governor. There were the special meetings of the IMF "Committee of Twenty", at which he formed a friendly relationship with M. Giscard D'Estaing, then France's Finance Minister. There were meetings of the African Development Bank, in which Nigeria is the biggest shareholder – in Abidjan, in Lusaka, in Rabat and in Dakar.

While he was a commissioner in Lagos, Shehu Shagari had not abandoned his interests in this own North-Western State, where he remained a Sokoto councillor, much concerned with local finance. He was also chairman of the *ad hoc* Sokoto Local Authority Committee "to combat Immorality and Extravagance" – an ambitious programme. This committee examined such matters as the practice of religious mallams taking away for "teaching" children who would later be lost in the cities, and proposed bye-laws to deal with this. It considered, too, the rise in the bride-price, and the making of "customary presents". Because of his association with both groups Shehu Shagari was a keen member of the Sokoto reconciliation committee which sought to improve relations between the settled farmers and the Fulani cattle herders. Neither this nor any other body could solve finally a problem which results from the meeting of two different modes of life. The committee, however, carefully analysed the causes of conflict and suggested means, such as the prohibition of cultivation, by Fulani as well as farmers, of grazing areas.

As well as his mission to Saudi Arabia as Amirul-Hajj (described in Chapter 13), Gen. Gowon gave him another task not strictly related to his duties as Commissioner for Finance.

He was chairman of the *ad hoc* Cabinet Committee on the "dual status" of Lagos – as a federal and a state capital. This decided that the Federal Government should take over responsibilities in the city which the state government could not discharge, rather than subsidising the state government further to meet them.

Just before he left the Ministry of Economic Development and Reconstruction Alhaji Shehu also undertook a mission abroad which showed him the great influence which post-civil war Nigeria could have in Africa. In October 1971, accompanied only by Mr F. O. Olufolabi, then a medium-ranking officer of the Ministry of External Affairs, he went to Kampala and Dar-es Salaam. The task given to him by Gen. Gowon was to persuade the new ruler of Uganda, Amin, still basking in the favour of Edward Heath, and the veteran Dr Julius Nyerere of Tanzania, who so recently had backed the secession in Nigeria, that whatever the origins of the dangerous dispute which had grown up between them, they must curb it. They must withdraw their troops from their common border, where there had been skirmishes, and end their argument over Uganda's representation at the East African Community, an organisation which at the time Nigeria regarded as an example to Africa.

When the Nigerian mission arrived in Entebbe it was told that Amin was out of town and there was no news of his movements. Later in the morning a lunch party at the house of Nigeria's acting High Commissioner, Mr J. F. Ajayi, was inter-rupted by the news that Amin was back and wanted to see the mission at 2 p.m. Lunch ended abruptly. It was an hour, however, before Amin, sporting a huge colour photograph of Pope Paul VI behind a settee on which he gave audience, actually saw them. He still felt it necessary at that time to consult ministers and civil servants, some of whom were with him when he finally received the Nigerians. It was said that Amin took over twenty minutes to study a letter from Gen. Gowon and other documents offered by the Nigerians, while President Nyerere later completed the same exercise in a few minutes.

125

Alhaji Shehu now recalls that although Amin had loudly proclaimed the dangers of a Tanzanian invasion of Uganda, Kampala appeared free of war fever. Amin's case was that Nyerere was training supporters of President Obote, whom he had displaced, as guerillas and saboteurs, and that this was the only danger to peace. In the end Amin agreed to accept mediation from Gen. Gowon or President Kenyatta. He also explained that a mysterious delegation which he had announced he was sending to Dr Vorster in South Africa would not go. This delegation was intended in some unexplained way to help freedom fighters and to question Dr Vorster on his own ground. Alhaji Shehu was reported to have expressed Nigeria's relief at the cancellation of the delegation; but also to have stated bluntly that in such delicate matters an African state should leave no room for doubt about its intentions.

The interview with Dr Nyerere, who had no ministers or civil servants with him, on the following day, was much longer and much more difficult. It seems, however, that the firm insistence of Alhaji Shehu that Nigeria saw some action, such as withdrawing forces a specific distance from the border, as essential to show his intention of keeping the peace, impressed Tanzania's President.

How serious the dispute really was is uncertain. Amin had not yet shown his character fully. But Dr Nyerere, who has since in fact invaded Uganda, was at the time deeply concerned about the fighting in his southern neighbour, Mozambique, and was unlikely to risk a war with an African neighbour, for whatever reasons.

Alhaji Shehu Shagari's mission, however, can be counted a success. The relatively junior Nigerian representative had shown that even with such men as Dr Nyerere and Amin, his polite and patient determination can achieve results.

Appointments of federal commissioners were for three years. In 1974 Gen. Gowon offered Shehu Shagari an extension, which he accepted, the only invitation of this kind, it was said, which Gen. Gowon offered. This extension proved to be academic. On July 29, 1975, Gen. Gowon, then at the OAU meeting in Kampala, was removed by a bloodless coup organised by senior army officers, who then installed Brigadier, later General, Murtala Muhammed as Head of State.

The accusations against Gen. Gowon included not only his abandonment of the 1976 date for the return to civilian rule, but the ineffectiveness of his government, and the corruption of some of his state military governors. All civilian commissioners, federal and state, were dismissed; but Murtala Muhammed invited Shehu Shagari to become Nigeria's High Commissioner in London. This he felt he could not do, because of the arbitrary way in which the incoming military regime had dismissed him, although there were no allegations of misbehaviour against him. For the second time he returned from Lagos to Sokoto completely disillusioned with the national politics of Nigeria and resentful of his own treatment.

8

POLITICS NO MORE?

Freed from the pressure of the most important office he had yet held, with its nationwide and international responsibilities, the former Commissioner for Finance once again threw himself with enthusiasm into the educational and social affairs of his own state.

On July 1, 1976, Shehu Shagari was appointed by the Military Governor of the North-Western State, not yet split into Sokoto and Niger states, chairman of a new Sokoto Urban Development Authority (SUDA). The old city, slowly spreading into the countryside, was overwhelmed by its role as capital of a major state. Plastic containers and metal cans, cardboard and bottles, broken-down cars and abandoned equipment were now added to the traditional debris of mankind. Any open space, including the footways, became a refuse dump. Everywhere heaps of more-or-less offensive garbage awaited collection by the old local authority, which had neither the means, nor probably the will, to do anything about them. Drains were blocked throughout the city by refuse, debris, mud and stones. Even if clear they were unable to cope with the fury of rainstorms, which flooded the streets and dwellings.

Disposal of refuse was clearly the first task of any body charged with the care of the Sokoto urban area. This task was given to SUDA, which was reponsible for municipal services within a ten mile radius of the city centre.

The great central market at Sokoto had also been burned down. The normal chaos created by traders' stalls and hawkers, the roadside motor car and bicycle repairers, stacks of firewood and thatching, obstructively parked vehicles, and open-air cooking stalls, was now worsened by the absence of any major central area laid out specially for traders.

A new market was urgently needed. SUDA finally built it, at a cost, with its broad access roads and huge parking area, of some ₦24m. It is one of the biggest in West Africa, where markets are great social as well as commercial institutions.

After refuse disposal and the market, SUDA's main problem was the urban bus service. At the end of March 1977, for example, of the authority's ten buses only two were service-able. It was even feared that people might forget the very existence of the service. Replacement Bedford buses bought in the following months proved woefully inadequate; they were soon replaced by satisfactory Leylands.

A related problem was the provision of school buses. Alhaji Shehu Shagari was chairman of the *ad hoc* committee consider-ing this service. The problem was not so much the vehicles as the users. It was at first assumed that the service would be con-fined to children of government employees. The state govern-ment, however, thought it impossible to justify a subsidy for such a limited class of users and in 1977 the service was made available to all (the Universal Primary Education programme had started throughout the country) at a fare of 5 kobo each way. SUDA, wisely, unlike London Transport, sold tickets in books.

To clean up Sokoto, vehicles and labourers were not enough. Serious disease in Nigeria is mostly the result of dirt as well as poverty. The people had to be made aware of the danger refuse posed to their health, and of the likelihood that the annual flooding which they dreaded would be made worse if they blocked the drains. Once again Alhaji Shehu became chairman of an *ad hoc* committee – Operation Keep Sokoto Clean – which was in action within hours of its appointment by the state governor. Refuse vehicles were hired or bought, labourers were recruited, and a publicity campaign launched. While the task remains formidable today the refuse *is* regularly collected in Sokoto's streets and properly disposed of; people *are* more ready to use the SUDA receptacles for their rubbish, while still reserving the right to use the roadsides and vacant spaces. Although the competition is not keen – since a city like Ibadan, or even Lagos itself, is notorious for filth – Sokoto is today regarded as the cleanest major city in the federation, even if, like all the others, it still lacks a modern sewage system. As recently as January 1982, at a meeting in Sokoto, the Federal Minister of Housing and Environment complained that in many states refuse collection was "ineffective" and equipment for it was "in a continuous state of disrepair".

In March 1980, Alhaji Shehu, now President, had the pleasure of formally opening the great SUDA market. Its 50 acre area includes a lorry park for 400 vehicles. All the 6,000 stalls, built in rows, some with rounded and some with flat roofs, have concrete floors. There are abundant water and sanitary facilities, and, since it proved impossible to devise an economical system for providing each stall with light, there are a number of floodlights of the kind familiar at football grounds. There is, too, a most attractively designed mosque. A number of trees have been planted on the previously cleared site and, as elsewhere in the city, there are well-kept flower borders.

The market is clearly zoned into some sixteen areas for different commodities – meat, fish, textiles, groceries, etc. – and for different crafts. It is sad that the intricate task of establishing which traders were stallholders in the old market, and are thus entitled to places in the new, was not completed until long after the formal opening. When the traders did move in, their wares included, as well as the traditional textiles, grain, meat, scent, portable battery-television sets from Japan, powerful radio receivers assembled in Lagos, electric fans of all kinds and even umbrellas from Shanghai. Later some traders were to complain that the stall rents were too high; but the market remains SUDA's great monument.

In all SUDA activities the chairman was a tireless leader, always attending meetings – even during a Constituent Assembly recess – earnestly considering the tenders for a primary school or for a refuse vehicle, inspecting sites and listening to complaints. The authority's budget, by the standards of local government in Nigeria, was considerable. Recurrent spending in 1978-9 was estimated at almost a million naira, mostly provided by the state government. Yet the chairman, who might earnestly scrutinise a ₦13,000 tender for two refuse vehicles, had recently handled a national budget of five and a half billion naira. And the authority's office, near the new market, has remained a one-storey bungalow.

The general manager of SUDA was J.R. Muggeridge, a younger brother of the famous Malcolm, who shares some of his asperity. He was, however, one of those British officials who found working in independent Nigeria, and perhaps particularly in Sokoto, very congenial, and he designed the new market. He had managed a body similar to SUDA in Kaduna. With him, until he retired, Alhaji Shehu worked closely and cordially.

SUDA's chairman was faced, as operators of public transport are, with the problem of setting fares at a level which people could and would pay, while trying to make the service self-supporting. This proved no more possible in Sokoto than in London – Sokoto having the overwhelming additional problem of poor maintenance of vehicles and unavailability of spares. The school bus service had an additional problem. Usage was considerably less in the morning, when so many parents could take the children to school in their own cars, than in the afternoon – a problem of affluence.

SUDA was a hybrid body, designed to meet the particular problems of a rapidly expanding city, and affording its chairman valuable experience in handling such problems. Its responsibilities included planning beyond the metropolitan area – a failure to plan had left the old airport runway no room to expand and had allowed building dangerously close to it. Sokoto's new, international, airport, by contrast, is some seven miles from the city centre and the university's permanent site is even further out. Inside the metropolitan area, the ten mile radius from the city centre, SUDA was responsible for developing and actually running services. But for the market it called on Scott Wilkinson Kirkpatrick as consultants; it was never itself adequately staffed for such a task.

While he was chairman of SUDA, Alhaji Shehu was also patron of the "Yabo People Association". The Yabo district, which includes Shagari, then had some 150,000 people and 360 villages and hamlets. In 1975, appealing to friends all over the Federation for assistance to the association, he described the area as poor, lacking water and suffering from depopulation, and referred to the dispensary built at Shagari through self-help. The response was considerable. For example, from Chief Abiola, later to be a leading colleague of Shehu Shagari in the National Party of Nigeria, came a Volkswagen ambulance to be based at Yabo.

If in 1978 Shehu Shagari had not been "drafted" back into high politics, he might have become a well-known business-man, though not one of those Nigerian millionaires who flourish through companies they own and direct themselves. This was the heyday of "indigenisation", when, by federal government decree, all foreign-owned companies had to have a minimum Nigerian participation in their shareholdings, ranging from 60 to 40 per cent. These companies were looking, at the time, for Nigerian directors, as were many government-sponsored bodies. Alhaji Shehu Shagari's commercial experience was confined to directorships in the now Nigerian-controlled companies, whose former owners overseas were known as "associates". The companies saw in the former Commissioner of Finance, who had been twice cleared of any misbehaviour in office, a man with the experience they needed.

Nigerian friends also felt that such directorships kept him in national public life, whatever his political intentions or Sokoto responsibilities. He received far more offers of directorships than he could possibly accept. He is not commercially-minded; but in a country where almost everybody of all ages, both sexes, and all ethnic origins, is by nature a trader, he felt that such directorships would give him a valuable new experience. As President, he has indeed found that this brief connection with commerce has been of help.

132

His best-known commercial appointment was as chairman of Peugeot Automobiles Nigeria. In 1975 the company began production at its Kaduna plant, making up "kits" imported from the French associate, with a slowly increasing proportion of locally-manufactured components (the slogan "assembled in Nigeria by Nigerians" was not very exciting). Shehu Shagari was appointed chairman in 1976, in succession to Alhaji Ahmed Joda, and took the job very seriously.

Peugeots have long been popular in Nigeria. In 1980, partly because of the protection for locally-assembled vehicles, the company sold over 50,000 cars – more than double the sales of Volkswagen, then the only other car assembly firm in Nigeria, which Peugeot overtook in 1976, and far more than any imported make. In particular Peugeot almost monopolises the huge and growing taxi market.

Originally the "kits", on which, rather than on its return from its Nigerian investment – 40 per cent in the Kaduna plant – the French company has made its profit, were flown into Kano. Because, after a period of acute congestion, the ports had become under-used, the Federal Military Government in 1979 insisted that the Peugeot cargoes should come by sea and go up to Kaduna by rail. Perhaps, however, resentment that Nigeria Airways could not do the job which the French airline, UTA, was doing played a part. The company made dire prophecies of pilfering, but the government was adamant. By this time Shehu Shagari had resigned the chairmanship – and the government's decision has never been reversed.

With its light commercial vehicle production as well as its cars, the company had 40 per cent of the total Nigerian vehicle market by 1979, when it employed over 3,000 workers, a number which has since risen. Shehu Shagari recalls that the main problems they faced when he was chairman were the military government's controls, which restricted the prices the company could charge, but were often ignored by dealers, and the power failures which affected all Nigeria's industries.

He talks little, however, about this experience. One feels that the role of non-executive chairman, in spite of its perquisites, such as a house in Kaduna and another on Victoria

Island, Lagos, suit him as little as would the role of ceremonial President – it is too impersonal and remote from the real problems of the organisation. In any case he was essentially the representative of the Federal Military Government, which had 35 per cent of the company's shares. He found his inability to challenge technical points made by the French management irksome, particularly in the matter of Nigerianisation of the staff, although he was impressed by the warmth of his reception at the French headquarters of Peugeot.

More to his liking, perhaps, was his membership of the board of Cadbury Nigeria, which produces a wide range of products including Schweppes mineral waters under licence, biscuits, Bournvita, and even Jeyes disinfectants. This was a less impersonal operation and more firmly based in Nigeria. On his visit to the Cadbury headquarters at Bournville his views were listened to carefully. He was a director, too, of Nigerian Dredging and Marine, which has a Dutch associate, of International Housing Nigeria, with an American connection, of Roads Nigeria, the contractors, and of Associated Industries. Finally he was on the board of PZ Industries, the successful manufacturer of detergents, refrigerators, etc., and associate of the Manchester-based Paterson Zochonis. His friend Alhaji Shehu Malami, Sarkin Sudan Wurno, is chairman of this Nigerian company.

He was a conscientious attender of board meetings, and did his "homework" for them. But in a country where trading is second nature for the great majority, he seems to be exceptional. It is not that he finds commerce distasteful, in the manner of some British colonial officials, or that he fails to do all in his power to further the interests of enterprises of all kinds in Nigeria. He is simply not interested in making or accumulating money for himself and his family beyond their reasonable needs. This he showed when he attempted to resist the National Assembly proposal that his salary as President should be raised from ₦20,000 – the figure he proposed – to ₦25,000, the figure originally proposed by his party. Even the higher figure falls far below many commercial salaries in Nigeria, and compares poorly with Mrs Thatcher's £32,000;

As Federal Commissioner for Finance, Alhaji Shehu Shagari in his office on 28 August 1972 explains the new currency.

The Commissioner for Finance launching the 5 kobo and 10 kobo decimal coins on 3 July 1972 at the Central Bank.

The Finance Commissioner paying a visit to the historic Badagry Township with other Commissioners.

The Managing Director of the International Monetary Fund, Mr Pierre Paul Schwitzer, paying a courtesy call on the Commissioner for Finance.

but the legislators wanted it so that all political salaries, including their own, could be raised. When he failed to have his way, Alhaji Shehu at once allotted the extra ₦5,000 to four charities, including the Nigerian Red Cross, with which he had worked when he was at the Ministry of Economic Development and Reconstruction, and the Nigerian Society for the Blind, for which, many years ago, he was prepared to become a full-time worker. He was also, incidentally, showing his confidence in such voluntary organisations. He maintains this practice, selecting different charities each year.

The highest income he has ever had in a single year was ₦43,167 – and that was quite exceptional, even though it would have been considered derisory by hundreds of Nigerian businessmen and lawyers, including many of his "radical" political critics. Nor have his net "assets" as declared at various times, including his accession to the Presidency, been impressive. There is the house in Sokoto and the house in Shagari, although the farm there, in spite of his investment in it, is not a realisable asset. Like most people in a position to do so he leased a plot from Lagos State Government on Victoria Island, the new expensive suburb of Lagos. All paid the market rent; but it is surprising that they did not realise that there would be, as there was, a hostile reaction among those not so fortunate when details of the transactions were made public.

There was, too, a plot in the industrial estate at Port Harcourt which has cost him a lot in bank charges. There were a few thousand shares; and that was it.

The Port Harcourt plot, indeed, he never even saw, and no longer owns. For it was presented to him when he was Federal Commissioner of Finance by the then Rivers State Government. Governor Diete-Spiff argued that he had been of such assistance to the fledgling state that he should be an honorary citizen; and for that to be possible he had to have a piece of land in the state. The State Government also named a street after him. With a bank loan Shehu Shagari had a house built on the land, but sold it to help to finance his election campaign. Contractors financed development of the Victoria Island site, and themselves draw the rent until their costs are met.

Shehu Shagari's North-Western State was affected, as were all states, by the determination of the Murtala Muhammed government in 1975 to "purge" (the word generally used) the public services. It was not, however, only officials suspected of corruption who were "retired". It was difficult to know at the time precisely who made the choice, and it was later officially admitted that there could have been mistakes. The grounds for retirement, however, included incompetence, laziness and lack of ability to lead. Some officials were suspected of having falsified their ages so that they could remain in their jobs after retirement age. The term "deadwoods" was popularly used to describe all these unfortunate officials. The retirement of the head of the North-Western State's civil service and of five Permanent Secretaries was announced by the Governor on September 7, 1975. Six weeks later about seven hundred other officials were removed – mostly because they were over age – from the state and local governments, including about a hundred from Sokoto local authority.

In 1976 Sokoto was separated from Niger to become a new state, one of the seven then created, bringing the total to nineteen. Already short of staff, the "purge" had deprived it of some experienced people. Yet, pleased though he was at the creation of the new states, Shehu Shagari was still determined to accept none but purely local government office.

At the end of 1976 elections were held for the new "local governments" which the military regime had set up. These were intended both to establish a democratic basis for administration in Nigeria and to introduce a degree of uni-formity into local government. At the time local government had almost ceased to exist in many parts of the southern states, while in the northern states the big emirates, such as Sokoto, not only were able to provide a wide range of services but still, for many millions, represented "the government". The new authorities were to be elected, although military governors could, as they did in northern states, nominate a proportion of members, and no party affiliations were per-mitted. The Federal Government itself would ensure that they had adequate funds to man a wide range of services, an innovation in Nigeria.

Shehu Shagari stood for and was elected to the Yabo Local Government in which Shagari was included. He intended to use the office of councillor to further the local interests of his people. In fact he had taken the first step on his return to national politics. For members of the local governments were to elect the majority of the members of the Constituent Assembly (CA) which was to examine the draft constitution for civilian rule, to be established in 1979. This constitution had been prepared by the Constitution Drafting Committee (CDC) set up by the military regime in October 1975. Shehu Shagari was one of the CA members elected from Sokoto.

9

RETURN TO POLITICS

In the Constituent Assembly Shehu Shagari was at once regarded as a "senior statesman". He was, for example, secretary of the Assembly's powerful "Steering Committee". Almost all the important surviving politicians of the era before 1966 were members of the Constituent Assembly – MCAs – although not Dr Azikiwe or Chief Awolowo. Indeed so readily did members of the former legislatures reassert the parliamentary practices they had been following a dozen years earlier that young reporters, alarmed by the shouts of "Order, Order", the interruptions to speeches, the chants of "Hear, Hear" and the general informality of the proceedings, wondered if, after all, Nigeria was ready for a return to democracy. Their elders, however, explained to them that this was all part of the give-and-take of any democratic assembly. And so seriously were the proceedings taken that visitors in the public gallery were not allowed to take newspapers in with them, not because it was feared they might use them as missiles, but so that they had nothing to distract them from listening to the debate.

The Constituent Assembly met in Lagos on October 6, 1977. It was formally dissolved in September the following year, although it had presented the constitution it proposed to the Head of State some weeks earlier.

Before the assembly met, the draft which the CDC had delivered to General Obasanjo in September 1976 had been very extensively discussed throughout the country in symposia and other gatherings, in the newspapers and on radio and television. Shehu Shagari had joined in this national debate with views published in the *Daily Sketch* in November 1976 – he was already called a "frontline politician". Then he declared his support for an executive President elected by the whole nation, who could be a truly national, not sectional, leader. He also championed the division of power between the executive, the legislature, and the judiciary, and the end of the former division of influence, if not power, between a President and a Prime Minister. He commended, too, the proposal that ministers should be chosen from outside the legislature. Many of Nigeria's political problems under civilian rule, he said, had arisen because of the competition among legislators for ministerial appointments. Under the system now proposed a member of the legislature would simply be a representative of his people; you would go to the legislature "as a law maker and not as a job seeker".

The CDC draft did imply complete abandonment of the Westminster system under which Nigeria, like most British colonies, had become independent. There would be an executive President elected by the whole nation, who would select his ministers from outside the national legislature. Such a system is usually referred to as "American". But in contrast to the US constitution the CDC draft, as adopted by the Constituent Assembly, imposed on the federal government social duties such as provision throughout the country of equal opportunities for education. The constitution was also regarded as an instrument for fostering national unity, with its emphasis on the need for the President, in making appointments, etc., to have regard to the country's "federal character".

Some members of the CDC had urged the inclusion of socialism as one of the country's fundamental objectives. The majority felt this to be unrealistic for a state so commercially minded as is Nigeria. In the end the constitution provides that the state will "manage and operate the major sectors of the economy" – while protecting the rights of individuals to participate in these sectors. The constitution, as finally promulgated, also includes a formidable catalogue of "fundamental human rights" which the courts must protect.

Shehu Shagari's views on a new constitution were not, however, inspired only by the publication of the CDC draft or the imminent meeting of the Constituent Assembly. In what was now Sokoto State, as everywhere in Nigeria, the type of constitution needed to end the disasters of the "First Republic" was widely discussed. Shehu Shagari had been chairman of a committee of notables set up in Sokoto in February 1977 to consider the CDC draft in detail through sub-committees to which sections of the constitution were allocated. His own special interest was allocation of federally-collected revenue between the federal government and the states – an issue which was to loom large in Nigeria's politics during his presidency.

In a speech he gave at the Advanced Teachers' College in Sokoto in 1977 before the Constituent Assembly had met, Shehu Shagari maintained that a country could not have a "national ideology" if it also had, as Nigeria was to have, a multi-party system. It was possible, for example, to imagine the emergence of a party which opposed the concept of a government managing and operating the major sectors of the economy – yet that concept was embodied in the CDC draft constitution (and indeed retained in the constitution in its final form).

At about the same time, commenting on the CDC draft to an "orientation" course for members of the National Youth Service Corps, he questioned the idea that the proposed President could become a "dictator". Why, he asked,

in spite of our past and present experiences as a sovereign nation [do] we still entertain fears of so remote a possibility as the emergence of unbridled dictatorship, albeit through the ballot box, to descend upon this large, difficult, and complex society of diverse peoples, cultures and religions and impose its will with impunity? No; anyone who knows Nigeria well will agree with me that there just cannot be such a possibility in the Nigerian situation either now or in the foreseeable future.

In the Constituent Assembly Shehu Shagari re-emphasised the points he had made in the *Daily Sketch* about the importance of an executive president. "It is a tragedy", he said, "that up to now in our chequered history we have failed to produce a single national leader" to "transcend ethnic and sectional differences". An elected executive president "would provide an ideal symbol" of national unity and national purpose, "the like of which we have never experienced in the past". Nigerians would, he declared, having survived so many crises, "overcome passions, emotions, sectional affections. We shall rebuild our nation on firmer foundations".

Shehu Shagari himself had at this time no intention of filling this role, having decided, as he was to announce publicly when party politics were made legal in September 1978, that he could best serve his country as a Senator. Others, however, were already seeing him as the Nigerian most suited for the role. And it was in the Constituent Assembly that the movement was born which was to take him to the presidency.

Shehu Shagari also told assembly members that an essential role of the presidency was to strengthen national unity, and that they must therefore cast off their fears that an executive presidency opened the way to dictatorship. In any case, "I for one would not hesitate to vote for dictatorship if it was the only means of uniting and knitting together the diverse peoples of this country into a strong nation".

Throughout the months of the Constituent Assembly's deliberations Alhaji Shehu took part in debate after debate. Sometimes, as in the issues of revenue allocation and the executive presidency, he was dealing with the fundamental principles of the constitution. He was also interested in a multitude of lesser matters. He suggested, for example, that neither the Minister of Finance nor the Minister of Internal Affairs need be, as well as the Minister of Defence, a member of the National Defence Council as was proposed, since the President was very clearly in charge of defence. His advice was followed. The staffs of the legislatures, he maintained, should have access to promotion in the general government service, or their prospects would be too limited. In any case, what would happen to them if the legislatures were suspended by a coup?

He suggested that the draft constitution seemed too compli- cated for ordinary citizens to understand – in fact, when it finally became available for sale, it was a best-seller in Nigeria, being widely hawked by street traders, perhaps the only time that such a publication has had such a success. He asked for a definition of "pecuniary interest"; was a cocoa farmer MP prohibited from taking part in a debate on agriculture? He supported the granting to the President and governors of the power of creating ministries; the legislatures had the power of granting or withholding appropriations for ministries.

Shehu Shagari criticised the failure of the draft to deal adequately with land matters; to guard against revolution, he maintained, there must be justice in the distribution and use of land. In the end the constitution protected citizens only against official expropriation of their "property" – including their right to land – without compensation or just cause. Reviving one of his interests from the time when he was first Federal Minister of Economic Development, he urged the inclusion in the constitution of the status of the Niger Delta as a "special area" – now, in fact, an unrealistic idea. He suggested, unsuccessfully, that to some degree the size of the states' populations should affect their senatorial representa- tion. In the end each was represented equally in the Senate by five members.

In a discussion of the proposal that registered parties should be assisted in their election campaigns by federal government funds (which was authorised by the 1977 Electoral Decree), Shehu Shagari said that it was, in Nigerian conditions, un- realistic for parties to rely only on members' subscriptions. A nationwide party might need for its campaigning some 350 vehicles, many boats, and bicycles. Perhaps a party would need ₦10m for an election campaign. A party in power might also have an unfair advantage. Shehu Shagari saw nothing wrong in rich men underwriting party expenses; it could be seen as a contribution to democracy, provided it was open.

Referring to the creation of new states Shehu Shagari complained that in Nigeria they could think only of "subdivision". In the United States they had been interested in expansion. He wondered if it was realistic to treat all states as of equal importance constitutionally (they are now so treated).

The issue which produced the greatest dissension in the Constituent Assembly, to the dismay of those who looked forward to a Nigeria greatly different from the one they had known, was the CDC's proposal that there should be a new Sharia Court of Appeal at the federal level, parallel with the new Federal Court of Appeal. In Nigerian states which so decide, Sharia courts hear cases concerning Islamic personal law, and some states have Sharia Courts of Appeal. The CDC decided that it was necessary to "enable persons aggrieved by decisions of the State Sharia Courts of Appeal" to make "a further appeal to a higher court established for the Federation". Under certain circumstances appeals would lie from this Sharia Court of Appeal to the Supreme Court.

This CDC proposal may not have been unanimous but it seems to have excited no particular opposition in the committee's discussions. The CDC had met in private, but the proceedings of the Constituent Assembly were publicised continuously; and here the proposal produced from some non-Muslim members the accusation that it would confer on Muslims a favoured status under the constitution. There were suggestions that if there were to be a Sharia Court at the federal level, there should also be an ecclesiastical court of appeal for Christians – although there were no specifically Christian lower courts. Some MCAs from northern states, notably Kano and Kaduna, found the remarks made about supporters of the Sharia proposal by its critics so distasteful that they began to waver over their previous appeal for an executive presidency. A non-Muslim President, they feared, if he followed the line of the non-Muslim MCAs, might use his power to the disadvantage of Muslims. This was a far-fetched apprehension, but it illustrates the damage done to the Constituent Assembly's harmony by the controversy over the Sharia Court of Appeal.

The strongest critics were members from two states, largely

non-Muslim, whose territory had formed part of the former Northern Region and in which there had been considerable opposition to the former Northern People's Congress (NPC) – Plateau and Benue.

Shehu Shagari, while supporting the Sharia proposal, attempted conciliation. The issue, he said, was controversial only to those "who imagine it to be so". Muslims had made many sacrifices in the cause of national unity. They were not asking for Islamic law to be applied in criminal matters, and no non-Muslims would lose any right or advantage if the proposal was approved.

In December 1979 Shehu Shagari addressed a passionate appeal to the Constituent Assembly not to allow the Sharia issue to ruin the great hope which they should be offering Nigeria:

> This nation expects a lot from this honourable House. We must not let the country down. We must demonstrate to the nation, nay to the world, that we are here to re-build the nation on a firm and sure foundation and we are determined to succeed. We cannot afford to fail as our predecessors failed in 1967 to produce a constitution.

Unbelievably, he had to repeat this appeal four months later. In the meantime some ninety "pro-Sharia" MCAs had walked out of the assembly in April 1978, and had even queried its legitimacy. These members were not content to accept a compromise put forward by a sub-committee, whose chairman was the veteran and highly respected Yoruba former senior civil servant and diplomat, Chief Simeon Adebo. He suggested that judges learned in Islamic law should be appointed to the Federal Court of Appeal to hear Sharia cases.

Gen. Obasanjo himself appealed to those who had walked out to return. They did, but were unable to alter the Constituent Assembly's decision that there would be no Federal Sharia Court of Appeal. Instead, the new Federal Court of Appeal would hear cases from state Sharia Courts of Appeal, and for this purpose, the Federal Court of Appeal would include judges learned in Islamic law. At the same time,

144

instead of "ecclesiastical courts", it was agreed that appeal could be made from state courts to the Federal Court of Appeal, on cases arising out of "customary law" in those states which recognised traditional jurisdictions.

Many predicted that the "Sharia issue" had simply been pushed into the background in this way, and that it would emerge again under civilian rule. Some Muslim MCAs certainly threatened to raise the issue again after the return to civilian rule. They seem not to have done so, partly because, as Shehu Shagari himself suggested, very few people in the northern states aggrieved by a decision of a state Sharia Court of Appeal would be anxious to pursue their cause to a court in Lagos. To that extent the Sharia issue was artificial. It still almost wrecked the Constituent Assembly, and could arise again if "north-south" antagonisms were allowed to become important.

The other main issue which excited controversy in the Constituent Assembly, as it still does in Nigeria, was the creation of new states. Many members felt that the assembly was entitled to name new states which it decided should be created. That was an unrealistic view, since the assembly was only advisory, and could not make executive decisions. The definition of new states would have been an executive decision, as opposed to a definition of rules for their creation. It was decided that the assembly could make no definitions, but it approved the labyrinthine procedure for the creation of new states proposed by the CDC.

The Constituent Assembly made certain other changes in the CDC draft. It increased the number of seats in the House of Representatives, for example, from 350 to 450, and restricted the National Assembly to the use of the English language. The CDC had suggested fifteen years as the period before an election during which a conviction for corruption would disqualify a candidate. The Constituent Assembly decided that the starting date for the period should be October 1, 1960, the date of independence. It rejected the draft's elaborate proposals for a Public Complaints Commission.

The Supreme Military Council, for its part, also made

changes in the Constituent Assembly draft. It restored the CDC proposal that Nigerian languages could be used in the legislatures. It shortened to ten years the period before an election during which a conviction for corruption would disqualify a candidate from standing. It rejected the provision that the composition of the armed forces should be related to the population of each state, preferring a simple statement that the forces should in their composition reflect Nigeria's "federal character".

In general, however, the Supreme Military Council's changes were technical in nature, or were intended, as was the prohibition on the maintenance of bank accounts abroad by holders of public offices and legislators, to minimise corruption.

The constitution finally promulgated gave Nigeria a system which owed little to the Westminster example. Representative Nigerians, most of them elected to perform this task by their local councils, had freely designed or approved a system of government which they believed would suit Nigeria's special circumstances, and help to avoid the extravagances which had caused the first civilian system of government to founder. The constitution, Shehu Shagari himself fervently hoped, would show that Nigerians could "overcome passions, emotions and sectional affections". It would "rebuild the nation on a firm foundation".

As a good federalist, Shehu Shagari has always seen the central importance of "revenue allocation". In all federations the division of centrally-collected revenue between the federal government and the component units excites political controversy. In Nigeria's case the controversy was heightened because the nineteen state governments depend almost entirely on federally-collected revenue. Local governments also get most of their revenues not from funds they raise themselves, or even from the states, but from allocations made to them directly by the federal government.

The other two "tiers" of government, however, do not depend on the whims of the federal government or on political decisions for the amount of their allocations. These are made

146

according to a formula established by legislation, to which the federal government must conform. The formula has been changed from time to time down the years. At first the emphasis was on "derivation" – the principle that revenue should be allocated according to its region of origin. This was by stages altered to an emphasis on need, as measured chiefly by population, and on "equity" and "even development". The predominance of oil revenues in federally-collected revenues – the percentage rose from 43.6% in 1970 to 82.1% in 1973-4 – and the vast increase in the disproportion between revenues collected by the Federation and those collected by the States, required an elaborate formula. The CDC in its draft constitution offered no formula. It suggested, instead, a meeting of federal and state representatives to work out what Shehu Shagari criticised as a "stop-gap" arrangement. He was speaking at a symposium, in March 1977, organised by the *Daily Times*, to discuss the CDC draft. In this he spoke at length about revenue allocation.

As a former Federal Commissioner for Finance, Shehu Shagari emphasised that the sometimes arbitrary and haphazard methods used by the military in revenue matters would be impossible under a civilian government. Because of the likelihood that some state governments would be of a different political complexion from the federal government everything must be "clear-cut"; very little discretion should be left to individuals.

Claiming that revenue allocation in the past had been "the bane of Nigerian politics", Shehu Shagari urged a clear demarcation between federal, state and local government responsibilities; the CDC draft allowed too much "overlapping". The tendency of the Federal Military Government to "grab" functions from state governments had reduced the states to "mere puppets". The coming Constituent Assembly must draw a "bold line" for these responsibilities, and the different tiers of government must then be given by statute the funds to carry them out. The importance of federal grants for state government finances must be heavily reduced, so that state and local governments did not depend on the "whims

147

and caprices" of federal government functionaries. Grants should be used mainly to ensure "even development".

Alhaji Shehu was convinced that population was the only real basis for an allocation formula. He particularly ridiculed "derivation" as a basis for a formula, explaining that logically it would mean not that a state in some areas of which oil happened to be produced would be favourably treated, but that only those precise areas where oil was actually produced should benefit. He was also careful to emphasise that in their allocations to local governments state governments should follow the principles used by the federal government in its allocations to them. Shehu Shagari was to repeat to the Constituent Assembly what he told the *Daily Times* symposium. No oil, he emphasised to the Assembly, was found in Benin, capital of the oil-producing Bendel State. "Derivation" had made sense when most revenue came from agriculture. Oil, however "just happens" and is "God's bounty". People in the areas which actually produced oil were entitled to compensation for any adverse consequences of that production.

Shehu Shagari suggested that an expert commission should at once be established to produce recommendations to put before the Constituent Assembly, which was to meet seven months later. The federal military government did, in fact, appoint a "Special Committee", with Professor Aboyade as chairman. Its report was available for the Constituent Assembly. Shehu Shagari, however, was deeply disappointed by its recommendations, which he greeted on the floor of the assembly "with dismay". They flouted the committee's terms of reference, and had invented "abstract" and "absurd" principles for revenue allocations. The experts "had made a frantic effort to remove the problem of revenue allocation from the understanding of the ordinary man in order to make its operation the exclusive preserve of technocrats".

That seemed fair comment on a report which said that all principles previously tried for revenue allocation had failed, but that its own five new principles could succeed. The new principles included "equality of access to development opportunities", "absorptive capacity" and "fiscal efficiency";

principles which, as Shehu Shagari said, would be extremely difficult to turn into statistics. No formula, he declared, which completely ignored population, equality of states, and derivation, as the Aboyade report's formula did, could work in Nigeria. In the end the Constituent Assembly, like the CDC before it, gave up the task of working out a revenue allocation formula, and left it to the National Assembly which was to be elected in 1979 (cynics said that many MCAs could not understand the Aboyade recommendations, but were reluctant to admit it).

So one of Shehu Shagari's first and most important tasks as President was to be the presentation of a bill to the National Assembly embodying the ideas for a revenue allocation formula which he had three years earlier put before the Constituent Assembly. The formula gave due weight to population and introduced the new principle that the Capital Territory, where the new federal capital of Abuja was to be built, should have a share of revenue guaranteed by legislation, in order, as Shehu Shagari had told the Constituent Assembly, that "its financing is insulated from the vagaries of future politics". The President's bill did not have an easy passage, and was briefly "the bane of Nigerian politics". With minor amendments, however, it was finally passed and represented the major legislative achievement of the first years of Shehu Shagari's presidency.

The 111 members of the assembly who wanted the names of four new states to be written into the constitution were the major springboard of the National Party of Nigeria (NPN), says Dr Chuba Okadigbo, Special Adviser on Political Affairs in President Shehu Shagari's office.* Technically the formation of a political association remained illegal until September 21, 1978, the day after the Constituent Assembly had been formally dissolved. In fact, throughout the period of military rule politicians had met for discussions under various pretexts, although the Constituent Assembly provided the first real opportunity for people from all over the country to engage

*The Rise of the NPN (Ejike R. Nwankwo Associates, 1981).

149

in national political debate. The "Committee of Friends", for example, kept alive, if at times only in Lagos, the spirit of the former Action Group of Chief Awolowo; and although some of his lieutenants deserted him for other new parties, the Committee of Friends, with Chief Awolowo as undisputed leader, emerged as a fully-fledged political party, the Unity Party of Nigeria (UPN), as soon as the ban on parties was lifted.

The "pro-Sharia" group of MCAs came largely from the northern states, and included some who were later to be bitter opponents of the NPN. Before the Sharia affair there was what might be called the northern states consultative group in the assembly; its secretary was Alhaji Abubakar Rimi, who was to become PRP Governor of Kano State. This group, which sometimes met in Shehu Shagari's Peugeot company house on Victoria Island (which he could still use), had been making overtures to MCAs in other groups as well as to outsiders whom they regarded as "like-minded" and having a national outlook. Chief Akinloye, the Yoruba who was to become chairman of the NPN, was among these.

The Sharia argument, as one leading northerner put it, meant that the effort to build a national movement had to start all over again. The controversy about the definition of new states in the constitution was, therefore, in some ways useful as it brought together MCAs from different parts of the country. As Dr Okadigbo says, the National Movement, which was to blossom into the NPN, really derived its co-hesion from this controversy, since supporters of the new states came from all parts of the country.

Many southern MCAs, as well as some, such as the late J. S. Tarka, from a non-Muslim northern state, realised that no party could hope to win the presidency in Nigeria unless it represented an alliance between the former "north" and the former "south". The break-up of the former north into first six, and then ten, states, had ended the political domination of the Federation by the Northern Region. Yet this had not altered the fact that the majority of Nigerians lived in the northern states. The heirs of the old NPC – who were the core of the northern group in the Constituent Assembly – could now justly say that their objectives were national, even if they wanted still to protect the interests of northern states. They were essential allies for ambitious southern politicians not committed either to Chief Awolowo or to Dr Azikiwe. There were enough of these to make the National Movement truly national.

The National Movement became, in effect, a political party when in August 1978, at a meeting in the quarters occupied by the MCAs in Lagos, five representatives from each state came together to agree a plan to establish a party to fight the 1979 general election. Their opponents ridiculed these politicians as being reactionary and "deadwoods". They themselves may have been mistaken in claiming that they were the only politicians of "timber and calibre". Nor did this claim help them to disown the title "conservative" (no more a political handicap, as it turned out, in Nigeria than in many other countries). They certainly represented, however, a national complexion such as Nigeria had never known in a political party.

The MCAs who founded the National Movement knew that, even if the assembly was a convenient birthplace for a party, its success could only be guaranteed in the states. The Movement established "steering committees" in each state, and launched branches in all main cities. Dr Ibrahim Tahir, a young lecturer at Ahmadu Bello University, was at this time acting as general secretary, with the veteran Alhaji Aliyu, Makaman Bida, formerly lieutenant of the Sardauna of Sokoto in the Northern Regional government, as interim party leader – he was not a member of the Constituent Assembly.

The constitution of the NPN, drawn up after nation-wide consultations, carried the motto "one nation, one destiny". Among the objectives listed was the promotion of "mutual respect for and understanding of the religions, cultures, traditions and heritage of all the various communities of Nigeria". The party machinery reflected the federal structure of the country, but membership was to be individual. The constitution insisted on the representation of women at all levels in the

151

party. The only provision, however, which surprised some Nigerians concerned the relationship between the party and the government. "The policies and manifestos of the party", it said, "within the framework of the constitution of the Federal Republic of Nigeria shall be supreme."

In all the preparations for launching the party Shehu Shagari, still intent only on becoming a Senator, was active in many parts of the country. For example he was, with Malam Aminu Kano, who was still in alliance with his former political adversaries, and the late J.S. Tarka, the main speaker when the National Movement was formally launched on September 16, 1978 at Ankpa, among the Igala people of Benue State. He was also contributing papers on aspects of policy with which the National Movement, whether or not its candidate won the presidency when it transformed itself into a party, would have to be concerned.

Few parties had made more careful preparations for taking over power than did the NPN, into which the National Movement was transformed after the ban on party politics was lifted. Its "Presidential Transition Committee" examined minutely most aspects of government activity and produced papers on them. The chairman, Alhaji Ahmed Joda, seems even to have helped to draft Shehu Shagari's inauguration speech as President.

Perhaps the most important of the committee's papers was its report on the economy. It advised the incoming administration against indulging the political desire to demonstrate that it was not bound by the decisions of the military regime. On the other hand it urged the lifting of the ban on air freighting machinery, parts and raw materials, saying that the decision should be left to those who paid the cost. It called in question other proposals in the military regime's last budget, and was concerned that some of them would deter investment without conferring any benefit on Nigeria. It urged a reduction in official holdings of bank shares. Inflation and unemployment, it emphasised, could be alleviated only through increased production, an objective which should govern all fiscal and other economic problems.

The paper ranged widely – for example it questioned the cost and operation of the "Comprehensive Import Supervisory Scheme" (generally called Form M). Many of its recommendations – and those of similar papers – have not yet been implemented; some may prove to have been mistaken. But the NPN could not be accused of failure to prepare for the responsibility of government.

The Nigerian People's Party (NPP), for which eventually Dr Azikiwe was to be the presidential candidate, had a less easy beginning than either the UPN or the NPN. One of its original components was the National Union Council for Understanding, into which Alhaji Waziri Ibrahim, a former federal minister and now a very rich businessman who was not himself an MCA, tried to recruit MCAs. Another constituent was "Club 19", mostly former NCNC members of the Constituent Assembly – although the name was intended to suggest support in all nineteen states, it was thought that the group had little standing in some half-a-dozen. The Organisation of Nigerian Unity was a caucus of former Azikiwe supporters. Other groups also joined the NPP. Its original leader, however, Alhaji Waziri, insisted that he should be both the party's chairman and its presidential candidate. This led to a split and the formation by Alhaji Waziri of the "Great Nigerian Peoples' Party" (GNPP). He was bottom of the presidential poll, but considering that his was an entirely new party, not associated in people's minds with any former party, his votes were well spread throughout the country, while he won control of two northern states which the NPN might have been expected to win.

Mass support for the People's Redemption Party (PRP), which was to become the fifth registered political party, was based largely on the former NEPU support in Kano. The party, however, also embraced some small radical groups elsewhere in the country, and many radical intellectuals in northern states. Its presidential candidate, Malam Aminu Kano, claimed that he parted company with the NPN late in September 1978, because that party aimed to restore the power of traditional rulers, particularly the emirs, against whom he had conducted his campaign a quarter of a century earlier. In fact most of the changes he had demanded had been brought about under the military regime – the emirs had lost their law courts, their prisons and police and now had only an honorific role in local government, even if, in the emirates, a practical role survived for some traditional officials.

Others claim that Malam Aminu felt that the job of publicity secretary which the NPN offered him was unsuitable for an "elder statesman" like himself. The anti-NPN intellectuals in the northern states, many associated with Ahmadu Bello University, Zaria, welcomed the leadership of a man with the reputation and experience of Malam Aminu, and the PRP was launched in Kaduna on October 21, 1978. The PRP's victories in Kano and Kaduna States were the NPN's greatest disappointments in the 1979 general election. Aminu Kano's loss was a serious blow to the party, although the PRP itself was later to be deeply split, and there were constant rumours that Aminu and his supporters would return to the NPN.

Elections in Nigeria are costly, as is the maintenance of a countrywide party organisation. The funds which, under the constitution, the Federal Electoral Commission disburses to parties "to assist them in their responsibilities" are too small – and are paid too late – to enable them to mount general election campaigns, and to ensure that their supporters turn out at all five stages of a general election. In the Constituent Assembly Shehu Shagari had estimated that a party might need ₦10m for an election. Ordinary subscriptions from members could never provide the funds. So, he frankly advised, let the rich pay.

Certainly in the case of the GNPP, and to some extent the UPN, the leader himself was sufficiently rich to ensure that adequate funds would be available to their parties. PRP was probably the party worst off financially, even though some Kano merchants may prudently have hedged their bets by subscribing to its funds. The NPP has rich supporters, but they do not seem to have been particularly generous towards the party.

The NPN's great strength in this regard is that it has a large

154

number of rich supporters, so that it does not depend on one man, certainly not on its presidential candidate; and the rich supporters do pay up and assist the party.

For example, before the National Movement had been transformed into the NPN, it was decided that a Lagos headquarters should be ready for the new party. A house on Victoria Island was offered by one businessman. It was found to be unsuitable and another businessman then offered a block of four flats for the purpose. Two other supporters offered to turn these flats into offices. Chief J. S. Tarka offered the party the use of his house in Hampstead, London. Other businessmen who were not seeking office, but who in some cases could not have been unmindful of the possible advantages of association with a party which might control the federal and some state administrations, offered substantial sums.

Indeed there was later to be an occasion when the readiness of rich supporters to come forward publicly with large sums for a new party headquarters may even have damaged the party's standing. The headquarters proposed for the NPN at the new federal capital of Abuja is also on a lavish scale. It cannot be compared, however, with the splendours of the headquarters of the Ivory Coast's ruling party at the President's birthplace, Yamoussoukoro, or even the structures built for Dr Nkrumah's party in Ghana.

In 1982 the Federal Electoral Commission presented to the National Assembly accounts of the five political parties for the period from their registration to the end of 1979, accounts which FEDECO is by law required to submit annually. The Commission praised only the NPN for keeping proper books. UPN, it said, had not produced proper accounts for its subventions to state offices, nor had it followed the procedure for determining the percentage of bad debts allowable. GNPP did not keep proper books for the year. It should give "full explanation of the discrepancies in its cash and balances"; GNPP's annual accounts could not be said to have portrayed the party's proper financial position. FEDECO agreed with the auditors that NPP failed to keep proper books and records; "for example, except in a few cases, invoices and receipts were not attached to support expenditure". PRP (the report applies to the period before the party split) did not submit its accounts at all. FEDECO also wanted all parties to keep a register of "anonymous" donations, to be made available only to the Commission, or to any auditor authorised by it.

10

THE PATH TO THE PRESIDENCY

In September 1978 the military regime permitted "party politics" to return formally – politicians, we have seen, had never in fact completely given up their activities. Shehu Shagari at once declared in his Sokoto house that his ambition now was to be elected a Senator in the first "round" of the general elections, due to be held in July the following year. While the pre-1966 Nigerian Senate had little power and no prestige, under the new constitution the Senate would in many ways be more powerful than the other (not "lower") house of the National Assembly, the House of Representatives. It alone would approve, for example, many important presidential appointments, such as those of ministers and ambassadors. It would have equal power with the other house over all legislation, including financial legislation. Moreover, since there would be only five Senators from each state, each of the 95 Senate members might carry more political weight and have more opportunity for expressing his views than could each of the 449 members of the House of Representatives.

Like other members of the National Assembly, a Senator would not be a member of "the Government", a position Shehu Shagari now wanted to avoid for the rest of his life, in spite of his prominence in the Constituent Assembly. He could not forget that twice inside a decade he had been arbitrarily and unceremoniously removed from high national office, although his own conduct had subsequently been proved to be blameless. He still wanted, however, to have influence on government politics nationally. A Senator, he considered,

157

whether belonging to the same party as the President or not, would be an independent legislator, free to support or oppose the Executive's measures as he saw fit, subject only to the constraints of party discipline. These, in the Senate at least, Shehu Shagari did not expect to be rigid.

It is certain that he looked forward to this prospect with satisfaction. Already, however, members of the new National Movement, which was transformed into the National Party of Nigeria (NPN) when parties were legalised, were saying that they saw him as the only presidential candidate who could both unite their party and appeal to the whole nation, which would form, as the constitution prescribed, a single constituency for the election of the President. "We will draft him, if he doesn't agree", they declared – and not only privately. A year later, after he had accepted the presidential nomination for the NPN, he was to explain to a journalist of the Kaduna-based *New Nigerian* what had changed his mind. He simply had not realised how great would be the pressure "from many quarters" to which he would be subjected.

So determined were those in the NPN who saw him as the only possible candidate to "draft" him that some Sokoto people even asked the Sultan himself to join in persuading him to accept the nomination. Sarkin Musulmi – the "last gentleman" as he has been described – natually felt it improper to make such a political request, which, had it come from him, Shehu Shagari could not have refused. But the genial Sarkin Kudu, the Sultan's eldest son, who was more ready to be interested in party matters, as well as the future President's old friend, Alhaji Aminu Tafida, then discussed the matter with Shehu Shagari in Sokoto.

All this was in 1978, when the date for the parties to nominate presidential candidates was near. Shehu Shagari, however, was unimpressed by the arguments of his two friends, although they pressed them for some three hours. He recalls that he even flew back to Lagos from Sokoto without paying his customary call on the Sultan, in case the ruler should, however indirectly, make some reference to the matter.

158

Then came the respected Makaman Bida, the senior surviving member of the Sardauna of Sokoto's last Northern
Regional cabinet. He was too old now himself to seek office,
but he was soon to become Grand Patron of the new NPN. In
Lagos he talked to Shehu Shagari for hours. The new movement, after considering its electoral prospects in different parts
of the country, had decided that it was the northern states
which should this time provide the presidential candidate; the
eastern states would provide his vice-presidential partner;
and the western states the party chairman. So the Makama
urged Shehu Shagari to be one of the three potential candidates from the northern states whose names should be submitted to the forthcoming NPN national conference in Lagos,
which would make a final choice.

Shehu Shagari was satisfied that he had persuaded the
Makama that he had no presidential ambitions; but Makaman
Bida persisted. When Alhaji Shehu soon afterwards went to
Kaduna, the wily old politician summoned him, to say that
now he himself was being called an unworthy lieutenant of the
late Sardauna, since he could not persuade this "young man"
to follow his advice. Did Shehu Shagari wish him to go to his
grave (in fact he died in 1980) under such a charge? In any case
delegates of the movement from both the eastern and western
states had come to him, the Makama said, to ask what would
happen if, since the presidential candidate was to come from
the northern states, no candidate proposed from these proved
acceptable to the national party convention as a whole? So,
said the Sardauna's old lieutenant – a short, bearded, and very
tough traditionalist – did Shehu Shagari want to endanger the
whole basis of the new party? For, he was confident, Shehu
Shagari and nobody else from the northern states would win
general acceptance as a candidate.

So obdurate was Shehu Shagari's resistance that he was
even pursued to Paris, where he had gone for a Peugeot
company meeting, by pleas to accept the presidential candidature. He was also pursued to London's Churchill Hotel,
which, in the days before party politics became legal again in
Nigeria, and for some time afterwards, seemed for a time to be

159

a more important centre for meetings of Nigerian politicians than anywhere in Nigeria itself.

Sokoto people everywhere continued to urge him to let his nomination go forward. On the day after his talks in Kaduna with the Makama, a Sokoto delegation at last told him directly that he would be "drafted". This time the delegation made an impression on him; for they made it plain that if he refused the presidential nomination he would not have their support for any other political office – including, presumably, that of Senator. So he could never again have any influence in government policies.

In a rearguard action he said that he would allow his name to go forward to the preliminary NPN meeting at Kaduna, which was to select the presidential candidates from the northern states who would go before the Lagos NPN convention. If, however, at the first round at Kaduna he failed to get the highest vote, he would drop out. He would also require some time, if he won the nomination, to decide whether to accept it. "This was the most trying period I have ever gone through in my life", he told *New Nigerian*.

So once more Shehu Shagari's reluctance to seek office, this time the highest, was overcome by others. It is difficult to understand his consistent under-estimation of his own capacity. He has never sought high office; it was always been thrust upon him, although, as was said of Abraham Lincoln, "he will not be bullied, even by his friends". His own ambitions have been for useful but narrow offices; even in education he never sought promotion. Other Nigerians have seen his worth, and their communities' or their country's needs. His supporters today would say of him, whatever their disappointment at the limited achievements of his adminis-tration, that, as was also said of Lincoln, "if he is not the best conceivable President he is the best available". Is he, perhaps, the only freely-elected President in history who resisted his own nomination? Nominated in Kaduna, however, he was, at the head of six candidates who would appear in Lagos (there had been complaints that the number originally proposed, three, might restrict the choice of Kaduna delegates to candidates from the most northerly states; and the six did include men from the former "Middle Belt", J. S. Tarka from Benue and Sola Saraki from Kwara State). In the subsequent voting at the NPN convention at the Casino Cinema, Yaba, Lagos, in December 1978, the first ballot gave him just under the 50 per cent vote he needed for outright nomination by the 2,245 delegates. The question of his withdrawal, however, never arose; for the two runners-up at once agreed to withdraw, giving him an unopposed nomination. He was greatly helped by the requirement that each presidential candidate should address the convention for five minutes on the subject "My idea of the Presidency". He asserted his reluctance to accept nomination and repeated his conviction that there were better candidates. His vision of the presidency as a means of service to all Nigerians, however, seemed to have persuaded even the many delegates who knew little of him personally that here was a man to appeal to all Nigeria – which is the chief task of a presidential candidate.

After the withdrawals he could only accept gracefully – and both the runners-up were later given appointments by him as President. Alhaji Maitama Sule, a 50-year old Kano man who had been an NPC Federal Minister, became Nigeria's UN Ambassador; and 45-year old Malam Adamu Ciroma, from Borno State, who had been editor of *New Nigerian* and Governor of the Central Bank, became Minister of Industries. Another presidential aspirant, Professor Iya Abubakar, became Minister of Defence.

After the legalisation of parties the establishment of some 53 was announced. After splits, mergers, alliances, etc., some seventeen applied for registration with the Federal Electoral Commission in December 1978. The Commission decided that only five, including the NPN, met the conditions for registration, and so for the right to contest the election, laid down by the constitution.

There was no doubt from the start that in each of three of the other four registered parties the leader, who was also the party's founder, would be its presidential candidate. There was at first some doubt, however, about Dr Azikiwe's readiness to stand for NPP. Indeed there were earlier rumours that the National Movement might invite him to stand as its presidential candidate, with Shehu Shagari as his running mate – and possible future replacement.

The NPN was the only party to choose its presidential candidate by vote from among a number of aspirants. The decision that this time the NPN candidate must come from one of the "northern" states, however, was criticised both inside and outside the party. Many felt that the NPN policy of what the critics – but not the party itself – called "zoning" for all party positions, could encourage the very divisions inside Nigeria which those who had devised the new constitution had attempted to overcome. And while nobody accused Alhaji Shehu Shagari himself of tribal, religious or party bigotry, it was not forgotten that the leader of the old NPC, the expression of northern regional identity, the Sardauna, also came from Sokoto.

The President himself – who after all, had tried to reject the opportunity which this gave him personally – explains that the "zoning" arrangement was intended to ensure that the national constitution-makers' intention was fulfilled. For, he maintains, in Nigeria the government cannot leave to chance the distribution of anything – industries or social services as well as political offices. As party politics returned it was necessary to ensure that no part of the country should feel "left out" of a party claiming nationwide support. "Nigerians are not yet politically mature enough to consider only purely democratic processes ..." he stated. These processes, if unrestricted, could result in too many offices in a party going to one area. In Nigeria those who could contrive a majority might monopolise everything if there were no formal restraints.

So, believing that no area should be "left out", the NPN had decided on this division of responsibilities. The principle was applied to other appointments. The President of the Senate was to come from one group of states, and the Speaker from another. Shehu Shagari himself, since the vice-presidential candidate was to come from the eastern states, invited an Ibo lady, a much respected educationist, to join his "ticket". She, with great commonsense and modesty, told him that a woman was no greater an electoral asset in her part of Nigeria than in his; so the choice fell on Dr Alex Ekwueme, from Anambra State, well known in Nigeria as an American-trained architect, but politically an unknown quantity and personally unknown to Shehu Shagari. In office he has proved to be a great success.

The division of appointments inside the NPN makes sense. An Ibo candidate, for example, although the scars of civil war have been remarkably healed, was unlikely to win the presidency for any party in a nation-wide ballot. Originally at least, it was also intended that no NPN party functionary would also hold a government job, so that functionaries might exercise a power exactly parallel to that of the government. In practice, however, this has not happened, and it probably never could.

The principle of allocating public offices to particular areas was sound for another reason. There is no point in pretending that the core of the new movement from which the NPN came was not formed by the surviving leaders of the Sardauna's NPC. Yet if the old NPC might be at the party's centre, during the Constituent Assembly's debates, and the discussions following the raising of the ban on party politics, politicians who had previously belonged to many groups, some antagonistic to the former NPC, like the United Middle Belt Congress (UMBC), throughout the country rallied to the new movement. They included Chief J. S. Tarka, former leader of the UMBC, Chief Enaharo, a leader of Chief Awolowo's Action Group, and Dr Kingsley Mbadiwe, formerly of Dr Azikiwe's NCNC. They saw that at last Nigeria might for the first time have a truly national party; this NPN proved to be.

Because he was persuaded by party men to stand, and, unlike the other four presidential candidates, was not his party's "leader" (nobody in the NPN was given this title) or founder, some who knew little of him assumed that the President-elect would prove to be the creature of the NPN party machine. This certainly, before and during the election, semed to be a powerful influence, having united in a nation-wide organisation so many disparate elements. That view, however, ignored the very nature of the NPN, which was and

163

is a coalition. It therefore depended, and depends, on the one man who could give it credibility and unite it. The President-elect also had had more experience of public office, most of it at the top, than anybody in Nigeria. In Alhaji Shehu Shagari it was no amateur politician whom the party had chosen as its standard-bearer.

The names of all five presidential candidates were to be found in the "Elder Statesmen" section of the Nigerian *Who's Who*, by virtue of their long service in pre-1966 civilian politics and the important posts they had held. The constitution pre-scribed a minimum age for presidential candidates of 35. At the time of the election, however, the youngest of the five candidates, Alhaji Waziri Ibrahim, was 53. Alhaji Shehu Shagari was almost a year older. Alhaji Aminu Kano, leader of the PRP, still enjoyed the radical reputation which he had earned in the former Northern Region; but he was 59. Dr Azikiwe, although extremely sprightly, was 74, and had been presumed to have retired from active politics when he accepted the post of Governor-General in 1960. Chief Awolowo celebrated his 70th birthday in the middle of the election campaign.

Civilian rule, it seemed, would be in no danger from brash inexperience. It was more likely to suffer because the label "old politician" was attached to all the presidential candidates, as well as to some candidates for governorships and the legis-latures. Some of Shehu Shagari's lieutenants, in particular, came into this category. While Nigerians were now heartily sick of military rule, the older amongst them recalled with little affection or esteem the period between 1960 and 1966, or even earlier, when the politicians first ruled. Now, however, such voters were probably ready to give the politicians another chance, confident that the lessons of 1966 had been learned.

The vice-presidential candidates, who would be elected with the candidates for the presidency, did something to lower the average age of the "tickets". They, too, included "old politicians". The NPN nominee, however, Dr Alex Ekwueme, was not one of these. Yet so little mercy do Nigerians give to their politicians that this was at once held against him.

At 46 he was the youngest of the presidential running-mates. Like Dr Ekwueme, the running-mates of the other three non-Ibo presidential candidates were Ibos. This was not a calculated device to show the world the extent to which the Ibos were now integrated into Nigeria's politics, but a simple recognition of political reality. There is no evidence, however, that voting was significantly affected by the presence of any of the vice-presidential candidates on their party "tickets".

Dr Azikiwe's colleague, the only non-Ibo vice-presidential candidate, was Professor Ishaya Audu, a distinguished paediatrician, formerly a Registrar at King's College Hospital, London, who had been Vice-Chancellor of Ahmadu Bello University. He came from a Muslim family in Zaria, in the former Northern Region, but had become a Christian. President Shehu Shagari invited him to become Minister for External Affairs when, after the 1979 elections, the NPN and the NPP reached an "accord" to ensure that, through a combination of the two parties' votes, the President could command a majority for his measures in the National Assembly. When, in the middle of 1981, the accord, which had never worked smoothly, was formally rescinded, the President asked Professor Audu to carry on. This he did.

During an election campaign which lasted eight months Shehu Shagari not only for the first time spoke to and was seen by hundreds of thousands of Nigerians. He himself saw more of the country than he ever had before, in spite of his enthusiasm for "touring" when he was a Minister. He lacks the physique to be a mass orator; but his honesty and sincerity are conveyed by his calm manner and measured tones. His main themes were those of his party's manifesto, particularly the need to help farmers to grow more food. He made, however, no promises to regret later. Alhaji Umaru Dikko from Zaria was his campaign manager. But he was also accompanied throughout by two men who have since earned some criticism in the party, but by whom he will always stand because of their devotion through these months, which were physically testing – Chief Akinloye, the NPN national Chairman, and Mr Mikail Prest, who was to become the President's

Chief of Personal Staff. He was much helped, too, by the journalist Chief Olu Adebanjo, who was to become Special Adviser on Information.

All five presidential candidates were given National Security Organisation (NSO) escorts by the federal government as soon as their nominations had been accepted by FEDECO, as well as police escorts in each state they visited. But the campaign seems to have been remarkably peaceful, enlivened not by clashes but by such features as Chief Awolowo's use of a helicopter.

In the election Shehu Shagari received more support

ITINERARY FOR THREE WEEKS OF
SHEHU SHAGARI'S CAMPAIGN TOUR

Friday	December 29	Lagos—Abeokuta	by road
Friday	December 29	Abeokuta—Ibadan	by road
Saturday	December 30	Ibadan—Lagos	by road
Sunday	December 31	Lagos free	by road
Monday	January 1	Lagos	by road
Tuesday	January 2	Lagos—Ife (University)	by road
Wednesday	January 3	Ife—Akure	by road
Thursday	January 4	Akure—Benin	by road
Friday	January 5	Benin—Calabar	by air
Saturday	January 6	Calabar—Port Harcourt	by road
Saturday	January 6	Port Harcourt—Owerri	by road
Sunday	January 7	Owerri—Enugu	by road
Monday	January 8	Enugu—Makurdi	by road
Tuesday	January 9	Makurdi—Jos	by road
Wednesday	January 10	Jos—Bauchi	by air
Thursday	January 11	Bauchi—Kano	by air
Friday	January 12	Kano—Sokoto	by air
Saturday	January 13	Sokoto	by air
Sunday	January 14	Sokoto—Maiduguri	by air
Monday	January 15	Maiduguri—Yola	by air
Tuesday	January 16	Yola—Kaduna	by air
Wednesday	January 17	Kaduna—Minna	by air
Thursday	January 18	Minna—Ilorin	by air
Friday	January 19	Ilorin—Lagos	by air
Saturday	January 20	Meeting of committee	

166

During Shehu Shagari's October 1979 visit to the U.N. Here in the White House after a state dinner Celia Tyson read Shehu Shagari's *Song of Nigeria*.

With King Khalid in Saudi Arabia.

nationally than had ever been demonstrated for a Nigerian leader. With 5.68m votes he was well ahead of the runner-up, Chief Awolowo, with 4.91m votes. His support was also far more evenly distributed throughout the country, although it was insignificant in Yoruba areas, including Lagos itself. Of Chief Awolowo's votes well over four-fifths came from Yoruba areas – Oyo, Ondo and Ogun States, Lagos State, which is also largely Yoruba, and Kwara State, which has a substantial Yoruba population. Awolowo also had a majority in Bendel State, part of the former Western Region when he was its Premier. Outside these six states he secured over 20% of the votes only in Gongola. In seven his vote was under 5%.

Shehu Shagari, while nowhere securing the over 90% of votes cast which his nearest rival won in two of the Yoruba states, or even the 80% his rival won in two others, had over 20% of the votes in 14 states. Nowhere was his support as low as the 0.75% or 0.64% of votes given to Chief Awolowo in the two Ibo states, or the surprisingly low 2.57% the UPN leader secured in Benue, where once his Action Group had been the ally and mainstay of the United Middle Belt Congress, which before 1966 was politically dominant in the area. In two states, Gongola and Kaduna, Shehu Shagari led the presidential voting, although in the elections for their governors men from other parties had been victorious. He led the presidential voting in nine states and came second in another nine. Lagos, however, which gave him only 7.18% of its votes, produced the anomaly of a President being placed third among the candidates in his own capital.

In general Shehu Shagari did somewhat better than his party, particularly in his own state, Sokoto. In "pockets" in states overwhelmingly hostile to his own party he had majorities. And – although this is not surprising since it took place at the end of the elections which were held over six weeks – the percentage of registered electors who voted in the presidential election was the highest of those voting at any stage. Only a third of registered voters, however, voted even at this stage. Alhaji Shehu Shagari won a third of the votes cast. So while he was clearly the choice of those who voted, next time it could be the verdict of those who did not vote first time, or have come on to the register in the meantime, which could decide who is to be President.

Why was the turn-out of voters so poor, if the figures of registered voters, now under question, can be believed?* When he was appointed Chief Electoral Commissioner Chief Michael Ani, a senior and very experienced civil servant (he was once Alhaji Shehu Shagari's Permanent Secretary), told a reporter that he was confident that the very complicated elections could be satisfactorily organised; but only if they were not held during the rains or during the Ramadan fast. They were held in the rains, and in Ramadan.

That, however, is not the whole story. The Nigerian Institute of Social and Economic Research (NISER) at Ibadan University has conducted a survey of the elections. This has not yet been published but the Institute has said that when published the survey would show that on the whole the elections had been free and fair, which was the impression of most observers, including this writer who observed much of it. Almost half a million electoral staff were needed, however, for 125,000 polling booths. There were almost 10,000 candidates for all the posts at stake in the election's five stages. It would be incredible if in a country which had known no general election for fifteen years – and the last one had been surrounded by controversy – such a huge operation could have been mounted without a hitch.

Ironically, it was in Lagos itself that the first stage of the elections, that to the Senate, was so badly organised, whether by accident or design, that the military government seriously considered a fresh election there. Only the realisation that defeated candidates everywhere would demand a similar re-run changed the government's mind. But even if the dominant group in Lagos was able at some stage to prevent its opponents

---

*A study of "Voting Behaviour" contributed by Dr Oyeleye Oyediran and Dr Oladele Arowolo to *The Nigerian General Election* (Macmillan, Nigeria) suggests that the imperfections of registration resulted in "inflation" of the figures, which were probably closer to 41 million than the official 48.6 million.

voting by closing polling stations and other devices, the NISER verdict is probably correct; misconduct did not significantly affect the election results.

This was the planting and weeding season in many areas. So farmers who genuinely intended to go to vote after the day's work was done might have felt that they couldn't be bothered. In some rural areas the booths were so widely spread that a voter might have to walk several miles to cast his vote. There was, too, much scepticism about the sincerity of the soldiers in handing over power; some people felt, most unjustly, that the whole exercise was a sham and the soldiers would soon take power again – a view reinforced by much ignorant comment abroad.

Throughout the country, however, the actual voting was conducted in an exemplary manner, voters queuing peacefully and quietly without any interference from party stalwarts. I myself observed Alhaji Shehu Shagari quietly standing in a line, mostly of women voters, before a makeshift booth in one of the narrow and tortuous lanes behind his Sokoto house. The police did not even think it necessary to put guards on party offices on election day.

More immediately important to Shehu Shagari, however, was the challenge to his victory made by Chief Awolowo and Alhaji Waziri Ibrahim, the GNPP presidential candidate, who asked the Electoral Tribunal to declare his election invalid. The issue turned on the definition of the constitution's requirements, intended to emphasise the "national" character of the presidential office, that a successful presidential candidate, where there were, as in this case, more than two candidates, must win not only the highest number of votes cast but "not less than one quarter" of the votes in "at least two-thirds of all the States in the Federation". The Electoral Tribunal found in favour of Shehu Shagari. Chief Awolowo and Alhaji Waziri then took the case to the Supreme Court.

Delivering the judgment of six of the seven Supreme Court judges that Alhaji Shehu Shagari's election was valid, the recently appointed Chief Justice, Mr Justice Atanda Fatayi-Williams, a distinguished legal scholar, and a Yoruba Muslim,

169

said that the President had secured the highest number of votes of any candidate, 772,000 more than the appellant, Chief Awolowo. His votes were also more evenly spread geographically; he had secured a quarter of the votes cast in each of twelve of the nineteen states. But in a thirteenth, Kano, he had secured 19.94% of all votes cast, while Chief Awolowo had secured 1.25% there. The Court upheld the view of the Electoral Tribunal that since 19.94% of all votes cast in Kano State exceeded a quarter of two-thirds of those votes, this constituted the necessary one quarter of this thirteenth state, thus satisfying the constitution's requirement concerning "at least two-thirds of all the states". This gave Alhaji Shehu Shagari the majority in "at least two-thirds of the states".

The dissenting judge, Mr Justice Kayode Esho, concentrated on a single point. How could one say, even for the purpose of an election, that a state consisted not of its entire land area and of its total population, but only of the votes it cast? The Electoral Decree, in speaking of "at least two-thirds of all the states" must mean, he said, the totality of any state, and so the totality of all the votes it casts, not two-thirds of those votes in any state.

This is a tenable case; but the other judges, with the exception of Mr Justice Andrew Obaseki, who did not, however, agree to grant Chief Awolowo the "relief" he sought, supported the view of the Electoral Tribunal forcefully put by Shehu Shagari's counsel, Chief Richard Akinjide, who became President Shehu Shagari's Minister of Justice and Attorney-General. Chief Akinjide claimed that since the number of states was not a multiple of three, and the framers of the decree, who were well aware that Nigeria had only nineteen states, had not stipulated that two-thirds of these must be taken to be thirteen, the Electoral Tribunal must follow the path of common sense and decide as it did.

The persistence of Nigeria's Commonwealth connection is shown by the use as his main precedent by the resourceful Chief Akinjide of the case of Magor and St Melon's Rural District Council and Newport Corporation, a 1952 decision by Lord Justice Simons.

Nobody asked whether, if for the purpose of the constitution only two-thirds of the votes cast in Kano should be taken into consideration, only two-thirds of the President's votes there should also qualify – which would have left him where he was. But equity and the interests of Nigeria would have suffered from any other than the decision taken. The figures showed that Chief Awolowo could not possibly have beaten the President in any nationwide vote. Submission of the issue to the National Assembly and the state Houses of Assembly, for which the constitution then provided if no candidate won outright in the first round, would have exposed those newly elected, if not entirely guileless, bodies to intense political horse-trading, and to the flourishing of bribes by supporters of the candidates.

In fact the framers of the constitution had simply not allowed for the possibility of a candidate securing such a narrow lead. And resulting from this case, as one of its last acts before leaving office, the Supreme Military Council amended this provision of the constitution. Now, if a candidate for the presidency fails to secure a quarter of all the votes cast in "two-thirds of the states" there will be a second, and if necessary a third, nationwide election, with no reference to the legislatures. The Supreme Court ruling on what "two-thirds" means, however, is now part of Nigeria's constitutional law unless and until the legislature changes it.

After the Supreme Court verdict both Chief Awolowo, a devout Christian, and Alhaji Waziri Ibrahim, a Muslim, declared that they placed their appeal "before Almighty God. The Almighty Allah will surely give justice to those who have been cheated". Dr Azikiwe, however, urged all Nigerians to accept the verdict.

Few voters studied any of the party election manifestos or were greatly influenced by them, particularly by their references to external affairs. It was said, however, that Chief Awolowo influenced voters in the western states by reminding them of the achievements of his Action Group government in the former Western Region, and by promising a minimum wage of ₦200 a month – a promise derided by his opponents

171

and not yet achieved. The manifestoes of all five registered parties were widely discussed, however, in the newspapers, and coverage of them by the official radio and television stations was thorough and dispassionate. Since they were later to be used at federal and state levels by politicians, both to measure their own achievements and to call in question those of their opponents, they were more important after the elections than during them. But no politician in power has been seriously embarrassed by the failure of his election performance to equal his election promises.

Although there were differences of emphasis in the manifestos, all demonstrated attachment to what can be called the "extreme centre"; all supported a "mixed economy" and "non-alignment". Not one pretended that Nigeria had unlimited resources which could support a spectacular welfare programme. All showed the same impatience with the failure of the economy, in spite of the surging oil revenues and the variety of Nigeria's resources, to improve the lot of ordinary citizens.

The differences in emphasis, however, were important. The NPN manifesto, to which President Shehu Shagari has steadfastly been loyal, opened with the unanswerable claim that "Nigeria today is a country where too many things do not work as they should." The party, it said, intended to make them work. Fulfilment of this promise – with regard, for example, to some city water supplies, internal telephones, urban road maintenance, refuse collection and electric power – was still awaited halfway through the President's term of office. Food (which in the shape of corn, together with a house, had pride of place in the NPN election emblem) was the party manifesto's first topic. Measures proposed included abolition of Jangali tax on cattle, more credit for farmers, and other measures to make rural living more attractive and farming methods more productive.

The party promised incentives for foreign capital in industry. It would "review" existing price controls "to ensure that inflation is contained and goods are more readily available" – a promise some entrepreneurs would say has failed.

It promised support for OPEC (a constant problem now), a thorough mineral survey, and support for the Nigerian National Mining Corporation, "and other entrepreneurs", to exploit known non-oil mineral deposits. The party would "work towards" free education at all levels. Attention would be paid to the moral and "African indigenous" content of education. Autonomy of the universities would be preserved. Special attention would be given to technical education. Ultimately medical services would be free.

To remedy deficiencies in public corporations each would be headed by an executive of cabinet rank directly responsible to the President – a promise so far executed only partially, in the case of the most controversial corporation, the Nigerian National Petroleum Corporation (NNPC). International experts would be called in, and the "monopoly position" of some services would be reviewed. NPN urged "restoration of trade union independence", and free collective bargaining by unions organised democratically.

The NPN manifesto called for "harmony" between "defence needs, foreign policy and national economic development"; it also promised that nobody would be released from the armed forces unless there was a job for him. This promise recognised the general feeling that the armed forces, swollen over twenty times in size by the needs of the civil war, were far too numerous for Nigeria's present needs, but should not be hastily run down, thus releasing, perhaps to permanent unemployment, young men trained in the use of arms. The Nigeria Police would be expanded, the NPN said, and modernised, and "regular beat policemen" would be re-introduced – the first promise, but not the second, is being implemented.

The rule of law and the sanctity of the constitution would be preserved. In due course, state boundaries and creation of more states would be considered; this, we shall see, is one of the administration's major problems. Traditional rulers would be guaranteed "befitting functions and remunerations" – a vague promise which has caused some embarrassment.

Special attention would be given to the needs of youth,

particularly through a revitalised National Youth Council. Women would be encouraged to play a full part in national life. "State Homes" would be established for the aged, destitute and disabled. Tax relief would be given for contributions to these – but they are yet to be established. Sport would be encouraged, as would "public enlightenment".

Commitment to the OAU, the UN, and ECOWAS, would be the keynote of NPN's foreign policy. Cordial relations would be maintained with all friendly countries.

The late Chief J. S. Tarka, then the NPN's deputy executive vice-chairman, and a masterly political organiser, answering questions at a news conference in London before the elections, said that it was his own view that when Israeli forces withdrew from African soil Nigeria should again recognise Israel, which had a contribution to make to African countries in technology. This is an issue now raised from time to time in Nigeria, where, in spite of the break in diplomatic relations, Israeli firms still win contracts. Liberation of southern Africa was an essential part of the NPN programme, as was defence of the dignity of non-white people everywhere, he said. Nigeria would assist less fortunate countries. Chief Tarka promised "life more abundant" (a phrase made popular years before by Chief Awolowo) in a "balanced federation". The party did not want chiefs to have executive functions. There was no need for new taxes to finance their programme; they knew where the money was and could "dig it out". There would, however, be no magic change on October 1, when President Shehu Shagari would be sworn-in. Nor – Chief Tarka was, we must remember, speaking in London – would they give money to people for not working.

The manifesto and the NPN's organisation, Chief Tarka then claimed, were the result of twelve years of unpublicised work. Pensioned politicians, he said, obviously referring to Dr Azikiwe and Chief Awolowo, should stay out of politics. The armed forces, who on the whole had ruled benevolently, should be "depoliticised".

Too rapid economic change, Chief Tarka continued, would cause the quality of life to suffer; the NPN would use gains from economic development to improve the quality of social services, provide free health care, better housing, etc.

In the UPN's "Mid-term Political Report" issued at the end of the first phase of his election tour, Chief Awolowo declared that a UPN federal government would save up to ₦500m in the first year of its office. The money could be saved by checking extravagance and abolishing fringe benefits, "waste and sloppiness".

His and other statements by UPN party spokesmen showed a dislike of import and similar controls, not on doctrinaire grounds, but because they bred corruption.

The manifesto of the UPN, whose leader, Chief Awolowo, although celebrating his 70th birthday during the campaign, toured very widely, was said to be based on four principles: free education at all levels; free medical care; integrated rural development; and full employment. Of these principles free education has since received the most publicity. Chief Awolowo declared that the UPN had a detailed blueprint of its cost and possibilities. But the party's manifesto was sufficiently down-to-earth to declare that the school year might be changed so that children could help parents (most of whom were farmers) on the farms. (When the NPN government of Sokoto State did introduce this, UPN criticised the change.)

Curricula, the UPN said, would stress agriculture; schools would be modernised and local languages would be the medium of instruction in the early years. Secondary education would be free and compulsory for all who had completed primary education; but agriculture would still be the centre of education.

The UPN manifesto declared that the existing method of providing fertilisers, loans and other inputs to farmers would never succeed. Agriculture would not improve unless the land could be made to attract the younger generation. The UPN would tackle the problem through integrated rural development and would strengthen the farmers' capacity by a vigorous programme of co-operative farming.

Although Nigeria had had two decades of industrial development, the manifesto said, she still could not manu-

175

facture a nail without outside assistance. The party was concerned that around Lagos those of the few industries Nigeria had were of the import-substitution variety, which ignored local raw materials. Nigeria could effect even distribution of industries to arrest migration from rural to urban centres. Foreign capital investment would be encouraged in areas which immediately required expertise.

Dr Azikiwe, a notably inventive master of the English language, declared that "neo-welfarism" was the policy of his NPP. The party was no less keen than NPN and UPN to offer attractions to foreign investors. But, said the NPP manifesto, its ideology "embraces belief in private enterprise and profit motive, democratically regulated in the public interest, to avoid the exploitation of man by man and reinforced by state participation in the private sector". The NPP would take the emphasis off prestige projects and guarantee the ordinary citizens a better living. It would increase incentives for foreign investment, foster the transfer of technology, and so multiply jobs for Nigerians. An NPP government would invest only in industries where capital and manpower requirements were beyond the private sector, or where national security called for it. A system of adjusting wage rates without fuelling inflation would be devised. Interest rates would be reduced and credit facilities liberalised to attract investment and encourage the establishment of small businesses. Industrial peace would be promoted by inclusion of democratically elected workers' representatives on management committees of all enterprises. Balanced development of rural and urban areas would be ensured. Domestic savings and self-reliance in investment financing would be promoted. An environment "conducive to modest consumption" would be created.

Dr Azikiwe himself said that the NPP's taxation policy would be: "the more you earn, the more you pay and the less you earn the less you pay". He promised to abolish payment of income tax by Nigerians earning below ₦1,000 per year. In agriculture the NPP would transform "low-productivity small-scale farms" into successful enterprises through sustained

176

application of modern techniques, adequate support services, accessibility to markets, strengthening of extension services, and formulation of basic changes in farming systems and provision of incentives to farmers.

Nigeria Airways' monopoly would be ended, the NPP declared, and interested groups encouraged to compete on internal and external routes. The NPP would turn Nigeria into a "first-rate land, sea and air power, stronger than any other African country, so that it would be in a position to challenge South Africa should the need arise". A National Service Corps of school leavers, who would be given military training, was planned.

The one party which appeared to deviate from the "extreme centre" was Malam Aminu Kano's PRP. Its manifesto was published only a month before the elections began.

Development of the economy, it said, should be strengthened by ensuring that it was based on heavy industry, such as the planned iron and steel and petrochemical complexes. Management of concerns in which the government had a controlling interest, particularly banks and insurance houses, should pass immediately to Nigerians. A PRP government would increase the state shareholding in the oil industry. To ensure efficiency civil servants would not be allowed to run publicly-owned corporations. A PRP government would set up a N200m fund to finance establishment of worthwhile industries.

All teachers and medical personnel would have free training, and there would be free care for all under a national health insurance scheme. The party saw labour as a powerful ally in the "struggle for full national independence", industrial democracy and industrial development; it would enhance the status of the Nigerian Labour Congress.

The PRP was the only party to promise in its manifesto to create new states by name. These would be a Katsina State, an Abakaliki State, and an Oshun State comprising the old Oshun Division (one state in each of the former big three regions). A one billion naira revolving loan scheme for farmers would help modernisation of agriculture. Housing was seen by the party as a social service; but it planned to help to provide owner-occupied houses.

The PRP promised to accelerate releases from the armed forces; all affected would be absorbed into the police, customs and excise, and prison services.

More important than its manifesto, however, was the PRP's earlier statement of its "General Programme". This spoke of a "privileged few" who "roll in wealth devised from super-profits", from foreign business, kickbacks on government contracts, "price speculation and ill-gotten gains". It was clear that a "freer and fuller life" was not attainable "under the existing social order". A "People's Democratic State" would be established under the PRP. But in defining "the people" the programme included small and big businessmen, self-employed and professional people, as well as "traditional rulers with a social conscience". And it, too, allowed a place in the economy not only for Nigerian but for foreign private enterprise.

The PRP programme sounded most radical in its sector on external affairs. It linked "Zionism in the Middle East" with South Africa as "the bastions for imperialist strategy in Africa".

Since the PRP was the party most likely to exercise power only at state level – and that only in one or at most two northern states – and since its leader's strong views about the proper place of Emirs and their establishments in political life were well known, it was disappointing that neither from the manifesto nor from the programme was it clear what precisely the party would do about these rulers if it was in power in any state. In practice the deep split in the party in Kano, the state it won outright, and the confusion caused by its Governor's policy there towards the Emir, showed that this aspect of its policy was imperfectly thought out.

Alhaji Waziri Ibraham's GNPP was to win two states, Borno and Gongola. It was probably too early in the field, producing its manifesto in November 1978. This foreshadowed most of the policies advocated in other manifestos, with its emphasis on food production, on free education at all levels as soon as practicable, and on encouragement of Nigerian private enterprise. The manifesto also emphasised the GNPP's devotion to democracy, a free press (which meant sale to the public of government shares in newspapers), a multi-party system, and the exclusion from politics of ethnic and religious influences. It identified inflation as a main economic problem, and promised action to improve the performance of public utilities. It laid more emphasis than did other manifestos on development of health services; but its foreign policy section was a very short paragraph. "Hard work", it said, was the "foundation of development and affluence"; but it promised fairer distribution of wealth.

The voters' motives for supporting candidates or parties in the 1979 elections may never be clearly established. This writer, for example, found that a ward in the northern emirate of Daura in an otherwise solidly NPN area had voted for PRP because the most influential family there still believed that, over fifty years before, the then Emir had unjustly imprisoned their grandfather. For them NPN was now the successor Emir's party.

Obviously ethnic loyalties played a leading part. To a greater extent than ever before – to the dismay of some Yoruba intellectuals – this was true of the Yoruba areas, which gave Chief Awolowo support that they had never given him when he was their Premier. The same was true of Ibo support for Dr Azikiwe, and of Borno support for Alhaji Waziri Ibrahim.

Election manifestos, as we have said, played little part in these results. Perhaps, however, although here ideology and religion played a part, this was not true of Kano support for Alhaji Aminu Kano, since his opponent was also a Kano man.

In all cases, however, except for Lagos State, the voters, when they did not give him first place, as they did in nine states, gave Alhaji Shehu Shagari second place. In Nigerian terms this was an astonishing result. For the first time a politician in Nigeria had secured support which could be called "national". He had secured it not because he was a charismatic national figure, but because he had a reputation for honesty and commonsense, and had impressed the voters.

179

11

PRESIDENT OF ALL NIGERIA

If the framers of the constitution failed to make plain the definition of "at least two thirds" of the states for the purpose of the election of the President, because they had not expected a result nearly as close as that of 1979, the new system of government also provided surprises for the whole country. Nigeria, since 1952, had been used, at the centre and for the most part in the regions, to solid majorities in the legislatures, supporting without question the Prime Minister or Premier and his ministers. They had also experienced over thirteen years of military rule under which, reasonably enlightened though it was, any systematic criticism of the federal or state governments could be dangerous. The state governments, too, in spite of the governors' apparent immunity under Gowon, were mere agencies of the Federal Military Government.

Now, however, in spite of the vast power the constitution gave to the nation's "chief executive", the first executive President's own party held only about a third of the seats in each house of the National Assembly. Only seven state governors belonged to his party and he could no more issue orders to these than to any of the other twelve. He is ultimately responsible, it is true, for the Nigeria Police, a single force throughout the federation, and is in more than name Commander-in-Chief of the armed forces. The other "tiers" of government depend almost completely for funds on federally-collected revenues; but their allocations are mostly guaranteed by law. Even over local government the Federal Government has no control at all, although, in contrast to the system in Nigeria before 1976, it now provides almost all the funds for the local authorities. Nor has it any authority in matters of chieftancy.

Under the 1979 constitution state governments have considerable functions. They are responsible for primary education and share responsibility with the Federal Government for other aspects of education. They look after health services, agricultural extension work, and roads, except for federal trunk roads and feeder roads. They can sponsor scientific research. The Federal Government is responsible for major economic development and for direct economic relations with foreign governments or international bodies; but a state government can undertake economic development of any kind, except mining, within its boundaries, make contracts with foreign organisations and, under federal sponsorship, seek foreign loans or assistance.

The President's only ultimate sanction against a state governor – and it is hedged about with restrictions – is to declare a "State of Emergency" in a state, under which the National Assembly could supersede a state House of Assembly and the President exercise executive authority. A governor is also subject to the same legal restraints under the constitution as is the President – and to "media" criticism in other states, if not his own. One governor and one deputy governor have already been "impeached" and removed, although in each case a majority of the state legislature concerned was politically hostile to the accused official.

The apparent autonomy of the governors and the domination of a majority of state governments by parties opposed to the President is seen by some as threatening paralysis of the federal system. Others see the diffusion of power among all five registered parties as a safeguard for democracy in a continent where total exclusion from power has often tempted parties into conspiratorial courses. Nigeria, in spite of the nature of some of her state regimes, is far removed from the "one-party" system which many outside Africa suppose to be typical of African countries.

The states, however, provide another, quite different, problem for the President. The creation of new states was a crucial issue at the Constituent Assembly. Demand for division of the existing states into smaller ones has become a major feature in Nigerian civilian politics, cutting across parties. If the National Assembly supported the most insistent demands and was able to satisfy the intentionally involved provisions of the constitution concerning creation of states, there could be well over forty. The demand arises partly from the belief, strongly held by many groups, that their particular area is "neglected" by the government of the state where they now find themselves, and that they are discriminated against in official employment, etc., since another group is held to "dominate" the state.

For politicians of all parties, however, the creation of new States has great attractions. Each, regardless of size – unless the constitution is amended – would be entitled to five seats in the Senate, and to a federal ministry. Each would have a governor, commissioners (ministers), numerous state boards and representation in various federal organisations. Apart from any funds the Federal Government might feel obliged to provide as grants to a new state administration, each would be entitled by law to its share of federally-collected funds allocated to states, the main source of state finance.

Many Nigerian administrators maintain that Nigeria can neither finance nor staff new state administrations, particularly as it was only in 1976 that the number of states was increased from twelve to nineteen. Advocates of the new states, however, maintain that they would "bring government closer to the people" and stimulate development; in any case, they say, most of the states would still have populations greater than those of many independent African states.

The constitution, whose provisions about procedures for creating new states are not entirely clear, offers no criteria which the areas concerned must pass to qualify as states.

Concerned that, if politicians imposed no check on the new state demands, unviable units might proliferate – and in concert they can, whether he likes it or not, operate the constitution's provisions to create new states – President Shehu Shagari invited the parties to produce a realistic programme for state creation. How many states he had in mind is not known; but everybody agrees that a small number, perhaps five, are, if not necessary, perhaps inevitable. The parties, including the NPN, however, have been reluctant to commit themselves to a limit. The issue may complicate the 1983 general election. The President finally invited a committee of party representatives to consider the matter, rather like the military regime before him.

Further division of the existing states would make the Federal Government, in theory, even more powerful by increasing the number of its clients. If this meant, however, that an increasing proportion of a national revenue in decline was spent on administration, without a corresponding stimulus to productive economic activity, while the constituent units of the federation became even less competent to discharge their functions, the federation as a whole could be gravely weakened.

A parallel problem is the apparent determination of state governments also to "proliferate" local governments. Some of the units created by the last military regime are almost as big as some of the new states now proposed. The President persuaded the National Council of State to prescribe criteria for the creation of new local governments, but state governments are ignoring these in an effort to satisfy a public clamour for new local governments, which is based on the same alleged grievances as is the clamour for creation of new states. Moreover, local governments now have substantial funds guaranteed to them by the Federal Government.

The Secretary to the Federal Government, Alhaji Shehu Musa, warned a conference at Ife University that what he called the "unbridled proliferation" of local governments, which were being increased by "a weird system of permutations and combinations", might soon leave Nigeria with the "confusion, incompetence and ineffectiveness" she had before the 1976 reforms. The local governments proposed might dissipate all their funds on wages and salaries. Existing local governments were woefully deficient in their provision of services and the production of elementary data. There was little hope that new and smaller areas would "motivate and mobilise the masses towards self-help and purposeful development". The prospect of a combination of unviable states and unviable local governments is a daunting one. Both are due to the tendency of politicians for pandering to ill-founded local prejudices.

The new local government system was intended, smoothly and painlessly, to replace the system under which in many parts of the country chiefs played an important role in local government. In practice the system is scarcely operating after over two years of civilian rule. All elected councils, their terms having expired, were replaced by caretaker committees, since fresh elections were not deemed possible until the National Assembly had passed the new Electoral Law. So even before the new authorities have been able to assume any significance in the people's lives or to develop their organisation, state after state has carved them up into smaller authorities.

Whether this division is unconstitutional (a schedule to the constitution lists local government areas to define the areas of states, so that to change local government areas is to change the constitution) is yet to be tested. What is certain is that the aim of the 1976 changes, which were intended to produce local authorities big enough to maintain appropriate services, will be thwarted by the creation of much smaller units, even if these correspond to what the politicians deem to be popular demand. The simultaneous creation of new and smaller states and new and smaller local authorities poses serious administrative problems. The President can and does warn the politicians of this. He has no power to prevent it happening.

Formulation of new rules for dividing federally collected revenue between the three "tiers" of government, as we saw, was left by the Constituent Assembly to the incoming civilian government. Yet, if his success in getting the National Assembly to approve the formula he had himself proposed to the Constituent Assembly has been President Shehu Shagari's most significant legislative achievement, it tested his

184

diplomacy and powers of persuasion, and demonstrated the problems raised for a President both by the provisions of the constitution and by the political circumstances of the Shehu Shagari Administration.

One of the President's first tasks after his inauguration was to appoint yet another revenue allocation commission, Nigeria's eighth, to make recommendations for a new formula. The chairman was Shehu Shagari's old friend, Dr Pius Okigbo. On July 30, 1980, after eight months' work, it presented its report; these recommendations the President described in his budget for 1981, presented in November 1980. His own proposals, based on the recommendations, came to the National Assembly in the form of a bill.

Although its proposals were far simpler than those of the previous Aboyade Committee, the Okigbo Commission did try to refine some of the cruder concepts of revenue allocation. It suggested, for example, a "Social Development Factor", to be represented by primary school enrolment, to account for 15% of the money allocated to the states and local government. Out of this 15%, 11.25% would be shared on the basis of direct primary school enrolment; the balance of 3.75% would be shared on the "attributable basis of inverse enrolment which will be represented by the number of children of primary school age who are not in school" – an effort to help states still backward in education.

The main effect of the recommendations was greatly to decrease the Federal Government's direct share of revenue – from 75% to 55% – while increasing that of the other two tiers. Yet there was still a great outcry from state representatives – including those of the President's own party – for a much greater share. The House of Representatives demanded a major change in the President's bill, to give the states more; the Senate demanded lesser changes. Some legislators talked almost as though money spent by the Federal Government was "lost" to the states; but, as the President emphasised to them, the greater part of the revenue of the Federal Government was spent in, or allocated in grants to, the states. Nor is the individual citizen, although he may or may not prefer control of spending to be near-at-hand, concerned with the channel through which education, roads, water supplies, health services and the rest are financed. He is concerned with quality and quantity.

In accordance with the constitution, a joint committee of twelve members from each house met to reconcile their differences. The Senate proposals were finally accepted by the joint committee. So the Federal Government was to spend 58.5% of federally-collected revenue, the state governments 31.5% and local governments 10%. The Federal Government's 58.5% included 2.5% for initial development of Abuja, the new capital already under construction, and 1% for aid to "ecologically degraded" areas, principally those which might suffer from oil spillage, or damage from mining.

From the states' allocation, funds equal to 5% of all federally-collected revenue were divided among mineral-producing states on the basis of "derivation". Half of the remainder was to be divided equally among all states, 40% on the basis of population, and 10% on a new principle of "land mass". This last principle recognises for both state and local governments the extra cost per citizen of administering and providing services for sparsely-populated areas. There is great variety in population density among Nigeria's states, and in their areas. Borno, for example, with just over three million people, is 117,000 sq. kilometres in area; while in Imo a somewhat larger population live in only 13,000 sq. kilometres. Local government areas show similar disparities.

Of the 10% to local governments, 50% was to be shared on the basis of "minimum responsibility and duties", 40% according to population, and 10% also according to land area. The House of Representatives had wanted to reduce the Federal Government's share to 50% and to increase the share of state governments to 40% and of local governments to 10%.

Voting in the joint committee was very close; for example the proposed 58.5% for the Federal Government attracted 13 ayes and 11 noes. PRP and GNPP Senators, as well as those from his own NPN, supported the President's proposals. The Assembly's approval was particularly important as without it the Federal Budget for 1981 could not go forward, as it was based on the new formula.

The President immediately signed the Revenue Allocation Bill. Yet constitutionally he had been wrongly advised. Certain state governors took advantage of this to ask the Supreme Court for a declaration that the bill had not been properly passed. Delay could be of no benefit to the states, but the governors presumably hoped that further consideration of the bill would mean its alteration in their favour. The Supreme Court ruled that under the constitution a bill agreed by a joint committee had to go to each house of the National Assembly for approval. The President at once submitted a fresh bill to the National Assembly, which passed it quickly, so that it could become law on January 22, 1982.

President Shehu Shagari, however, had had to undertake, for the second time, a great deal of lobbying to get his bill through. Various amendments were approved by the National Assembly; in the end, as the result, one supposes, of superb lobbying by the President, a joint committee rejected the amendments, and then both houses passed the bill. The President made one small concession; he agreed that the 2.5% for Abuja should come out of the 55% for the Federal Government; but in return Abuja should in future be treated as a state – as the constitution provides.

Talking of this episode the President said that it emphasised a main difference between parliamentary and presidential government. In a parliament "the government is *there*"; in a presidential system legislators come to the government, the President, or he goes to them. Whatever happens he can take nothing for granted, not even the support of members of his own party, and must keep constantly in touch.

Nigerians were now seeing in full action that equality and separation of the three branches of government – executive, legislature and judicial – on which Nigeria's constitution is founded.

There have been other issues which emphasised the separation of the executive and judicial areas. The Federal Government suffered a defeat in the courts when the attempted deportation of Alhaji Abudurraham Shugaba Darman, GNPP leader in the Borno House of Assembly, on the grounds that he was a foreigner, was quashed – incompetence rather than malevolence was the cause of this debacle. Politicians constantly take to the courts issues on many of which the courts have no jurisdiction; but at least the politicians are showing their respect for the judiciary. On another issue, the right of the state Commissioners of Police rather than the Governors to issue permits for political meetings, the Supreme Court found in favour of the Federal Government.

The Courts, in other words, which began their new lease of life under civilian rule by having to adjudicate in the matter of the election of Alhaji Shehu Shagari himself, are playing their constitutional part. The President loses no opportunity of championing the judges, who are still called "My Lord" and wear wigs in court. He has particularly attacked what he called "a campaign of calumny" directed at those who ruled in his favour after the election. He also commended the Supreme Court, which alone can hear constitutional cases, for its decision that his assent to his Revenue Allocation Bill was unconstitutional.

The only measure which, to date, the President has failed entirely to get through a hostile National Assembly, is one which does him more credit than any of his successes. This was his bill recommending the salaries for himself, his Ministers, Presidential Advisers and other functionaries, and for Senators and members of the House of Representatives themselves. The legislators spent much time on this issue in the last months of 1979 and the first months of 1980. In particular they took evidence about their remuneration from people prominent in private business and in government corporations, in the expectation that this evidence might support their claims for rewards higher than the President recommended. This evidence showed, for example, that the general manager of the partly government-owned Savannah Bank, a commercial bank, received a salary of ₦30,000 a year, together with a company house and car. The Governor of the Central Bank, on the other hand, was paid only ₦14,700 a year, with official house etc., car, and servants' wages. The then managing director of the *Daily Times*, in which the Federal Government has a majority interest, was paid almost ₦34,000 a year, with a large entertainment allowance, house, car, servants' wages, etc. The managing director of the most important economic organisation in Nigeria, the state-owned National Petroleum Corporation, had a salary of only ₦20,360, with a car and driver, and wages for four domestic servants. Senior aircraft pilots earned ₦28,000 a year or more. Mr Christopher Abebe, then chairman and managing director of the United Africa Company of Nigeria, the Unilever associate, in which 60% of the shares are held by Nigerians, declined to give details of his remuneration; later the chairman of a joint special committee of the National Assembly claimed that Mr Abebe's salary was ₦58,800. Mr Abebe, however, mentioned that some senior UAC executives earned ₦30,000 or more.

The joint special committee, taking into account the ₦133,337 salary of the President of the United States, and his considerable expense allowance, wanted a salary for Nigeria's President of ₦52,870, with allowances far more modest than those considered necessary in Washington. All other public salaries, certainly those of members of the National Assembly, would be geared to the President's salary (Shehu Shagari had recommended ₦25,000 as his own salary). In the end the legislators, warned, for example, by the President of the Senate that there would be hostile public reaction if they voted excessive salaries and allowances for themselves and other public officers, decided on a salary of ₦30,000 for the President, although his allowances exceed this. All other salaries are geared to his. Pay for members of the National Assembly was ₦15,000, but they receive in addition consolidated allowances – ₦5,000 for senators and ₦3,000 for members – and constituency allowances of ₦49,000 and ₦24,000 respectively. Many members of the National Assembly have visited Washington to see how the legislature works there. They complain that, in spite of their allowances, they cannot afford the kind of assistance available to all US legislators.

The Secretary to the Government now gets the modest

salary of ₦16,000 and the Head of the Civil Service ₦15,500.

On learning that the National Assembly had voted him ₦5,000 a year more than he required the President announced that he was allocating this surplus equally among several charities: Nigerian Red Cross Society; First Aid Group; Jamaatul Nasril Islam Islamiya; Pacelli School for the Blind; Nigerian Airforce Officers' Wives Association; and Wesley School for the Deaf and Dumb. Each year, selecting different charities, he follows this practice.

Another bill which, surprisingly, was rejected by the National Assembly was one to establish an "Open University". The Administration had assumed that passage of the bill would be automatic. However, it opened up some ancient "north-south" antipathies. The Open University is intended to prepare for degrees through education by radio those who cannot get places in existing universities. Legislators from some northern states saw the plan as yet another means whereby people from southern states would go ahead of their own people, since, while large number of qualified people could not get university places in southern states, in their own states there was sometimes a shortage of such people to fill the places. The argument did not emerge clearly in public; the legislators preferred to concentrate on the fact that the new university was not mentioned in the NPN's election manifesto and that the Vice-Chancellor had been appointed and funds allocated for it before the Assembly had approved its establishment. In fact there are a growing number of people in the northern states who could benefit from the Open University: the President remains confident that in the end the measure will get through.

An example of the President's independence both of his party apparatus and of the military establishment was his decision, announced on October 1, 1981, that the former Gen. Gowon was now free to return to Nigeria. The former Head of State, who was in Britain, had been declared to be a "wanted person" in 1976, after the murder of his successor, Gen. Murtala Muhammed, in the attempted coup in February, although no specific accusation had ever been made against him and he had always declared his innocence of any association with the murder. The decision was the President's own. At the same time, on the advice of the Council of State, which, presumably, he invited, he ordered the immediate release of all serving terms of imprisonment as a result of their conviction for their part in the attempt.

There remained, and remains, the issue of the continued exile of the former Col. Ojukwu, who is still, in effect, a prohibited immigrant. This is a more complicated problem than was the Gowon case, since among Gowon's Plateau people the demand for his return was unanimous and continuous. The President had earlier ordered that the period of service under the secessionist regime of federal civil servants of "eastern states" origin, should now be counted for seniority and pensions. He also ordered that people convicted of currency offences under a retrospective decree of the military regime should be released. Reconciliation and legitimisation were his aims.

No civilian president taking office after over thirteen years of military rule can ignore the army as a political force. President Shehu Shagari certainly has not done that. Almost all officers, for example, who held government appointments under the military regime have been retired. The Nigerian Army was always sparing with promotions, so there was much room for manoeuvre. Yet Nigeria still has far fewer generals in relation to the size of her forces than have most countries, and there is promotion to spare. Above all, while the size of the army (though not of the much smaller air force or navy) has been consistently reduced, so that it is now some 100,000 below the civil war peak of some 230,000, its equipment is both more sophisticated and much heavier. Though it fought the civil war with armoured cars only, for example, 40 main battle tanks have now been ordered from Vickers, to be added to 65 Soviet medium tanks delivered in 1979.

It is assumed that the highly professional senior officers in all three services will be sufficiently devoted to their careers, and to improving the efficiency and the equipment of the services, to stay clear of politics. Nobody can answer for their juniors, but the size of the army still makes improbable the kind of "majors' coup" which happened in 1966.

An issue which is often raised with the President, particularly by those most affected, is the future of chieftaincy. In his speech in the House of Representatives on March 26, 1957, in which he supported the motion that Nigeria should become independent in 1959, Alhaji Shehu gave what he called a warning about the status after independence "of a very important section of the people of this country". He was referring to the traditional rulers, the chiefs and emirs. For independence, which was inevitable for Nigeria "ready or otherwise", would mean, he declared, not only transfer of power from the British to the people of Nigeria "but from the chiefs as well". The powers of the chiefs would "wane and dwindle"; where would they finally be? Unlike aristocrats in Britain and Europe, who had lost political power but retained their "mighty mansions" and their lands, chiefs and emirs in Nigeria owned no land or mansions; "all they have belongs to the masses".

It is no satisfaction to him that his words were prophetic. For it has been under his presidency that the institution of chieftaincy has suffered its greatest setback. For their own purposes the British maintained the institution, and in spite of strains, it survived the first period of civilian rule with resilience. Under the soldiers chiefs probably grew in influence.

The Constituent Assembly decided, no doubt rightly, that the institution would be permanently damaged if chiefs participated in party politics, or in administration at all, in a country ruled by parties. The executive functions the chiefs exercised in some parts of the country in local government had already been abolished by the new system which the military regime introduced in 1976. In the emirates, however, the emirs still appoint the District Heads, who remain an essential part of local government machinery, although after their appointment these officials become subject to the discipline of the elected local authorities. The Village Heads, an even more essential part of local government in the emirates, similarly continue to be appointed by the District Heads, although then also becoming subject to the local authorities.

The local government changes of 1976 allowed chiefs only a ceremonial role in local government; but they are entitled, in the manner of constitutional monarchs, to be informed about the activities of the local governments of their areas and to offer advice to the elected bodies.

In the constitution the only references to chiefs concern their membership of the National Council of State and of the state Councils of Chiefs. In the first body there is a chief from each state, chosen by the state Council of Chiefs. All governors, however, also sit in the National Council; so the possibility of independent action by their chiefs is limited. A state Council of Chiefs is concerned mostly with customary and chieftaincy matters, on which it can advise the governor. It may also offer advice to him on the maintenance of public order; but if, as could often be the case, a council felt that it was the activities of the governor's own party which constituted a main threat to law and order, the chiefs would find the point difficult to make.

Informally people still take their personal disputes to chiefs to settle; and they can still pacify angry individuals or groups. But lacking formal jurisdiction and powers of coercion they cannot play in matters of law and order the role they once did, and which many still expect them to play. And in vast areas of the countryside no substitute for them exists.

Chieftaincy matters are, under the constitution, entirely the affair of states. To this extent the undertaking in the NPN manifesto to maintain chieftaincy was somewhat academic. In practice the Federal Government itself can do nothing to maintain chieftaincy in a state whose government is hostile to the institution.

The main example during Shehu Shagari's presidency has been Kano. There the PRP, with its anti-emirate tradition, has used state power to attempt to diminish the standing of the Emir of Kano, one of the greatest traditional rulers. The state government has created new emirs in his domain, thereby raising up rivals to him. The creation is of doubtful legality; but if it were challenged in the courts, the state legislature could, no doubt, legalise it. No Kano Council of Chiefs yet exists.

The fact that the PRP in Kano is split into two factions, of which one appears to have resorted to serious violence against state functionaries to demonstrate its opposition to the state government's treatment of the Emir, shows how explosive such matters can be. But the anti-Emir faction of the party is firmly in control of the legislature. It is too late for those who feel, as does the President, that chieftaincy has much still to offer in the conduct of local affairs to reverse the trend which has become so clear in Kano. Elsewhere, though there have been some well-publicised disputes between governors and individual chiefs, conflict of the Kano kind has not yet erupted; and most governors would declare their devotion to the maintenance of chieftaincy. In the states of the south minor chieftaincy titles are still multiplied and the rich and influential are still ready to pay for the privilege of carrying a title. Yet totally bereft of political and administrative power, and for the most part influence, the institution is obviously undermined. If it is ultimately to be extinguished, it is to be hoped that the process will be more dignified than it has been in Kano.

In a freshly cleared forest area near the city of Onitsha in the east of Nigeria, the Pope during his Nigerian tour in February 1982 addressed a crowd estimated to number at least a million. At the suggestion, no doubt, of the Nigerian Roman Catholic bishops, he listed the evils which Nigerians should combat. These included "bribery, corruption, the embezzlement of public or company funds, extravagance and unproductive spending, neglect of the poor and friendless, the parade of wealth, nepotism, tribalism, political denial of the rights of the poor ...", and other evils which range the world.

The Pope did not suggest that these evils were peculiar to, or particularly blatant in, Nigeria. He was, however, echoing a speech the President had made only a month before at the Convocation of the new Jos University, a speech which newspapers called the "Sermon on the Plateau", and which led many to suppose that it would be followed by action against recognised wrongdoers in public life. Nigeria now, the President said, in many ways would not be easily recognised by those who knew her only in the days before independence.

For instance from one University College at Ibadan founded in 1948 we have progressed to seventeen universities. From three Colleges of Arts, Science and Technology in the 1950s, today we have many spread all over the country. The rise in number of other educational institutions, such as Secondary Schools, Primary Schools, Trade Centres, etc., has been no less impressive.

Places which knew no roads before

today have dual carriageways. Areas hitherto considered as deserts, today have green belts due to dams and irrigation projects. A country with only one port at one time can today boast of having no less than six ultra-modern ports and is in fact moving into the steel age.

Nigeria's progress in "ethics", however, was in no way comparable. Over the last decade "many in this nation, particularly among the elite, have become so materialistic that to them nothing matters except money and what money can buy. Such people have relegated morality to the background and the general tendency is to deprive our nation of its soul". A minority

often speak as if the nation is at war with itself and has made no progress except in those few areas which they ascribe to their own efforts. Others speak as if our country is nothing but a collection of ethnic groups ever hostile to one another, because to them, the more divided we are the more they reap the fruit of that division. This negative attitude of such people is very often reflected in their politics. In loss, they have shown bitterness and in victory a corresponding intoxication.

The "swing" to materialism and "ethnic politics" had affected attitudes to work and had contributed to "so much indiscipline in our society". This moral cancer had

eaten deep into the fabric of our institutions – educational, economic as well as political. In our educational institu-

195

tions, our students are inspired to go on rampage and vandalism. Such incitement to lawlessness sometimes, most regrettably, comes from their teachers and at other times from other elders outside the institutions. In our corporations, efficiency and probity are attacked by the same cancer. Sometimes delays and bottlenecks in the implementation of programmes designed for the benefit of the people are artificially created simply because personal or sectional interests are involved. In the field of politics, material considerations more than national interest are employed and determine the behaviour of some political actors.

Universities should be in the forefront of a new crusade, a "revolution of the mind".

Expectations raised by this speech were scarcely met by a minor reshuffle of ministers, aptly called by *New Nigerian* "night of the short knives". In the remaining period of Shehu Shagari's presidential term, the "revolution of the mind", if it happens, may be as important as the "green revolution".

NPN leaders claim that in the 1983 elections their party will improve on its 1979 performance. Its opponents, on the other hand, have asserted that an alliance of what they call the "progressive" parties i.e those opposed to the NPN, will be invincible. There has been much cynicism about this alliance producing an agreed presidential "ticket", and about any such ticket attracting more support than can the NPN's ticket. The non-NPN governors have assiduously used the term "progressive" to describe themselves and the regular and well-publicised meetings they have held. Such labels, however, mean little in Nigeria. Voters in 1983 may be much influenced by the performances of their state governments. The voting, however, is likely to follow broadly the 1979 pattern.

President Shehu Shagari has never felt threatened by any alliance of his opponents. He and the legislature are elected for four years, and they have to live with each other. So long as his measures are likely to enjoy popular support – as he believes they all are – his opponents in the National Assembly would be

196

unwise to impede them. He was unconcerned even when the "accord" the NPN made with the NPP after the 1979 elections, which seemed to assure a majority for his measures in the National Assembly, broke down in July, 1981. For the accord never really worked. In any case, he remained "chief executive", still facing the task of getting his measures through the Assembly. In spite of ill-informed comment abroad there never was, nor could be, a "coalition government" in Nigeria.

There is another opposition, of intellectual radicals, which has no formal link to any of the five registered parties. It seems to have small popular support but it is very articulate and includes a number of significant people. It is particularly strong in universities in the northern states. The Secretary to the Government of Kaduna State, for example, is one of this group.

It also has its martyrs. First is Alhaji Shugaba, whom the Federal Government failed to deport – himself probably rather conservative. Then there is Bala Mohammed, Political Adviser to the PRP Governor of Kano State, and a distinguished Marxist scholar, who was killed in a political riot in Kano in 1981. The NPN's critics claim that it instigated the riot and planned the murder because the victim was a radical. The police, this group claims, ignored the violence. Farmers in the Bakolori irrigation project in Alhaji Shehu's own Sokoto State, who were shot by police during disturbances there, are claimed to be victims of officially-inspired violence. Recently there was the West Indian lecturer at Ahmadu Bello University, Dr P.F. Wilmot, whose intended deportation (presumably on the grounds that he was improperly, as a foreigner, interfering in Nigeria's politics) the federal immigration authorities bungled.

This group is nation-wide. It includes, for example, the distinguished writer Professor Wole Soyinka. The complete freedom with which they are allowed to express their views hardly justifies their accusations of "fascism" against the Federal Government and the President, whom they dismiss as the reactionary representative of the rich and privileged, or their allegation that the Nigeria Police, one of their particular targets, connive in political violence against "radicals".

It is Shehu Shagari's custom not to reply to personal political attacks in kind. Apart from his distaste for vulgarity he does not see why these attacks should receive the added publicity his replies would give them. In an unexpectedly strong attack on his political opponents at the NPN annual convention in November 1981, however, he accused them of "cowardice, failure and inadequacy". And he condemned their then rumoured plans to form a united front against the NPN to fight the next elections. "Our political opponents delude themselves into believing that by grouping their various parties they can somehow evolve a new political force which can beat the National Party at the polls." In an obvious reference to Chief Awolowo, the UPN leader, Shehu Shagari said that this "ganging-up" was determined by the ambition of a single person who, realising that his own party was not capable of putting him in power, wanted to ride upon the backs of other, weaker, parties. "Whenever a group of men or parties conspire to fight just one man or party, that is indicative of cowardice, failure and inadequacy of each and every member of the conspiring group." The "path of honour and truth is distinct from the path of gang-up and conspiracy; the path of courage and wisdom has no room for strife and rancour", he said.

President Shehu Shagari is in a much stronger political position than to be satisfied with the claim, at the end of his first four-year term, that he has survived. True, his Administration's legislative record will not inspire the average voter. It is typical of it, perhaps, that the first bill submitted by the President to the National Assembly was one to establish a Ministry of Science and Technology. At the signing ceremony the President explained that the new ministry would "stimulate the nation's interest in the sciences". That, no doubt, is important; but it would not swing votes over to the NPN.

Yet this is the President's style. He does not seek popularity. He attempts only what he thinks needs to be, and can be, done. He has poured scorn on the cult of "dynamism", quietly asking, "dynamism for what?" A full account of his steward-

The President at Lagos Central Mosque during the 20th Independence Anniversary 1980.

Throwing "pebbles" at Satan during the Hajj at Mina. Forty-nine pebbles are thrown at three sacred pillars by each pilgrim. In popular legend the pillars mark the places where Satan appeared to Abraham and his family and attempted to dissuade them from sacrificing Ismael, as ordered by the Lord.

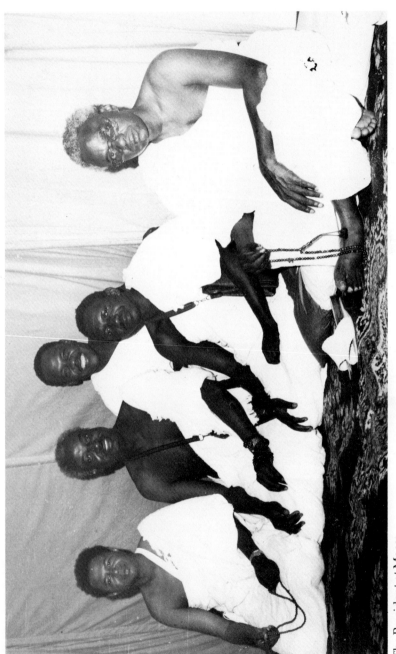

The President at Mecca.

ship even up to the point when the manuscript for this book was finished would occupy more pages than are intended for the whole book. It would, however, record for the most part, so far as domestic affairs are concerned, few exciting new developments or enterprises. It would, instead, discuss efforts to honour his election pledges, to reform the administration of existing enterprises, to make government machinery more efficient, to establish satisfactory relations between the President and all state governors, to improve the quality of education, to make his party more effective (a task which, during his visits to states, has sometimes kept him up very late indeed).

All this, however, adds up to something very important for Nigeria. In his person President Shehu Shagari is healing the old north-south division which was, even more than revenue allocation, the "bane of Nigerian politics". If he succeeds in this, and in establishing the presidency as the focus of national unity, he need not refer to his legislative record to claim support.

12

NIGERIA AND THE WORLD

At the banquet for him in Buckingham Palace's gilded ball-room on March 17, 1981, guests settled down after the Queen's own speech to hear what they expected to be a routine reply by Shehu Shagari. He was beginning his state visit to Britain, and on such occasions visitors do not usually extend the thinking or disturb the consciences of their hosts. In his quiet but clear voice Alhaji Shehu courteously thanked the Queen for her hospitality and for the elaborate ceremonies which had marked the day. Then, equally courteously, he made the points he was to make throughout his visit. What the London *Sunday Times* described as a "glittering multitude" were jolted into reality as the Queen's guest declared that because he and other Nigerians admired British democracy, they expected Britain to adopt towards South Africa and the "horrible state of affairs there" policies which were not only morally right, but were the only ones which could benefit the Western world.

Among those hearing this forthright message were the Prime Minister and the Leader of the Opposition, the Arch-bishop of Canterbury, the Lord Chief Justice, Ministers, Generals, and such businessmen as the chairman of Shell. The tone in which it was delivered and the sincerity of the speaker gave force to the message. The President, who belongs to a people who are proud and independent and for whom colonial rule in West Africa was a mere interlude in their history, does not need prompting from anybody to make him reject totally the evil notion of racial superiority.

The state visit would not have been possible if there had

been no Zimbabwe settlement a year earlier. Now President Shehu Shagari was appealing to Britain to apply the "tact and diplomacy" which made that settlement possible, to the problem of Namibia – South-West Africa. Britain was a member of the five-power "contact group" which under UN auspices was trying to negotiate independence for the territory which, as the President always emphasises, is a UN Trust territory illegally incorporated into South Africa. (The group's activity was for a time paralysed by the change of administration in the US, but its members have always been careful to inform President Shehu Shagari of their progress or lack of it.) He also hoped that "at the appropriate time" Britain would contribute to the emancipation of South Africa by imposing economic sanctions.

At 10 Downing Street the President made the same points, and at his news conference. Sanctions, he said, represented the only non-violent means of bringing pressure on South Africa. If they failed armed struggle was inevitable, as was the triumph of the oppressed. Mrs Thatcher believed she could get South Africa to negotiate; "I wish her luck".

In long private meetings with Mrs Thatcher and Lord Carrington, too, the President emphasised his concern over events in Namibia and over the "collusion and connivance" of the Western countries, which alone enabled the South African system to survive. The London *Times* noted that at Downing Street the British leaders had been unable to give the President much satisfaction. They were anxious, however, for "every nuance of favour" from him.

Of the comments made in Britain on the President's views, one was particularly cogent. In the pages of the *Sunday Times* the newspaper's then political editor, Hugo Young, devoted the whole of his column "Inside Politics" to the Buckingham Palace speech, which he called "polite but firm". He ridiculed the explanation given by some of the British side that the speech was intended for domestic consumption in Nigeria; the President had, instead, brought back into British politics

a subject which many diplomats, not to mention Conservatives, rather hoped had gone away; what, exactly, Britain proposed to do about her South African connection ... Behind the ceremonial decorum he gives us warning that a choice must be made, probably soon. It is a choice for which the British are totally unprepared.

Mr Young, however, was probably wrong to say that Alhaji Shehu's speech represented a bad week for the Foreign Office. They, or at least the Africa Department, were probably pleased that the President so clearly expressed views which they advance, without success, to other British government departments.

During the visit another episode emphasised the part now played in international affairs by the politics of racialism. The President was asked during his news conference by a journalist from an Irish newspaper what he thought of the proposed Irish rugby tour of South Africa. Shehu Shagari replied that any sporting organisation which defied African opinion would forfeit African goodwill. Politics and sport could not be kept separate, as Mrs Thatcher herself had shown by her attempt to secure a British boycott of the Moscow Olympic Games. Later the same day the Dublin *Evening Herald* made its main report the refusal of the Guinness company in Dublin to assist two of its staff to take part in the proposed rugby tour. The report quoted President Shehu Shagari, and said that a Guinness representative had explained that the company knew how Nigerians would view any participation in the team, and the effect it might have on the company's £11m investment in Nigeria.

The heads of some other companies have got the message. Even the London *Daily Telegraph* observed that Britain "cannot afford carelessly to jeopardise trade with Nigeria and probably the same holds true for America".

Before his state visit to Britain Alhaji Shehu made a visit, his first as President, to the United States. His main purpose was to address the UN General Assembly; but President Carter, in the midst of his election campaign, invited him for a one-day visit to Washington (in the hope, some alleged, that this might

NIGERIA AND THE WORLD

influence the Black vote, unlikely though this seemed). Alhaji
Shehu left the Americans in no doubt about Nigeria's stand
against the apartheid South African regime. He felt no urgent
need, unlike many other world leaders at the time, to see
Mr Reagan, then campaigning vigôrously on the Republican
ticket. Nigeria was speaking to the United States, not to a
particular person. Her message was the same, whoever was in
the White House.

Alhaji Shehu did, however, inform Mr Reagan that he
would be available to see him in Washington, an invitation of
which the future President did not take advantage. President
Shehu Shagari considers that the White House and State
Department files must make Nigeria's stand so clear on many
issues – particularly US attitudes to South Africa – that no
meeting between him and President Reagan is necessary to
define it further. The two Presidents finally, in fact, met at the
Cancun "summit" conference in Mexico.

This does not mean that President Shehu Shagari has not
been dismayed at the evidence of the Reagan Administration's
attitude to South Africa, which is based on the view that
the worst, if not the only, political vice is communism or
even tolerance of it. Of that the South African government is
certainly not guilty, so Mr Reagan takes a somewhat indulgent
view of its race policies, which others deem intolerable, but he
thinks are merely mistaken. Shehu Shagari realises that
no UN mandatory sanctions against South Africa are possible
while the Reagan Administration is in power in Washington
or the Thatcher Administration in London. He emphasises the
contrast, however, between Mr Reagan's and Mrs Thatcher's
readiness to apply sanctions to the Soviet Union because of
events in Poland, and their total refusal to contemplate such
action against South Africa. Although he had himself publicly
condemned Soviet aggression in Afghanistan, Shehu Shagari
drew the same contrast when Mrs Thatcher attempted to
impose a boycott on the Olympic Games in Moscow.

Nigeria's relations with the United States reached their
lowest point during President Shehu Shagari's visit to Britain.
So concerned was he over reports of President Reagan's

intention of offering arms to the UNITA rebels in Angola that he felt it necessary to send his External Affairs Minister, Prof. Ishaya Audu, to Washington from London.

At his London news conference Alhaji Shehu expressed his disbelief that reports of President Reagan's intention could be true. It was indeed difficult to believe that even a leader as unversed in international affairs as Mr Reagan could contemplate such folly. No doubt his British hosts had suggested privately to Shehu Shagari that, however disquieting were the reports from Washington, Mr Reagan should be allowed some time to find his international feet. In the end Alhaji Shehu seems to have decided that he could take no risks and must bring home to the new US Administration quickly and directly how serious a view Nigeria took of its plans. So Mr Reagan's Administration had, rather sooner than he expected, the opportunity he had spoken of in a letter thanking the Nigerian leader for his congratulations on his inauguration, of meeting officials of the Nigerian government to discuss "issues of mutual interest". The External Affairs Minister was despatched to make plain to Washington Nigeria's disquiet.

Dr Kissinger's complete failure to recognise the facts of the Angolan situation several years earlier had led to an open rift with the Nigerian military government. At that time, Nigerians pointed out, it was American and South African support for the opponents of the MPLA which had caused the Angolan nationalist movement to look for Soviet surrogate support. Yet it was now precisely this presence of Cuban troops which Mr Reagan used as an excuse for trying to make Angola a testing ground for an anti-Soviet strategy.

Many African governments are unhappy about the role of Cubans in Africa. But not one would support overt intervention by the US to sustain a movement which, even if it does have some internal support, is South African-backed and seeks to overthrow an African government recognised by most countries in the world. Assistance to UNITA could produce only the opposite result from that intended.

Mr Carter, too, had irritated President Shehu Shagari a year earlier by sending Mohammed Ali to Lagos to discuss a boycott of the Olympic Games because of the Soviet invasion of Afghanistan. Although Mohammed Ali, a self-invited guest, had been mobbed by the Lagos crowds during the President's inauguration some months before, the President declined to see him.

It is surprising that the Americans should have expected anything else. Apart from the tactless choice of this envoy, Alhaji Shehu saw the proposed boycott as politically futile, and as certain to attract insignificant support. Nigeria, in any case, would never line-up in what the Americans had turned into a crude big-power contest. She voted for the UN General Assembly resolution which in effect condemned the Soviet aggression in Afghanistan. But in Lagos, if not in Washington, other, if less internationally significant, recent examples of aggression were remembered which attracted no American condemnation. There were, notably, South African incursions into Angola, French intervention in Chad, and the activities of Mr Foccart's mysterious successor, Mr René Journiac, who had just died in an air crash.

Perhaps the State Department expected that Soviet violation of the territory of an Islamic country would arouse particular antipathy in Nigeria. Certainly individual Muslims – but not only Muslims – expressed their outrage at the Soviet action and there had been lively debates on it in Nigerian newspapers. No Nigerian government, however, would allow it to appear that its foreign policies are affected by religious considerations; Nigeria is a secular state for whom aggression is aggression, whoever the victim.

If the Lagos response to US initiatives over Afghanistan had been cool, the response to British suggestions that Nigeria might adopt a stronger stand towards the Soviet Union were even cooler. For the Zimbabwe issue had not then been resolved in a manner which seemed to President Shehu Shagari – himself recently elected in the most complex election Africa had known – to give effect to the principle of majority rule, and hence Britain was seen in Nigeria as bereft of moral authority in such matters. Soviet control of Afghanistan concerns Lagos no less than Washington or London. But it cannot supersede the African issues which dominate Nigerian thinking on external affairs.

The crusade against South African racism is at the centre of Nigeria's foreign policy, and is the long-term objective to which the President attaches the greatest significance. Yet other external issues, many much nearer home, constantly thrust themselves forward for his immediate attention and often for his decision. He has been, for example, Chairman of the OAU "Good Offices" Committee, whose concern is the conflict between Somalia and Ethiopia. Nigeria has a contingent in the UN force in the Lebanon, which has suffered casualties and could embroil Nigeria in Middle East tangles. Nigeria is a very important member of the United Nations, and she has constantly to decide her stand there on a great diversity of issues, such as the "Law of the Sea".

Shehu Shagari himself decided that Nigeria should take advantage of the Lomé Convention between the EEC and the African, Caribbean and Pacific countries (ACP), to which she is a party. Although Nigeria, under the military regime, had taken a lead in the negotiations for the convention, she had made it known that she was not interested in its main "aid" provisions. The President decided that Nigeria could use these. After a disastrous visit to Lagos by Mr Claude Cheysson, then the EEC Commissioner directly concerned, had failed to produce results, Nigeria formally announced her intention to produce, as do all ACP countries, an "indicative plan" for co-operation with the EEC.

As one of the most important, and most genuinely "non-aligned", countries, Nigeria has also to pay attention to the sometimes mystifying politics of the non-aligned movement. She is an obvious port-of-call for leaders of liberation movements and the like, although President Shehu Shagari will not permit any Nigerian interference in the domestic affairs of other countries. He upholds the OAU principle that, for better or worse, the frontiers bequeathed to Africa by colonialism must be scrupulously respected unless any change in them is agreed by the countries concerned.

Nigeria now enjoys more international influence than ever

before, partly because she is the most populous country in Black Africa. Her military forces, although in numbers they have been considerably reduced since the civil war, are also still Black Africa's biggest, and their equipment is constantly being improved. Her influence is also partly based on her recognition of her responsibilities to her neighbours, and her ability, at least until recently, to afford to other African countries considerable financial help, and to invest in their enterprises – the iron ore project in Guinea is an example. Nigeria has contributed ₦62m to the African Development Bank's development fund, which makes interest-free loans to poorer countries.

Nigeria has always been, and still is, the moving spirit behind the Economic Community of West African States (ECOWAS). Established in 1975, largely under the sponsorship of Gen. Gowon, its object is to create from the territories of sixteen states a great area of free trade and free movement stretching 2,000 miles from Mauritania to Nigeria, with a population expected to exceed 200m by the century's end, and to develop the region, particularly the poorest parts, through co-operative self-help. For Shehu Shagari, as for Gowon before him, one significant achievement of ECOWAS could be to help West Africa to overcome the inherited economic division between the "anglophone" and "francophone" states, although in Nigeria there is still suspicion of the close association with France of some ECOWAS members and of the various economic groupings, such as the Conseil de l'Entente and "CEAO", which survive among francophone countries.

The headquarters is in Lagos and because of the failure of some member states to pay their subscriptions Nigeria has had to give ECOWAS an interest-free loan of ₦500,000.

Nigeria also belongs to a wide range of regional bodies in West Africa, such as the long-established West African Examinations Council. She is always anxious to be a "good neighbour" and never uses her strength to claim "hegemony". She can, however, sometimes be over-sensitive to suspected "slights".

207

In the wider continental problems, African countries have to recognise – whether graciously or ungraciously – the leadership of Nigeria. In the Organisation of African Unity (OAU) President Shehu Shagari was, for example, the main influence in preventing the organisation from breaking up over the matter of Morocco and the Polisario movement in the Western Sahara, during the OAU "summit" in Sierra Leone in July 1980. Then a number of OAU members wanted to recognise Polisario as the government of Western Sahara, which would have led to the departure of Morocco, which claims Western Sahara, from the OAU – and other countries would have followed. Shehu Shagari's patient diplomacy, which lasted far into one night, was the main factor in preventing any hasty action. He emphasised that what OAU wanted was to stop the fighting on African soil and to prevent outside powers from interference in an African affair. Recognition of Polisario would only worsen matters, as the Moroccans would intensify their efforts to control the Western Sahara, while outside countries would then also feel free to help Polisario directly. A referendum in the territory remained the only answer. Unhappily, although Shehu Shagari has had to make more than one journey in this cause since, it again seemed likely, in February 1982, when a Polisario delegate was seated at an OAU conference (giving the movement de facto recognition), to disrupt the organisation. Through their supply of arms to the contestants, the Americans and the Russians are also interfering in an African affair.

Nigeria's most immediate foreign policy problem, however, is on her own borders. She has been, both under the military regime and under Shehu Shagari's Administration, the main OAU mediator between the rival factions in Chad, her vast northern neighbour, whose area is one and a half times that of Nigeria, but whose population is estimated to be only some five million. Nigeria's geographical position and military resources make her the obvious mediator. Her own interests, however, also dictate that she should do all in her power to bring peace to a country from which refugees pour into Borno State, and whose instability could prove infectious. More-

208

over an OAU failure in Chad could mean the return of the Libyans, who had been invited there by the interim President, Goukhouni Weddeye, to deal with threats from the Habre forces. On the promise of an OAU "peace-keeping" force President Goukhouni was induced to ask the Libyans to leave – which they did remarkably quickly.

President Shehu Shagari has himself directed Nigeria's policy in Chad. Although formally it is an OAU operation, he, rather than the current OAU chairman, has, since becoming President, been regarded by other African countries as the man to be consulted about developments there. He has had to take a direct interest in the details of the operations of the OAU peace-keeping force sent in temporarily after the Libyan withdrawal. The OAU officials appear to have been either ineffective or unavailable in Chad, and West African countries urged Nigeria to intervene again there, if necessary on her own. A Nigerian, Gen. Ejiga from Benue State, was appointed Force Commander and Nigeria provided three-fifths of the troops.

Nigeria provided much else. The Nigerians themselves have had to supply both rations and transport for the Senegalese. They had to take water by air from Maiduguri in Borno State to Ati, 600 kilometres to the north-east. And even if they had all the equipment and means of communication they wanted, the policing of such a vast area is probably an impossible task.

The Nigerians, however, have not had the logistic assistance from outside for the OAU forces which they had expected and which they deserved. Gen. Ejiga has complained that he had no centrally controlled air supply squadron. Separate support services for the different contingents, he said, hindered effective control. For various reasons the contingents from Togo and from Guinea which were originally expected to join the OAU forces never materialised. For a time both Egypt and the Sudan, although OAU members, supported the Habre forces; both later established relations with Goukhouni.

President Shehu Shagari has publicly expressed his irritation that President Goukhouni will not negotiate with Hissene Habre, in spite of his own military impotence, because he expected the OAU force not to "keep the peace" but to fight for him. It was suggested that the OAU should invite the UN to participate in the operation. For President Shehu Shagari Chad has been his most difficult problem. If he feels obliged to withdraw his troops the consequences could be serious. If he left them there to try to perform a hopeless task, he could clash with his military advisers.

With her eastern neighbour, Cameroon, Nigeria's relations have been uneasy. This is partly because Cameroon has never accepted the incorporation in Nigeria, as a result of a plebiscite, of the former UN trust territory of Northern Cameroon, which had been administered with Nigeria since German Kamerun was divided after the 1914-18 war. There has also been constant tension over the southern part of the ill-defined southern frontier between the two countries because of harassment of Nigerian fishermen by Cameroon gendarmes. President Ahidjo is, like President Shehu Shagari, a Fulani. The two presidents, therefore, could be expected to be on close terms. This did not prevent relations between their countries becoming dangerously strained in March, 1981. The circumstances were never fully established; but Cameroon forces in the coastal area killed five Nigerian soldiers who were, according to Nigerian sources, inside Nigerian territory.

A wave of patriotic excitement swept through Nigeria and Shehu Shagari was under much pressure to "take action". There were demands, some from radical quarters, for military reprisals by Nigeria. There were, naturally, some troop movements in Nigeria in connection with the incident; but in Cameroon it was alleged that the Nigerians were planning to invade not in the area where the shooting had taken place, but in the north in the direction of Garoua.

It was naturally assumed in Nigeria that France, although President Mitterrand had just taken over, was behind the Cameroon Government's intransigence. All Nigerian attempts to extract an apology and compensation from Cameroon failed at the start. The most Ahidjo would concede was a joint commission to examine the issue.

Nigerian suspicion of French connivance at the Cameroon government's attitude was strengthened by the apparent fore-

knowledge French representatives had of moves in the operation. France has a defence agreement with Cameroon. She also
has considerable interests in Nigeria. It was, some Nigerians
think, a careful balancing of these two factors which induced
Ahidjo to climb down.

Shehu Shagari's careful handling of the delicate negotiations with Cameroon, and resistance to Nigerian demands for
military action, finally brought success. The President refused
to attend the 1981 OAU summit in Nairobi because, although
Nigeria had referred the matter, correctly, to that organisation
for action, little or nothing had been, or seemed likely to be,
done to condemn Cameroon. It was president-to-president
exchanges, rather than OAU mediation, which worked. In
January 1982 Ahidjo came to Nigeria as Shehu Shagari's guest,
and spent some time with him in Sokoto. Cameroon had
agreed to Nigeria's demands and now the two Presidents
announced plans for cooperation of many kinds.

Nigeria has had longer and closer links with Ghana than
with any other African country. Relations between the two
countries, however, have often been strained, notably in the
days when Dr Nkrumah was asserting his leadership of Africa.
Ghana returned to civilian rule only a week before Nigeria,
so the two Presidents were natural allies. President Limann is
the first northerner to be head of state in Ghana. Moreover,
Ghana's critical economic problems, the result of two decades
of mismanagement and corruption, obliged her to seek help
from Nigeria.

Gen. Obasanjo had arranged to supply oil on concessionary
terms to the Ghana military government, but these terms
were abruptly withdrawn when the Rawlings regime executed
Ghana's senior officers in 1979. During a state visit to Lagos by
President Limann in early 1980 President Shehu Shagari
agreed again to help Ghana. By the end of 1981, however, the
country's financial position was so desperate that President
Limann flew to Lagos, almost without notice, on Christmas
Eve to explain that Ghana could not pay her oil bill to Nigeria –
estimated to be over $90m – even on the concessionary terms.
Nothing, however, was signed, and when President Limann

was overthrown, Nigeria, so far from extending credit, insisted on normal terms for oil purchases. Ghana could not meet such terms – which meant that oil supplies from Nigeria ceased. After an interval Libya temporarily filled the gap.

Nigeria did not "recognise" the Rawlings regime. On the other hand, she did not withdraw her High Commissioner, on the grounds that it is countries, not individuals, who are "recognised". Shehu Shagari did not attend the celebrations for 25 years of Ghana's independence in March, 1982.

Clearly President Shehu Shagari is strongly critical of President Limann's overthrow. The general view in Nigeria is that the Limann Government was properly elected and that President Limann, like President Shehu Shagari, would have submitted himself for re-election in 1983. Instead of offering himself as Ghana's saviour for a second time Flt Lt Rawlings should have entered politics in the ordinary way. Even Shehu Shagari's strongest critics took this line, and joined in denunciation of military coups.

Relations with the new Ghana regime, however, were made much worse by Rawlings' allegations that Nigeria – with US support – intended to invade Ghana to restore Limann, and by the close links he established with Libya. President Limann, it was presumed, had appealed for help to Shehu Shagari, as well as to other West African heads of state. Nobody, however, was prepared to intervene in the domestic affairs of a neighbour. Difficulties were expected to arise if and when Rawlings attended any international gathering at which other West African heads of state were present. Nigeria had refused to allow Staff-Sergeant Doe of Liberia to attend the OAU "economic summit" in Lagos in April 1980. In this case, however, Liberia's head of state, the widely-travelled William Tolbert, had been brutally murdered.

Because of Ghana's economic crisis many Ghanaians have sought work in Nigeria. There are a large number of teachers, for example. Nigerians, however, tend to exaggerate the number of Ghanaians working – or being unemployed – in Nigeria. They complain too that Nigeria is being swamped by immigrants from other West African states. Under the

ECOWAS agreement movement of people among West African states is now, in theory at least, very free and people from poorer countries do look to Nigeria as a promised land. Nigerians themselves, however, still travel in large numbers in other West African countries, and often settle abroad. As the secretary-general of ECOWAS has explained, this is not a one-way traffic.

With one neighbour relations have improved immeasurably during Shehu Shagari's presidency. The tyrannical and corrupt President Macias Nguema was overthrown in August 1979, in Equatorial Guinea, the former Spanish Guinea, part of which is the island formerly known as Fernando Po, lying just off the Cameroon coast. At the time Nigeria had virtually cut diplomatic relations with Nguema because of the vicious way in which Nigerian immigrant workers had been treated in Fernando Po, where they had formed the majority of the plantation labour force. In 1976 they were withdrawn by the Federal Military Government.

So great an improvement took place in the relations between the two governments after Nguema's overthrow that in January 1980 an Equatorial Guinea mission asked Shehu Shagari's help in framing a constitution. The new President, Obiang Nguema (not a relation of the ousted dictator) during a state visit to Nigeria presented a "shopping list", which included office equipment, to his host. Many other requests to Nigeria to help to restore the economy which Nguema had wrecked have come from the new government. Within a month of coming to power President Obiang Nguema had also gone to Lagos himself to renegotiate a labour agreement.

When asked what made conferences of Commonwealth Heads of Government different from other international gatherings, Shehu Shagari immediately replied "the absence of interpreters and their paraphernalia". That meant that discussion could be both informal and frank, and that partici-pants were in no doubt about what others meant. He appreci-ated that the Commonwealth was a forum rather than an agency for executive action. It was now, however, so repre-sentative of mankind that it was a forum of special value.

213

His own first major speech to Commonwealth Heads of State at the Melbourne Commonwealth conference, in October 1981, the first he had attended, was certainly frank. Inevitably it concerned southern Africa, but he concentrated on Namibia and South African incursions into Angola. After the independence of Zimbabwe and the Portuguese territories, which South Africa had tried to prevent, apartheid and South African control of Namibia were the "unfinished business" of the region. Of the new independent states sharing frontiers with South Africa, five were Commonwealth members. South Africa's leaders, however, had drawn no lesson from the independence of these countries. The President reminded the conference that the Kingston conference in 1978 had said that the Heads of Government looked "to the time when the Government and people of Namibia might be welcomed into the Commonwealth". They could not afford to "wait indefinitely for independence to come to Namibia". The Commonwealth must help to breach the impasse; otherwise Africa could be "engulfed in an East-West global power struggle".

Shehu Shagari said that by moving the Finance Ministers' meeting from New Zealand because of the South African rugby tour there, the Commonwealth had shown its stand against apartheid. And he congratulated "the good people of New Zealand" on their opposition to the tour, sharing their hope that "the good land of New Zealand has seen the last episode of dining with the devil that will be allowed to despoil it".

He assured the conference, too, that Angola would require no Cuban troops if the South African threat was removed. Angola's President had assured him personally that he needed these troops only to protect his country against savage aggression. President Reagan's views on the subject, concluded Shehu Shagari, were incomprehensible.

The South African Government, however, one fears, remained unimpressed by speeches, however sharp and well-phrased, made at international gatherings. Such speeches may produce diminishing returns.

Limited success has attended much of President Shehu Shagari's devoted diplomacy in Africa. Some of the problems with which it has been concerned seem to be almost insoluble. How, for example, can King Hassan and Polisario be reconciled, particularly if they are sustained by outside forces? Perhaps in this case the best that can be hoped for the time being is that this conflict will not be allowed to undermine the OAU, and that Shehu Shagari's efforts to save the organisation will be rewarded. President Goukouni seems bent on self-destruction and to be ready to fire on his rescuers. Col. Gaddafi will remain impulsive and unpredictable. Ethiopia and Somalia will maintain their belligerence. Shehu Shagari, however, has patience and determination. Nor does he hold unrealistic expectations about the wisdom or discretion of some of his African colleagues, many of whose countries are heavily in default in their payments to African continental or regional bodies. Perhaps he can still find comfort in that mission ten years ago when he persuaded Amin and Nyerere that they must draw back from the brink. He can certainly claim that the diplomatic efforts of Nigeria and her President have all been directed towards Africa's peace and unity.

13

TOWARDS ECONOMIC FREEDOM?

In the 1979 election the average Nigerian voter, as Dr Ladun Anise of the University of Ife puts it,* may have behaved "irrationally" with respect to measuring "his potential or actual political pay-offs" – or his standard of living. The voter concentrated instead on parochial political attachments. In any case, Dr Anise argues, the election manifestos did not really offer the voter any great choice of economic alternatives.

In the middle of President Shehu Shagari's 1979-83 term of office, it appears that in the next general election the voters may again attach more importance to matters such as the creation of states or the ethnic or family origins of the candidates than to economic affairs. Yet Nigeria is a country where a high proportion of citizens have long expected governments to confer economic and social benefits on their supporters.

If the voters do take economic performance into account when they go to the polls again, it may be the record of the state governments rather than of the Federal Government which will matter. Over 80 per cent of state funds come through the Federal Government. Most of these, however, belong to the states by right, rather than by courtesy of the Federal Government. Direct federal spending, for example on universities and major industries, defence and the police, and even on housing, is vast, and can significantly affect living standards in a state. But a state government, because it provides schools and clinics, rural roads, housing, services to

*The Nigerian 1979 Elections (Macmillan Nigeria, 1981)

farmers, rural electricity, water, and many kinds of assistance to businessmen, seems closer to people.

Whether or not the voters in 1983 will again behave as Dr Anise says they did in 1979, they must to some extent be influenced by their view of their own and their country's economic state. How rich, or how poor, *are* Nigerians now in comparison with people elsewhere in Africa and the world, and in comparison with their own past standards?

Statistics in the annual World Bank's *World Development Report* show that Nigeria's Gross National Product (GNP) was, in 1979, the equivalent of $670 per caput, and had been increasing during 1960-79 at an annual average rate of 3.7 per cent. This made Nigeria 56th in *per caput* GNP among the 124 countries the report lists. All such figures must be treated with caution. Dr Douglas Rimmer, for example, has estimated that if the real local purchasing power of the naira, rather than the dollar, was used as the index, the figure could be doubled.†

In Black Africa, however, it seems, of the major countries only the Ivory Coast ($1,040 in per caput GNP, which is increasing at 2.5 per cent) was, in 1979, better off than Nigeria. Among Nigeria's neighbours Cameroon ($560 per caput) alone approached her. Her northern neighbour, Niger ($270 per caput) had a negative growth rate. Benin, to the west ($250 per caput), had a growth rate of only 0.6 per cent. And Chad ($110) had a negative and rapidly falling growth rate. These countries were among the world's poorest. Some African countries with populations of under one million, on the other hand, including Mauritius, the Seychelles, and above all Gabon, had a higher GNP per head than Nigeria. Ghana's GNP however, once far higher than that of Nigeria, had fallen to $400 per head, and Ghana's growth rate was negative and her economy was in ruins.

How rich then are Nigerians? If we look outside Africa, or even to North Africa, the picture is not encouraging. Nigeria's 1979 GNP per head of $670 was well above India's $190; but it was far below the $1,120 of Tunisia, the $1,370 of Malaysia,

---

†*Nigeria since 1970* (Hodder and Stoughton)

Brazil's $1,780, Singapore's $3,830, or Czechoslovakia's $5,290. And Nigeria's figure was insignificant compared to the UK's $6,320 or Switzerland's $13,920. In any case the ordinary Nigerian, faced with inflationary prices, particularly for food, soaring rents, crippling transport prices, and inadequate services, would not be impressed by figures showing how well, or badly, he compared with people in other countries.

Clearly oil alone puts Nigeria ahead in GNP in Black Africa. Nigeria's 1979 GNP average, for example, represented an increase of $250 over the World Bank's 1977 figure. This rise, however, and the size of the GNP itself, owed so much to oil earnings that it is impossible to draw from it any reliable impression about individual standards of living. Any survey of real standards, as opposed to the simple division of the GNP equally among a population estimated in 1979 at 82.60m, would show many millions of Nigerians to be among the poorest of mankind. Yet, unlike the mass of people in countries like Upper Volta, no Nigerian now is doomed to a life of poverty, so many are the routes to some kind of prosperity. It is still not true of Nigeria, as was recently said of Ghana, that "the poverty of the poor" had become "the greatest barrier to their becoming rich". Inequalities in income between individuals have increased significantly. Those between regions, areas and communities, Dr Rimmer is confident, have decreased in recent years – and these are the differences which in Nigeria matter politically.

Some 55 per cent of Nigeria's working population were farming in 1979. This figure, if slightly higher than that for Ghana, was much lower than that for Cameroon, the Sudan, and even the Ivory Coast (79 per cent), and had fallen significantly since 1960. It was still almost ten times higher than the figure for the richest countries. In these, even in the very important exporters of agricultural produce such as New Zealand, Denmark or the Netherlands, the rural workforce is under 10 per cent of the total. The proportion of agricultural workers in a country's workforce seems to be in inverse proportion to agricultural productivity.

The average Nigerian is also worse off for medical care than is, for example, the average Ghanaian. Although the Nigerian figure fell remarkably between 1960 and 1977 from 73,710 to 15,740, the ratio between a physician and his prospective patients left Nigeria far behind Ghana (5,430) or Madagascar (10,240). Only 20 countries are shown by the World Bank figures to have a higher ratio than Nigeria, while 37 had a ratio of 1:1,000. The figures for nursing staff give much the same picture.

An average life expectancy of 49 years also puts Nigeria behind Lesotho (51), India (52), Kenya (55) or Sri Lanka (66); and far behind countries such as Poland (72), Ireland (73) or Hong Kong (76).

Educational statistics, although scant in the World Bank report, put Nigeria in a much better light. Universal Primary Education, although it strains the states' finances, is now almost a reality in Nigeria, where primary school pupils number well over 11 million. In states controlled by Chief Awolowo's UPN universal secondary education, whatever its quality, should soon also be a reality, while great advances in secondary education are being made elsewhere. The 17 universities, including two in Oyo State, will be joined by six more to give at least one to each state. An Islamic University is also proposed, while tens of thousands of Nigerians also still follow courses of all kinds in many countries abroad. Nigeria's version of the Open University, when the National Assembly approves it, will offer university education both to older people and to those who cannot now find university places.

In general, however, the average Nigerian's standard of living cannot be said to reflect his estimated share of the GNP which oil has produced.

The UN projections of Nigeria's population, which make it reach a "stationary" 450 million in the year 2105, or about three times the present figure, if not fanciful, cannot be called reliable; and the trends on which they are based could be reversed. The possibility, however, of such a population growth means that to produce food for this multitude is now, and will increasingly be, the main and most difficult respon-sibility of Nigeria's Federal Government. Shehu Shagari's

Administration recognises this responsibility. The "Green Revolution", one of the main planks of the NPN manifesto, sets out to make Nigeria self-sufficient in basic food within five years from October 1979, and a crop exporter in seven. These are ambitious targets but they are being approached in so many ways that the President himself is confident that, if the weather is kind, they can be met.

For years, however, Nigerian agriculture has been "stagnant", although large sums have been devoted by the Federal Government to its development. To spend oil earnings on importing food is not in itself harmful. If it helps to contain inflation and improve nutrition this is an excellent way of spending these earnings. Yet for a country still largely agricultural to spend some ₦1.5bn a year on importing food indicates a very serious deficiency in its agriculture. Moreover, Nigeria's farms are also failing to produce some of the crops to process which factories have been established, notably groundnuts.

In 1980 staple food production rose by only 0.3 per cent. It was clear that the vast and varied official efforts to stimulate food production, mostly directed at individual farmers, had yet to yield the returns expected. The President's confidence, however, that the "Green Revolution" has really started and will produce results remains strong. ₦300m is being spent under the programme in Sokoto State and ₦265m in Kano State. Similar amounts are being spent in each of the other States. The eleven "River Basin Authorities" are also important agencies for farm improvement. Yet while Nigeria must spend oil revenues on developing agriculture, money is not the only answer. A recent World Bank report showed that for all the food crops studied, Nigeria's cost of production far exceeded that of other African countries. The World Bank, too, has itself emphasised that Nigeria did not attach sufficient importance "to cost-recovery and a financially self-sustaining agricultural sector", even in the World Bank's own agricultural schemes which affect thousands of farmers. The Bank also questioned the wisdom of spending as much as $20,000 per hectare, as Nigeria does, in major irrigation schemes, the price of the crops from which, unless subsidised, will be far higher than the price of imports.

For the President the steel industry is the most important agency after agricultural development to ensure Nigeria's economic independence. In countries like Britain, where the steel industry is regarded almost as a museum piece, it is difficult to imagine the excitement which greets the erection of steel plants in the course of industrialising. President Shehu Shagari shares fully the enthusiasm with which Nigerian newspapers greeted his commissioning of Nigeria's first steel plant, the Delta complex at Aladja in Bendel State in February, 1982. Nigeria, he said, "has taken the first significant step towards true industrialisation. We have also taken our first confident and steady step towards technological freedom". The Aladja plant, built at a cost of ₦1.3bn by West German and Austrian contractors, will supply with billets its own rolling mill as well as three independent mills in widely separated locations – Oshogbo, Katsina and Jos. In the meantime, work proceeds on the biggest steel plant, the Ajaokuta complex on the Niger river in Kwara State, whose ultimate cost could exceed ₦5bn. This will also have a rolling mill, but it is designed around a blast furnace, whose output of some 1.3m tonnes a year will not be available until 1985.

Other steel projects are under consideration. The Indian consultants, MECON, are preparing a feasibility study for a "heavy section-cum-rails" plant. Sokoto State is planning a bar-rolling plant with an annual capacity of 60,000 tonnes. MECON is examining plans for another federal plant to produce "flat" products. And so it goes on.

There is no fear that all this projected production will exceed Nigeria's requirements. Will it, however, amount to the "industrial revolution" which Shehu Shagari hopes? There are suggestions that the Ajaokuta plant is outdated even before it has been constructed, because the process used at Aladja had not been developed when Ajaokuta, for which the feasibility studies were first commissioned in 1958, was planned. Aladja uses natural gas, of which Nigeria has unlimited quantities, whereas the Ajaokuta furnaces would need coking coal, whose availability in Nigeria has to be proved.

There is no doubt that protection of the local industry will make steel more expensive for Nigerian buyers, partly because of the uneconomic dispersal of the plants for political reasons. Restriction on imports may deprive users of certain types of steel which the Nigerian industry could not provide. There is no doubt, however, that the President sees the steel industry not as just another industrial development, but as a symbol of economic independence. Yet raw steel is itself worthless. Will Nigeria develop plants to fabricate it, into vehicle bodies, railway rolling stock, armaments, the needs of the construction industry, ships, and a variegated engineering industry? That is the test.

Annual federal budgets in Nigeria are the President's budgets. They are the most important indicators of the country's health. Because of the central importance of government expenditure and official directives for the economy they are also a powerful influence on that health.

The budget for 1982 (Shehu Shagari has altered the fiscal year to make it correspond to the calendar year) reflected the new uncertainty in the position of oil producers. In August the previous year, partly at least because of Nigeria's unrealistic price policy, exports almost ceased, but production had climbed back to 1.7m barrels a day towards the end of the year. This was a satisfactory recovery, but a considerably lower production rate than the rate of some 2.1m barrels a day projected as an average for the period of the 1981-85 development plan. Because of the fall in revenue resulting from the fall in oil production the total capital budget for 1982 was reduced by some 15 per cent, to ₦7.5bn, and some ₦1.6bn out of this was "reserved" until it was certain that there was revenue to meet it. Estimated recurrent expenditure rose less than the rate of inflation. It was hoped to raise over ₦2bn in external and ₦500m in internal loans. The chronic deficits run by state governments, however, are likely to increase during the year.

The President could nevertheless reassure Nigerians about the fiscal health of the Federal Government. Less reassuring is the rate of inflation. Alhaji Shehu gave no figure in his budget message but it is generally thought to be well into double figures. Yet, since government spending is the main cause of "overheating" in the economy, the fall in federal expenditure may in fact help to reduce the rate of inflation. The balance of payments, too, gives cause for anxiety. The import bill rose steadily in 1981, averaging ₦1.2bn monthly early in the year but reaching ₦1.5bn in December. And even if the bulk of imports are capital goods and supplies for industry, food accounted for 10 per cent of the bill. The budget proposals included several for slowing down or reducing imports. They had, however, nothing in common with panic measures introduced by the military regime in 1979 in the face of far less serious falls in oil revenue.

The uncertainty of future oil revenues has led to a revision of the 1981-85 Fourth National Development Plan, the most important economic proposals which the President has laid before the National Assembly. The expenditure originally envisaged was ₦70bn. Private investment during the period was expected to be some ₦11.5bn, a figure which seemed to most people to be an underestimate. Under the Third Plan, Shehu Shagari told the National Assembly when presenting the new one, only just under ₦23bn of a projected ₦43bn was actually spent. That was, however, four times the amount spent under the 1970-74 plan with which he himself had been connected, and was a considerable achievement. Even allowing for inflation, the estimated expenditure for 1981-85 is at least double that actually achieved in 1975-80. The President emphasised that staff shortage would continue to constrain public investment. This time, too, the emphasis was not on vast projects handled by foreign contractors and consultants (steel projects are carried over from the Third Plan period). The emphasis now is on improving rural living standards and the efficiency of small farmers. For this Nigerian staff are essential, and people of the right calibre and experience are rare.

Planned investment during the period is expected, the President told the National Assembly, to generate overall growth of some 7 per cent annually in real terms, a rate which compares favourably with the average under the second and third plans. About 13 per cent of total investment by federal and state governments would go to agriculture, which was expected to generate an annual growth of some 4 per cent. Governments would emphasise direct assistance to small farmers through extension services, provision of water and roads, and subsidies for fertilisers and the like. Large scale farming, however, whether by Nigerians or by foreign companies associated with Nigerians, would also be encouraged. The Federal Government might hold equity in commercial farming ventures. There would be tax relief for "pioneer" farming enterprises which would be allowed to import machinery duty-free and have an investment allowance of up to 10 per cent for losses. Foreigners are now allowed to own 60 per cent of the shares in an agricultural enterprise, in contrast to the 40 per cent they are allowed to hold in most other enterprises in Nigeria.

It was later explained by the Minister of National Planning, Mrs Adenike Oyagbola, that the ₦137m allocated to secondary education would be used mainly to reform the system and bring into existence in all parts of the Federation junior and secondary schools "to combine academic and vocational training". Technical education is allotted ₦354m and higher education ₦1bn. There will be seven new universities of technology, for example. There will also be seven more teaching hospitals. By 1985 student enrolment in Nigeria will exceed 100,000.

With one group of leaders who have great influence in the economy Shehu Shagari has established cordial relations. Before the return to civilian rule it had been expected that trade union leaders, strengthened by the new "streamlined" organisation given them by the military regime, would wish to assert their strength when the military ban on "industrial action" – which had always been ineffective – lapsed. In practice the union leaders have always shown great respect for the President. In March, 1982, they called off a major strike by power workers "out of respect for the Head of State". The union leaders, however, can feel content with what they have secured for their members under the civilian regime. In his March, 1980, budget the President promised a national minimum wage of ₦100 a month. The Nigerian Labour Congress had demanded a minimum of ₦300 and had produced cogent evidence to show that no family could live on less than this. In the end the National Assembly agreed on a minimum of ₦125. Inevitably this led to price increases which virtually cancelled the value of the wage increase, while making Nigerian industry even more uncompetitive than it had been. This is one of Nigeria's great economic dilemmas, which is likely to call in question all government development plans.

Nigeria has discovered painfully that oil, whose world prices were thought to be protected by OPEC, is after all only another raw material whose producers are almost as vulnerable to the world market as are cocoa farmers. The discovery reinforces Shehu Shagari's conviction, held for many years, that while it is futile for African countries to blame their economic woes on "our colonial past", there is a fundamental and inherent clash between countries which have experienced an industrial revolution and those whose main international economic role is to supply raw materials. The markets of the former govern the prices of the latter, while the raw material producers have little or no influence on the prices of the industrial goods they have to import. And while over 400 million people in poorer countries do not get enough food, industrialised countries spend $500bn a year on arms (an argument in danger of boomeranging, as Nigeria and other non-industrialised countries raise their arms spending).

Shehu Shagari does not attribute this imbalance to a "conspiracy" or to anybody's design. It arises inexorably out of economic circumstances. It has, however, significant political implications. For example, he says, the industrialised countries dominate world economic agencies such as the International Monetary Fund. They dominate the Security Council, the body which really matters at the UN. Poorer countries are affected even by the domestic politics of the richer. President Reagan's pledges to US voters, for example, perfectly proper in themselves, mean in the end that US contributions to the "soft-loan" affiliate of the World Bank are threatened. Such institutions should not have been allowed to become so dependent on the United States; but they have, and activities which depend on them can be disrupted by changes in US domestic policy. A similar, if less serious, consequence of a change in the domestic policy of a richer country was the decision of the Thatcher Government in Britain that overseas students, except those from the EEC, should pay full rates for their studies. Perhaps the British should not have allowed a subsidy for overseas students to become established; but they had, and the sudden change, in conformity with Mrs Thatcher's pledge, to her electors to cut public expenditure, was a considerable shock to affected students and governments. This was one of the subjects which, apparently, produced a certain asperity during the President's discussions with Mrs Thatcher in London.

It is his conviction of the importance of the imbalance between the industrialised and the non-industrialised world which has led Shehu Shagari to view the OAU economic "summit" held in Lagos under his chairmanship in April 1980 as the start of the "second phase of Africa's struggle for freedom", the struggle for "economic independence". That could be won only by the continent's economic unity and development of self-reliance. He did not expect speedy or spectacular results. Yet from all the examples of economic co-operation which Africa offered, from the African Development Bank to the Chad Basin Commission, he was confident, he told the Heads of State, that they could develop an African Common Market.

The average African today, the President told the twenty-one heads of state or government assembled in Cancun in Mexico in October, 1981, to consider matters arising out of the Brandt report, has ten per cent less food than he had ten years ago. He agreed that, particularly in agriculture and food production, responsibility for finding solutions belonged to the poorer countries themselves – a point made in the "declaration" issued after the Lagos OAU Summit. Technical aid from abroad, however, machinery, and items like fertiliser, as well as direct food aid, were essential at present. The services of bodies such as the International Fund for Agricultural Development – Nigeria's contributions to which, the President emphasised, were always paid promptly – were also essential.

Africa, Shehu Shagari told the Cancun meeting, needed help for agriculture for another reason. The world prices of her agricultural exports had fallen in real terms, while the cost of their production had risen. Action to improve these prices through international agreement was urgent. He reminded the gathering that they were discussing "how to revive the world economy". The attack on poverty in poorer countries was an essential part of the attack on unemployment and "stagflation" in richer countries.

If this case had been put by a leader whose incompetence, megalomania, extravagance and corruption had been largely responsible, as is true in so many cases, for his country's economic plight, it could be easily answered; "your wounds are self-inflicted". Nigeria is not guiltless. Hundreds of millions of dollars belonging to the marketing boards and allegedly held in trust for the producers of the commodities for which they were responsible were dissipated by politicians. Much other money has been dissipated in Nigeria. Yet Shehu Shagari, because of his own record, can make the case. He is, perhaps, its most effective advocate.

14

RELIGION FOR RULERS

In the 1981 Pilgrimage "Season" some 879,000 non-Saudi pilgrims made the Hajj – the Pilgrimage to Mecca in Saudi Arabia. Among these the Nigerians, just over 100,000, were the largest group, followed by 83,000 Egyptians. There were some 22,275 more Nigerians than in 1980, when Alhaji Shehu Shagari, as President, making his fifth pilgrimage since his first in 1960, was among the Nigerian group.

He was accompanied by a numerous entourage, including the Governors of Bauchi, Niger and Sokoto, the Emirs of Ilorin and Zaria, the Grand Khadi of Sokoto, and Alhaji Suleiman Takuma, national secretary of the NPN. But once the pilgrim enters Saudi Arabia (most since 1981 go through the new Jiddah airport, forty miles from Mecca and perhaps the biggest in the world) rank is forgotten. All must abandon for the pilgrimage period, between one and two weeks, their normal dress, however splendid, and any personal adornment, including wrist watches. They cannot even cut their nails or their hair. They must don the two seamless sheets of white cloth – a loin cloth and a loose shoulder covering – together with sandals and a belt slung over the shoulder with a pouch to hold necessities. They can wear no head-dress, even in bed.

This austere regime physically expresses the *Ihram*, a state into which the pilgrim may enter even before reaching Jiddah. A woman, who must be accompanied by her husband or a close relative, must wear white, with a head covering; her dress must be loose, concealing all except her face and hands.

Spiritually the *Ihram* means suppression of all aggressive

228

and disputatious attitudes, rejection of any acts of violence, even against insects and plants, and extreme austerity.

For Muslims the making of the Holy Pilgrimage is the "fifth pillar" of Islam – the other four are the five daily prayers, the declaration of the unity of God and acceptance of Mohammed as his Prophet, fasting during Ramadan, and the giving of alms. The Hajj and the attendant rituals reinforce the pilgrim's faith, signify atonement and enhance personal standing; but the universal use in Nigeria, and in some other parts of West Africa, of the titles "Alhaji" or "Alhajiya" for those who have made the pilgrimage is, the President himself declares, a "man-made" convention. The titles belong strictly only to those actually on the pilgrimage and lapse when the journey is over. One senses a parallel with the now out-moded use of "been-to" in English-speaking West Africa, to describe those who had studied abroad.

Above all, even if in recent years political dissension among Muslim states has impaired the ideal, the Hajj emphasises the world unity of Islam, now the religion of almost 1,000 million people, nearly a quarter of mankind. One pilgrimage in a Muslim's lifetime is considered obligatory. Further journeys gain further merit.

At one time the hardships, harassments and dangers encountered by pilgrims on their way contributed to the merit of the journey to Saudi Arabia. And so difficult was it still for ordinary pilgrims to make it that as recently as 1927 fewer than 100,000 non-Saudis made the Hajj in a year.

Islamic rulers of the ancient West African states had been making the pilgrimage for centuries. For most lesser people in what was to become Nigeria, it began to be feasible, however, only in the early years of this century, although Richard Burton records that during his visit to Lagos in 1861 he met several men who had "pilgrimaged to Meccah". Until recently the journey was made, and certainly with considerable hardship, by land and sea. Of the community of at least two million people of Nigerian origin who now live in the Sudan most are there as a result of their own, or their parents' or ancestors', failure to complete the journey, although no pilgrim is supposed to set off from home without the means to return.

Since the early 1950s, however, almost all pilgrims from Nigeria have made the journey by chartered aircraft. Now that is virtually the only route, although some rich Nigerians fly privately. So popular has the Hajj become that already by 1972-3 the number of Nigerian pilgrims had reached some 50,000. In 1975 a Nigerian Pilgrims Board was established to assist in caring for the welfare of pilgrims, and to regulate their transport and the agencies making arrangements for them.

Alhaji Shehu's elder brother, the Magaji, was the first Shagari man to make the Hajj, in a large party accompanying the late Sir Ahmadu Bello, Premier of the Northern Region, on one of his numerous pilgrimages. In 1979-80 some dozen Shagari people went to Mecca. Today the Village Head and the elders are enthusiastic about the new international airport at Sokoto from which the state's pilgrims can now fly directly to Saudi Arabia, avoiding the congestion, discomfort and chaos of Kano, for long the only pilgrim airport. The big new permanent pilgrim transit camp, lying on the road from Shagari to Sokoto near the airport, is evidence of the importance that the Hajj plays in Sokoto life.

In spite of the equality which the *Ihram* requires, the Saudi Arabian authorities are at pains to ensure that the most distinguished of the pilgrims, and certainly the Heads of State, are as comfortably housed as possible during the short days of the Hajj, when a total of over two million people must be accommodated in the Mecca area – which, but for these few weeks and the less crowded period of the "lesser Hajj", is a quiet backwater. While the Saudi Arabians have brought about remarkable improvements in the conditions under which the mass of humbler pilgrims live during these days, these conditions are necessarily rigorous.

President Shehu Shagari, however, understands the conditions very well. As he now wryly recalls, he has even shared with humbler Nigerian pilgrims the rigours of a quarantine camp. For in 1972-3, in spite of the burdens he was then carrying as Commissioner of Finance, he readily accepted General Gowon's invitation to become for that season

The Emirs of Zaria and Ilorin,
with the Governors of Sokoto
and Bauchi, accompany the
President at Mecca.

The President visit sick
children at Lagos University
Teaching Hospital.

President Shehu Shagari laying foundation stone for University of Sokoto.

"Amirul-Hajj", or overseer of the Pilgrimage; and on January 31, 1973, towards the end of the Hajj, he led a delegation to Saudi Arabia to study the problems.

In that pilgrimage season cholera had broken out in Nigeria. The Saudi authorities, uncertain whether they had been inoculated, put the first Nigerian arrivals into quarantine and for a time banned further arrivals. Alhaji Shehu took with him on his flight an undertaking to the King from his own Head of State that all Nigerian pilgrims would continue to be inoculated. But on their arrival in Jiddah he and his party were also placed in quarantine. Nigeria's Ambassador in Saudi Arabia, then Alhaji Bello Malabu, who had come to meet them, pleaded for them in vain with the Saudi authorities, and kept vigil outside their camp. But Alhaji Mahmud Gummi, who had been first Grand Khadi of the Northern Region, who was in the party and was well known to the Saudi ruler, succeeded in getting a message out to the King, which secured their release. They finally had a very satisfactory interview with the King, and presented General Gowon's message.

The Ambassador had reported that by this time over 28,000 Nigerians were left in Saudi Arabia out of the 50,000 who had made the pilgrimage. Half were living in exposed conditions around Jiddah airport, had no money left, and were in danger of starvation. Alhaji Shehu had earlier visited Kano, still the main departure point for pilgrims. There he gave the customary warning about using, and trading in, drugs (he was pleased to record later that the Saudi authorities had in this respect taken action against only one Nigerian – and he was not trafficking – during the 1972-3 season); and examined conditions for pilgrims at the northern Nigerian airport.

Nigeria already maintained, as she still does, strong medical missions in Saudi Arabia to look after her pilgrims during the Hajj period. From their staff in Medina Alhaji Shehu and his party learned of the particular hardships of the old, who easily succumb to the cold of the nights. There were Nigerian clinics, too, in Mecca and Jiddah, which had equally disturbing reports – some 2,000 patients came to each clinic each day, but Mecca reported daily deaths of as many as five to seven, some from road accidents. Nigerian External Telecommunications provides direct telephone and telegraph services between Saudi Arabia and Nigeria during the weeks of the Hajj season. It has offices at the three Nigerian medical centres as well as one at the Embassy in Jiddah and one in the Embassy's Mecca office. Radio Kaduna also sends a team to Saudi Arabia for the Hajj period, to send messages back to Nigeria from pilgrims.

Alhaji Shehu found the Nigerian welfare officers in Saudi Arabia to be of uneven quality and recommended an improvement in this respect. He also felt that pilgrims did not receive enough advice about the climate and similar matters before they left Nigeria. He was particularly impressed by the great concentration of humanity, over a million people, who gathered at Muna for the main Hajj rituals; but noted in his report that as this was only a temporary gathering it raised no serious problems. Some Nigerian States, Shehu Shagari found, did not use local Saudi "agents", who were, in any case, of doubtful value. Pilgrims come from almost all states of the Nigerian Federation, and the Yoruba people, whom many outside Nigeria suppose to be non-Muslims, are strongly represented among them.

Since that mission Alhaji Shehu has continued to urge the more radical recommendations he then made, but with little success. He thought that since, in his view, far too many Nigerians went on the Hajj, Saudi Arabia should introduce quotas for pilgrims; Nigeria herself could certainly not thus cut their number, but a quota imposed by the host country would have to be accepted by Nigerians. Fifty thousand flew to Saudi Arabia from Nigeria in 1972-3. This made Nigeria then the third biggest source of pilgrims, after Pakistan and Yemen; but so far from Saudi Arabia imposing a quota the number of Nigerians has since doubled.

In Nigeria, Alhaji Shehu suggested, there should be rigorous medical tests before pilgrims departed. Nobody under sixteen and no pregnant women should go on Hajj. No known bad characters should go either (Nigerian security sends officers to Saudi Arabia for the period of the pilgrimage). Alhaji Shehu also found that Nigerians could only get a limited number of the "courtesy cards" issued by the Saudi authorities to allow pilgrims to travel freely; and he found that too many pilgrims spent their limited funds on unnecessary "souvenirs" and the like, as they still do, and were often cheated.

Shortly after this Saudi Arabia mission the terrible crash of a Boeing 707 at Kano Airport killed dozens of returning pilgrims and disrupted services there; Shehu Shagari went to share in the grief of the bereaved. The Ambassador in Saudi Arabia warned officially that further consequent delay in repatriation from the country might lead to Nigerians rioting at Jiddah; but Nigeria Airways, as always, was opposed to sharing the lucrative pilgrimage business with other airlines, and the Ambassador felt obliged to charter Sabena aircraft on his own initiative. In the meantime, or so the Nigerian Pilgrims' Welfare Association claimed, the Saudi authorities had created difficulties in the way of landing Nigerian food for the stranded pilgrims, difficulties which the Amirul-Hajj overcame.

Alhaji Shehu's successor as Amirul-Hajj in 1973-4, Alhaji Femi Okunnu, a Yoruba lawyer, who was then Commissioner of Works and Housing, had much the same experience as had his predecessor on his inspection tour in Saudi Arabia. His report showed a total of ten doctors and thirty seven nurses in the Nigerian clinics. There were again a large number of destitute Nigerians.

The problems raised by the Hajj for Nigeria continue. The increasingly prosperous pilgrims use the pilgrimage, or are themselves used by richer pilgrims, to circumvent Nigeria's stringent import restrictions by bringing back goods, particularly textiles, to sell in Nigeria, thus inflating their "loads" for the return flight. Pilgrims also take out far too much luggage and attempts by the Pilgrims' Board to introduce a standard suitcase have had limited success. But in 1980, for the first time, there were no cases among Nigerian pilgrims of drug offences or currency rules violations. And now pilgrims can fly not only from Sokoto, Kano and Lagos, but from Maiduguri in Borno State and from Ilorin in Kwara State. In 1981, however, it was only at Sokoto, from which 7,000 pilgrims flew out, that they were all virtually in time for their flights. The Pilgrims' Board blamed Saudi delay in issuing visas in Nigeria for the delays at airports.

Alhaji Shehu has not intervened as President in Hajj matters, apart from ordering a cut in the cost of the Hajj for pilgrims. This in 1980 ranged between some ₦765 and ₦739, according to the airport of departure. He has a keen understanding, however, of the problems raised in the life of Nigeria by the deep-rooted institution of the Hajj.

Nigeria is a country which preserves a remarkable religious balance between Christians and Muslims. No better proof of this can be offered than the amendment made in 1981 to the Pilgrims' Board Act to allow the Board to look after pilgrims of all religious faiths when abroad. It is too soon to say how this arrangement will work in practice; but in theory at least, Christians going to the Holy Land, at Easter perhaps, will be entitled to ask the Pilgrims' Board for assistance.

Some people abroad may find such a development, under an administration led by a devout Muslim, surprising. Shehu Shagari's own faith pervades all his thoughts and actions. Islam, for him, as for all true believers, cannot be separated from politics or government, from education or from the law or its administration. That does not imply, however, any hostility to other religions. On the contrary, he has emphasised that "the worthy ideals of Islam are shared by other religions". Almost all religions "preach that man should be simple and humble and that as a matter of faith he should hold certain principles". Alhaji Shehu does not urge non-Muslim Nigerians to abandon their beliefs – although the number of Muslims in Nigeria is probably growing. He asks all of all faiths, instead, as he said in a message to Muslims marking the end of the Ramadan fast in 1980, "to respect the teachings of their faiths".

If Shehu Shagari sees no necessary conflict between Muslims and those of other faiths, he also denies the existence of contention between "progressive" and "traditional" (not "fundamentalist") Muslims. Whether he played a part in

234

drafting it or not, the speech delivered in 1977 at the University of Nsukka, in the heart of Christian Iboland, by the Sultan of Sokoto when an honorary degree was conferred on the Sarkin Musulmi, perfectly expressed the President's views. The Sultan said that in Islam universal education was an established principle, dear to Shehu Uthman dan Fodio himself. The Prophet had also declared that "the ink of the scholar is holier than the blood of the martyr". Literacy was important, for example, for worshippers to understand their faith. Universal Primary Education (UPE), then coming into operation in Nigeria, was "only now beginning to catch up with a principle and practice enjoined by almighty Allah fourteen centuries ago". The Sultan's only reservation was whether UPE would produce "God-fearing, honest, patriotic and dutiful citizens". If it did "there may be a place in the mercies of Allah for those who have had the wisdom to formulate and implement it".

The Sultan, however, could not support "modernisation" for its own sake. Since the arrival of the Europeans in Nigeria "a medley of divergent and conflicting ideas have been preached as intrinsically, uniquely and exclusively properties of something called modern". Protagonists of such modernity sometimes advocated imposition of these ideas "over and above everything else that the people of Africa have conceived, thought, done or established in the course of our common journey with other races in the march of history".

Modern equipment, Sir Abubakar conceded, such as the tractor, had advantages over the hand hoe. But it had no moral or intellectual superiority.

In a Nigeria which was among the most materialistic of societies it was the aim of the "modern man", Sir Abubakar charged, to put "the pursuit of increasing material welfare above every other purpose". Such a man would organise society "only to facilitate material growth", he would favour the city and the growth of industry above the countryside and farming.

Christians, one supposes, would support the Sultan's attack on the idea that there is a necessary conflict between science and religion. Reason, he went on, was supreme in Islam; those who denied the beliefs of the religious were themselves merely asserting contrary beliefs. Their "religion is that of irreligion". In contrast to the modern man, the Sultan said, the scholars of Islam had stressed the duty of all to work and of leaders to create conditions for fruitful work, but only to serve the religious idea of the total welfare of the community. To this day "our rural populations use the agricultural activities of their village and district heads as a barometer of their own in such things as when to plant".

Nigerians, the Sultan concluded, could find in their indigenous traditions all the inspiration they needed for progress. They must never ignore their "own native creative genius". Progress consisted not in mere growth without regard to discipline or humility. Indigenous tradition taught the virtues of "the acceptance of limits and hence discipline, tolerance and self-control". He prayed that Nigeria's intellectuals would now turn their attention to these traditions.

The Sultan finally emphasised that while he had direct knowledge of only one Nigerian tradition he was confident that in what he had said he could speak for all. That is certainly Alhaji Shehu Shagari's view.

The great majority of Nigeria's Muslims belong to the orthodox Sunni mainstream of Islam – in contrast, for example, to the majority of Iranian Muslims who have adopted the minority Shia creed. The Nigerians follow the Maliki school of law in non-criminal matters – in criminal matters the same secular law applies to all Nigeria; and while on the whole very tolerant of other faiths and non-Islamic survivals in their own communities, Nigerian Muslims are generally regarded as conservative in their approach to their religion.

Of the great Islamic Sufi brotherhoods, the most prominent in Nigeria are Quadiriyya, whose main centre is Sokoto, and the newer Tijaniyya, whose main centre is Kano State. The division has some political significance, which in Kano State may have persisted even into the 1979 election; but it is less important than the general unity of Nigerian Muslims.

Less important Islamic influences are at work. There

have been Mahdiyya movements with Khartoum links, Usmaniyya, and the Ahmadiyya movement, which at one time attracted significant support in Lagos and among the Yoruba, but is now regarded as heretical by orthodox Muslims throughout the world. But while the Central Council of Jama'Atu Nasril Islam, the most important component of Nigeria's central Islamic body, felt it necessary in Kaduna in 1980 to establish a special committee to review and harmonise the relations between Muslim sects and examine the causes of the recurring conflicts between Muslim preachers, the existence, and the representative membership, of the Jama'Atu Nasril Islam itself suggests that Nigeria could face nothing like the bitterness which, in Saudi Arabia, erupted into the seizure of the Great Mosque in Mecca by adherents of the Al-Masifatu sect in December 1979.

Just over a year after the Mecca events, however, Nigeria was shocked by an outburst of religious violence on a scale which the country had never before experienced. In the ancient merchant city of Kano perhaps four thousand people, including many policemen, were killed in riots which lasted eleven days and which were finally brought under control by the army.

The old part of the city, where, after many months of sporadic violence, the disturbances erupted, is almost entirely Islamic. Adherents of a fundamentalist Islamic sect were attacked by outraged Kano citizens because they were abusing Kano's "materialism" and physically molesting Kano citizens, and because they had proclaimed their intention of occupying Kano's Central and Fagge Mosques. The sectarians, who had established what amounted to a "no-go" area, proved to be both more numerous and better armed than either their opponents or the police had realised. Most sectarians were armed, as were groups who unexpectedly tried to come to help them from other centres in Nigeria's northern states, only with bows and arrows.

The brave efforts of the police to contain the violence – partly the result of outraged citizens taking the law into their own hands – were overwhelmed. Governor Abubakar Rimi of

Kano had to appeal to the President for help from the army. This was effective and speedy, and the President himself, for whom the episode was deeply painful, was then able to inspect the ruins left by the fighting. He at once appointed a Tribunal of Inquiry, under an Ibo judge, Mr Justice Anthony Aniagolu, to examine the causes and course of the violence.

The sect leader, Muhammadu Marwa, was killed in the fighting. He had been deported, on the strong recommendation of the then Emir of Kano, Alhaji Sir Muhammadu Sanusi, from Kano to his native Cameroon as far back as 1962, on the ground that he was a "security risk". After his return to Kano he had again been warned about his inflammatory speeches. It was generally believed that his followers, who at the height of the disturbance numbered some 10,000, included a large number of "strangers", attracted to Kano from areas over Nigeria's northern borders, also almost entirely Islamic. They were, perhaps, escaping from the Sahel drought or the Chad civil war, and were ready to fall under the influence of those denouncing the evils of a society which some may have found inhospitable.

Because of the suggestions that "light-skinned" strangers were prominent among the Kano sectarians, fingers were pointed at the Libyans. Colonel Gaddafi chose this moment to turn his embassy in Lagos into a "People's Bureau" – without obtaining the sanction of Nigeria's Ministry of External Affairs. People sent by Tripoli to take over the Lagos embassy had only visitors' permits. The Nigerian government did not ask the Libyan Ambassador and his permanent staff to leave – but they did. Nigeria retained her own embassy in Libya, but could not accept the "People's Bureau". The External Affairs Ministry was already incensed at the undiplomatic behaviour of Libya's Ambassador, a man born in Nigeria; and the President and his ministers were concerned about the presence of Libyan forces in Chad.

Shehu Shagari may, indeed, be the only Muslim statesman who has clearly explained to Colonel Gaddafi that his external policies have no necessary connection with Islam, and may, because of their aggressive aspects, actually run counter to its precepts. The two leaders met in Chad's capital, Ndjamena, in July 1981, when the question of OAU troops taking over from the Libyans there was under discussion. It is said that Gaddafi assumed that Nigeria's President would see Libya's activities as advancing the frontiers of Islam, and so would approve of them. President Shehu Shagari had to explain that in the world today Islam would indeed spread, as it was spreading in Nigeria, but only through peaceful means; to advocate aggressive proselytising was non-Islamic. And, no doubt to the surprise of a man who permits no democracy in his own country, the President explained that he could not in Nigeria's then mood, caused by suspicion of Gaddafi's expansionist intentions, go to Tripoli to continue the discussion – which seems to have fascinated the Colonel – or make any move which might appear to favour Islamic over other influences in Nigeria. Nor could he now simply accept back the former Libyan Ambassador without proper formalities.

The Kano Judicial Tribunal, however, decided that there was no evidence that the Libyans – or any foreign influences – were behind the disturbances (some Nigerians had even, in an extraordinary confusion of roles, accused the Israeli secret service of responsibility). The Tribunal found, it is true, that about a fifth of the almost one thousand people arrested after the disturbances came from neighbouring countries. Most came from Niger, and nearly all were illegal immigrants. But the episode showed how difficult it is to isolate Nigeria from unwelcome currents in world religions.

The Inquiry strongly criticised the local authorities in Kano – including the Governor, the immigration authorities, and the police and security services for laxity and for failure to realise the extent of the danger posed by Muhammadu Marwa and his followers, although they had received warning enough, and Kano citizens were incensed by the terrorism practised by the sect. The Kano State House of Assembly before the disturbances had even refused to accept a motion urging action against the sect on the ground that this might alienate supporters. The response of the President, who trusted the army leaders not to make political capital out of this demonstration of the civilian regime's need of their help, as well as the response of the army (the air force helped with "spotter" aircraft) in this Kano crisis, however, earned them much respect. But, for Shehu Shagari, the intolerance and violence of the sectarians are abhorrent, and alien to the precepts of Islam.

Indeed, the sect responsible for the violence is probably better defined as "anti-Islamic" than as "fanatic" or "fundamentalist"; for the Judicial Inquiry, which included Muslim members, found that Muhammadu Marwa's followers engaged in the systematic killing of hundreds of Kano Muslims, and were so bigoted as to declare that anybody who read any book except the Koran must be regarded as a pagan. But behind the followers' attachment to Marwa and total contempt for all law and authority in Kano – including the authority of the nominally "radical" PRP Kano State Governor – there also lay a disturbing alienation from Nigerian society. Many of the followers, the Tribunal's report emphasised, "did not own more than the clothes they wore"; they "did not have much to lose".

There was no evidence that the Kano disturbances led to similar events elsewhere in Nigeria, although minor troubles in Jos had some connection with them. The efforts of Nigerians from other northern states to come to the aid of the sectarians, however, must cause concern. The Tribunal's report also listed over thirty cases of more or less serious clashes between Islamic groups in Nigeria's northern states in 1978-80. It noted the serious consequences for law and order of religious intolerance in these groups. In particular it drew attention to the sometimes violent intolerance of the Moslem Students' Society, with its headquarters in Lagos, in Nigerian universities, and the attachment of some of its leaders to an "Iranian-type" revolution.

Such intolerance, whether on the part of one Islamic group against another, or of Muslims against adherents of any other religion, Shehu Shagari finds not only hateful in itself, but contrary to the spirit of Islam. This spirit, as Shehu Shagari understands it, is perfectly expressed in a book published in

1978, of which he is co-author, whose lofty ideals are in heartening contrast to the squalid realities of the Kano upheaval.

The President must be one of the few heads of government who set out a complete philosophy of government at a time when he had abandoned any idea of exercising political power himself. With Mrs Jean Boyd, a teacher and a Hausa scholar with long service in Sokoto, Shehu Shagari is the author of *Uthman dan Fodio*.* This short work, written in 1966 and 1967, is designed to make available to young people the teachings of the Shaikh and his disciples, based on the Holy Koran and the Sharia Law, and the character of the leadership he had exercised in the years before, during, and after the Jihad, whose nature we examined briefly in Chapter 1. The authors hope that their readers will relate the book's lessons "to the conduct of affairs in Nigeria today". Certainly Shehu Shagari himself always does exactly that, and takes the book's philosophy of government as his own.

Apart from the purely religious and moral teaching of the Shaikh and his followers, their precepts and principles of government and details of administration are, indeed, relevant to "the conduct of affairs today". Very important in *Uthman dan Fodio* is the extract summarising "The Essentials of Good Government and the Obligations of Leadership", advice given at their request, in a book written in Arabic, to followers of the Shaikh who in 1807 were establishing a new administration for the Kano Emirate, by Waziri Abdullahi, the Shaikh's younger brother. The advice may now seem obvious; but it was given in 1807 and is followed today by the President of Nigeria.

Rulers are told to make frequent "assessments" of their officials, particularly to see if they have acquired any "unexplained wealth". This should be confiscated – a hundred Commissions of Enquiry in modern Nigeria have been based on that principle. A ruler must always be accessible to listen to complaints from his people, which are likely to be about his

---

*Islamic Publications Bureau, PO Box 3881, Apapa, Lagos.

officials. He should avoid any appearance of favouritism – the oath the President took on October 1, 1979 included a promise to "do right to all manner of people" without "fear or favour, affection or ill-will". A ruler must not only be upright but must "let his uprightness shine before him as simple proof". He will be on guard against those offering gifts – "the man who pays for his title will extort what he has paid from the poor". Those he appoints must be qualified for their offices, whose authority must be clearly defined. A good ruler "roots out tyranny and protects his people against wrongdoers". A ruler must be dignified but never extravagant.

Similar injunctions are to be found in the works of the Shaikh himself, and of his son Sultan Bello. President Shehu Shagari sees no difficulty in following them, regarding them not as archaic relics but as living imperatives. Their modern approach is emphasised by references to such matters as the need for judges to visit prisons to see if their convicts are properly treated, and the appointment of "Public Complaints Commissioners" – the title used today in Nigeria for "Ombudsman". Throughout there is strong condemnation of bribes, corruption, nepotism, oppression of the weak by the strong, ostentatious display of wealth – indeed of all the evils which Nigerians now recognise in their society.

The Shaikh himself even emphasised the need for all measures of quantities to be uniform, at least in individual towns, and – a matter very topical in Nigeria – for precise allocation of responsibility among citizens for the disposal of refuse. The book tells us, too, of the very detailed Sokoto regulations about school hours and teachers' responsibilities (recent reports in Nigeria suggest that modern teachers do not measure up to these) and about the proper behaviour of pupils.

Perhaps *Uthman dan Fodio* gives a somewhat idealistic account of the administration of Sokoto City in the early years of the nineteenth century under Sultan Bello. The book, however, does not claim a high degree of sophistication in the government of the Caliphate ("there was no oil revenue, no systematic taxation; officials did not have monthly salaries");

but it emphasises that the theocratic as well as the political rulers were and should be interested in day-to-day affairs. Sultan Bello, who was an innovator in agriculture as well as in administration, wrote about medicine and established a garden for medicinal herbs. President Shehu Shagari has drawn strength in his presidency from the example of the first Sultan, as well as from the teachings of the Shaikh and the other Sokoto leaders.

The book also explains the attitude of the Sokoto scholars to the education of women. The Shaikh was a poet of distinction. But *Uthman dan Fodio* tells us of his poems only obliquely, by reminding us that it was his daughter Nana Asma'u who translated them from Fulfulde (Fulani) into Hausa. The erudition of this daughter, however, who herself wrote some fifty poems in Fulfulde, Arabic and Hausa, allows Shehu Shagari and Mrs Boyd to discuss at some length the Shaikh's attitude to the education of women.

He was most determinedly in favour of it. His daughters were highly literate, as was his granddaughter, Fatimayu. He condemned learned men for "abandoning" their wives and daughters "like beasts". And the remarkable Nana Asma'u established a school attended by students of both sexes; sexual segregation was enjoined, but girls could come out in public for education.

Today throughout Nigeria Universal Primary Education is intended to bring all girls into the system no less than boys, and Shehu Shagari himself has been no less concerned with the education of his daughters than with that of his sons – he keeps careful files of the school reports of all his family.

Among the President's fifteen children have been eight girls including the youngest, Saudatu, born in 1981. All have gone, or will go, to school. One, Zuwairat, is still at Girls' College, Sokoto; another, Mrs Hauwa Kulu Umaru, teaches in Sokoto. Others are also married. Maria, for example, is married to the Vice-Chancellor of Sokoto University, Dr Shehu Ahmed Said Galadanci; and Hauwa, the eldest, to a son of Magaji Muhammed Bello, who looks after family affairs in Shagari. Hadiza is married to a member of the Niger State House of

Assembly; and of the other two one is married to the General Manager of the Sokoto-Rima River Basin Authority and the other, Mrs Atika Mahe, to a Sokoto businessman.

Of Shehu Shagari's sons the eldest, Lt Bala, after doing mechanical engineering at Bristol Technical College, is in the Nigerian Army. He is an enthusiastic polo player like many Nigerian army officers – and many men in the northern states. Ahmadu and Abdurram are at Kaduna Polytechnic, Aminu and Musa are in the Federal Government College in Ilorin (one of a number of secondary boarding schools intended to bring pupils from all parts of the country together). At four years of age, Shehu Usman, and at three, Abdul Mutallib, are too young to go to any but a nursery school.

Shehu Shagari's first wife, Amina, whose father was a Fulani and mother a Hausa from Shagari itself, and whom he married in 1946, died thirty years later leaving five children. His second wife, Ige, whom he married in 1949 and whose father and mother came from the Royal Family of Sokoto, had three children. After ten years of marriage she was divorced. The President now has two wives. The parents of the elder, Hadija, are both "semi-nomadic" Fulani. Their clan has its own settled village in the Yabo area, where they concentrate during the farming season. But since this is a farming area they cannot take their cattle there. They establish, instead, a temporary "camp" in an uncultivated area not far away, where a small number of the clan "herd" them. When the farming season is over the clan resume their nomadic life, leaving behind in the village only the old and infirm. They move about with their cattle, which include Shehu Shagari's own, in search of grazing.

Shehu Shagari's younger wife, A'ishatu, whom he married in 1969, has had two young children. Her family are Fulani from Zaria. At Zaria Middle School the President himself briefly taught her father, now his father-in-law, Alhaji Ibrahim Dabo, who is now a senior official of the Zaria local authority – an unusual relationship for a son-in-law.

Like many successful Nigerians the President has also accepted responsibility as a foster father of a number of children, mostly relatives. They include Muhtari Shehu Shagari, a lawyer, and Abubakar Nuhu Shagari, who is a teacher in Sokoto, as well as a number of girls.

15

A PRESIDENT AT WORK

Few Heads of State or government face a more strenuous working day than the President of Nigeria. When he is in Lagos his day starts at 5.30 a.m. Then he makes the first of his five daily prayers. After taking a bath and having his breakfast, he is in his State House office before 8 o'clock. To greet him there are his personal staff: his doctor, the Chief of Personal Staff, Mikail Prest, the Chief of Protocol, the Chief Press Secretary and the Chief Speech-Writer. First there is mail to look at. It is Prest's job to go through this and prepare it for the President, summarising letters as necessary. Shehu Shagari treats his personal mail seriously. He tries to find time to read and to sign letters sent in his name, and would never sign a memorandum without reading it. There is discussion of the day's appointments.

Before the official visitors begin to arrive, at 10 o'clock, the most urgent files receive attention. The Press Secretary will have gone through Nigeria's score of daily newspapers and other publications, and will mention to the President anything which seems to him to require attention. The Chief of Protocol will discuss the day's arrangements. The speech-writer gets his instructions – but the President does most of his own drafting and the writer's main job is to liaise with the ministry or other body with whose activities a speech may be concerned, and to do research.

This small group and five others have the status of "Special Assistants" to the President. Unlike the presidential "Special Advisers", who have quasi-ministerial duties and whose number and terms of service are decided by the National

246

President Shehu Shagari with Governor Lateef Jakande of Lagos State when work on the Lagos overhead railway was started.

President Shehu Shagari presenting a National Award to the former Head of State, Gen. Olusegun Obasanjo.

Assembly – although the President himself names them – Special Assistants are purely personal appointees of the President. Most of his staff are civil servants and most of his work is done in association with them, particularly the present Secretary to the Government of the Federation, with ministers, or with Special Advisers. The personal staff, however, have a special place in the presidential constellation.

Mikail Prest is tall and slim, with an academic appearance. When the President appointed him in 1979 he was 43. His father, the late Chief Arthur Prest, was an Action Group Minister in Sir Abubakar's Cabinet with Shehu Shagari. He finally became a judge. The family comes from the Itsekiri people, that small but highly talented group whose capital is Warri, the Bendel State port lying between Lagos and Benin. Mr Prest's family has long been Christian, but he has become a Muslim. He is a lawyer and holds the almost ethereal qualification of a Diploma of the Institute of Air and Space Law. He came back to Nigeria to join Shehu Shagari's election team, in which he made himself so useful that the President, who had previously not known him, felt that such loyalty and application would be valuable in State House.

Another member of the team who came to the President's attention during his election campaign, for which the "manager" was Alhaji Umaru Dikko, who became Minister of Transport, was Charles Igoh, the Chief Press Secretary. Born in 1940, he was an experienced journalist, some of whose best work was as Sports Editor of the *Daily Times*. He has been a member of the staff of the National Sports Commission. An Idoma from Benue State, he is a graduate of the University of Lagos. He offered his services in 1979 as a press officer in the presidential campaign, and joined the State House staff in February, 1980.

Among officials very close to the President is the Chief of Protocol, whose job is little understood by those who suppose that it concerns only matters such as precedence on official occasions. In fact, the holder of this appointment, Alhaji Yusuf W. Sada, who comes from Katsina and was born in 1927, has many highly practical duties. He looks after the accommodation and arrangements for distinguished foreign visitors in government guesthouses, etc., organises transport for the President and his entourage, helps to arrange all public occasions in which the President participates. He is also concerned with security matters.

Alhaji Yusuf has had long experience in the diplomatic service, which culminated in his appointment as Ambassador in Bonn. Surprisingly, however, he is by profession a radiographer, with a qualification from Bristol University; he also holds a certificate in public administration from Pakistan's Administrative Staff College.

A Special Assistant with a qualification as unexpected is Alhaji Salihu Abubakar Tanko Yakasai. A Kano man born in 1926, he was a staunch supporter of Malam Aminu Kano's NEPU. He received a Diploma in Political Science from the Wilhelm Pieck Youth High Institute of East Germany in 1962. In 1979, however, he decided that the future belonged to NPN rather than NEPU, now reincarnated as PRP. NPN, in fact, did badly in Kano, but he was appointed one of the President's Special Assistants for National Assembly Liaison in Lagos. A colleague of Alhaji Tanko, who is also concerned with the President's liaison with the National Assembly, is Mr Archibong Archibon-Omon. A Calabar man, he is by profession a town planner.

As Special Assistant on Information there is Mr John 'Nnia Ugwu Nwodo, a young Ibo with an economics degree. Another Special Assistant with practical, if not academic, experience of economics is Alhaji Mohammed Buba Ahmed, whose concern is Nigeria's multifarious statutory boards. Before leaving the civil service he had become Senior Customs Collector. Later he was chairman of the federally-owned Superphosphates Fertiliser Company in Kaduna – he himself comes from Plateau State.

Finally among the Special Assistants are two late-comers. Abiodun Aloba, a Benin man born in 1921, was once, as the *Sunday Times's* columnist "Ebenezer Williams", not only the best-known journalist but perhaps the best-known man in Nigeria. He went off the boil and took various administrative jobs in journalism. Now, still a master of English (he avoided the handicap of a degree) and as sardonic as ever, he is the President's official speech-writer. The invitation to take this appointment surprised him as much as it did everybody else.

The latest Special Assistant, but certainly not the least, is Alhaji Osman Ahmadu-Suka. A large and impressive man, he has been brought in by the President to be head of the new, cumbersomely named, "Department for Monitoring Execution of Government Policies and Programmes". Alhaji Osman, a Sokoto man born in 1926, is one of the few northern Nigerians to have been educated at the famous Achimota School in Ghana, where he spent over ten years. He now has two sons at Harrow. He attended universities in Britain and the US, and after teaching experience joined the Foreign Service, finally becoming Nigeria's ambassador in the Netherlands.

His new department's obvious problem is staff with the right experience; for theirs is a delicate as well as a skilled task. They are expected to examine the routine work of ministries and government bodies as well as specific projects and policies.

Their head was soon able to identify from personal experience one of the routine obstacles to efficiency in the government. The department was allocated premises of its own off Awolowo Road, not far from State House; but financial indiscipline among the contractors delayed completion of these premises for over six months.

On the President's instructions plans for this new department were drawn up by Alhaji Shehu Musa, Secretary to the Government, since it will complement the work of his own office in the general supervision of federal government activities. As the National Assembly might have questioned the appointment of another Special Adviser, the President, who regarded the job as urgent, decided that the head of the new department should be a Special Assistant; and, although he is now a politician, Alhaji Osman retains the personal rank of ambassador.

The President has also appointed a Special Assistant as

"liaison officer" in each state. These appointments have been keenly criticised, even by some NPN spokesmen in the states. It was thought that their holders, all party men, would act as presidential "spies". Politicians of all parties are fiercely jealous of state autonomy. One liaison officer in particular gained notoriety by claiming that he must have police outriders as he moved about on public engagements. There was also criticism of some of them on the ground that they were defeated election candidates coming to office through the "back door". In fact their task is to supervise and co-ordinate federal government activities in their states – and these activities are extensive, including, for example, a multitude of agricultural schemes, the work of the post office, labour affairs, federal housing, major roads and much else. The President is unrepentant about these posts. They are popular, he says, with federal officials in the states who like the presence of a presidential representative.

At Shehu Shagari's side at home and abroad, since he became President, is his ADC, Lt Colonel Isa Usman, a genial infantryman from Gongola State. The army authorities attached him to the President before he was "sworn-in". The arrangement was intended to be temporary both because at the time the Supreme Court had not ruled on the legality of the presidential election results and because Major Isa, as he then was, had been posted to the Nigerian High Commission in India as Defence Adviser. After he had been "sworn-in", however, the President, showing that deep loyalty which he always displays towards those who serve him, rejected other names submitted to him and insisted on retaining Col. Isa as ADC. He, whatever effect the appointment might have on his military career (he has done the course at the Jaji Staff and Command College), was happy to remain the new Head of State's ADC. Unfailingly he ensures that the President has the correct papers – or gifts or awards – on all public occasions, sorts out the problems which arise even during the best-organised events, liaises with the Chief of Protocol and the security men – even helping Shehu Shagari to manage his sword now that he has decided to wear the appropriate cere-

250

monial uniform as Commander-in-Chief of the Army, Navy, or Air Force when protocol requires it.

At home and abroad, too, even on the Mecca Pilgrimage, never far away from the President is Alhaji Dr D. Sarki Tafida, his Chief Consultant Physician, who is also in charge of the State House clinic. A Zaria man born in 1940, he was a pioneer student at the University of Lagos Medical School. He did post-graduate work at Newcastle and Liverpool, and after medical teaching posts in Nigeria returned to Newcastle to work at the Royal Infirmary.

Most of the files which reach the President's desk come through the office of the Secretary to the Government, Alhaji Shehu Musa. He was formerly Permanent Secretary in the Federal Finance Ministry. Under the constitution the Secretary to the Government, who is appointed by the President alone and can be dismissed by him, need not be a civil servant (the office of the Head of the Civil Service is technically part of the President's office). Many NPN stalwarts felt that this was an ideal job for a thrusting politician, in which he could galvanise the federal government machine; an analogy was drawn with the office of Prime Minister. The President, however, decided that the first holder of this new office should be a civil servant who would understand the way the government machine worked, or didn't work, and would not be seen as a rival by ministers and advisers. Shehu Musa's office acts as secretariat for the President's cabinet and he attends its meetings. These take place weekly at the State House.

Shehu Musa sees the President each working day about noon as a routine. Before he comes, however, Shehu Shagari will usually have received a large number of callers.

Although there is considerable flexibility in the day's arrangements, his first callers will probably be important foreign visitors. These range from ambassadors presenting their credentials or saying their farewells to the leader of Namibia's Swapo. A visiting minister is by convention usually restricted to meetings with his Nigerian opposite number, but some slip past protocol by bringing with them what are claimed to be important "messages" to the President from

251

their own Head of State or government. Nigerian state governors, official delegations, Nigerian ambassadors, traditional rulers, members of Commissions of Enquiry, etc., must all be fitted in.

The routine of a State House day may be broken by the need for the President to attend an international gathering in Lagos – these have ranged from the Commonwealth Law Conference to the African Football Confederation. He attends the National Assembly in person to deliver his budget message. Committees and members of the National Assembly, and leaders of all its parties, are also constant visitors at State House. The President holds an occasional news conference, although he does not seek personal publicity and deprecates the habit of Nigerian newspapers of using his photograph on all possible occasions, and of radio or TV news programmes "leading" with an item about him when items which in his view are far more important should be given precedence. The Vice-President gives a regular monthly briefing for "media executives".

The President regularly meets his Special Advisers. Of these Alhaji Yahaya Dikko, whose concern is petroleum and energy, is in a position analogous to that of a minister. His main concern is the giant Nigerian National Petroleum Corporation; he is an electrical engineer and was the first Nigerian General Manager of the National Electric Power Authority. In effect the President is Minister for Petroleum and Energy, with Alhaji Yahaya as Permanent Secretary. A Special Adviser who was in a similar position is Chief Olufunmi Adebanjo, whose concern is information. There is a complete Department of Information, but only recently was a Minister appointed. A Yoruba, Chief Adebanjo is an experienced journalist and worked in the Washington Embassy. He, too, was prominent during the election campaign.

Three Special Advisers are concerned with economic and financial affairs. Chief Theophilus Akinyele, Director of the Budget as well as Special Adviser on Budget Affairs, comes from Ibadan. He is a former academic administrator and senior civil servant. Professor Chukwuma Edozien, who has an

American economics doctorate and is an Ibo, is one of the two Special Advisers on economic affairs. The other, Dr Joseph S. Odama, who comes from Kwara State, also has an American doctorate, and is a former university teacher.

There are two Special Advisers on Political Affairs, both Ibos. Professor Godwin Odenigwe is a lawyer, and holds an American Ph.D. Dr Chuba Okadigbo also has American degrees and is a former university professor. Thirty-eight when appointed in 1979, he is the youngest of the Special Advisers. The duties of these two are obviously the most difficult to define.

Only a few months older than Dr Okadigbo is Dr Olufemi Olaifa, an Ibadan man with high qualifications in veterinary medicine and surgery from many universities, including Oslo. His concern is statutory boards. There is, curiously, another "vet" among the advisers, Dr Bukar Shaibu, who comes from Borno, the great cattle state. He is MRCVS Liverpool and has had considerable experience in the regional and federal ministries. His concern is now national security, but the President has called on him to be chairman of the "Green Revolution" Committee. Finally the veteran Ibo politician and former federal NCNC minister, Dr Kingsley Mbadiwe, is Special Adviser on National Assembly Liaison. In view of the absence of an NPN majority in either house, some think that this task may call for more diplomacy than the 65-year old politician can command.

In a position similar to that of an adviser is the Minister of Police Affairs. The ministry in fact forms part of the Office of the President, who is ultimately responsible for all police matters.

In view of the key position steel holds in the Government's programme for industrial development, the Steel Development Department, headed by a Minister, Mallam Mamman Ali Makele, an economics graduate from Kwara State, is also in the President's Office. Similarly the Ministry for Capital Territory Development (Abuja), is in effect part of the President's Office. In both of these subjects the President takes a deep personal interest.

Dr Alex Ekwueme, the Vice-President, both carries more responsibility than personages in such a position often do, and has become closer to the President than might have been expected, since before he joined the* presidential election "ticket" the two were unacquainted. He is deputy chairman of the Council of State, the National Defence Council and the National Security Council. He is chairman of the National Economic Council, on which all state governors sit, together with the Governor of the Central Bank, and which has important functions concerning the Development Plan. He has been given special responsibility for statutory corporations, and has made official missions abroad on the President's behalf.

At about 1 o'clock each day Shehu Shagari likes, if possible, to hold a short discussion with Dr Ekwueme. If there is no formal luncheon, for example with Nigerian newspaper executives, he has a simple and informal meal at about 2 o'clock, and says prayers again. Then he tries each day to spend some time with his family – he has two wives and of his fifteen children some are still at school (I describe his family in Chapter 13).

Later in the afternoon he returns to the office to deal once more, with the help of his presidential assistants, with files. At about 4 o'clock he likes to return to his house. Again there are prayers in his private mosque, and a bath. For the rest of the day, unless he has to go out for an official engagement, he likes to receive visitors privately, or to read and to watch television. There is usually, however, little respite.

The NPN "national caucus" for example, meets him each Monday evening when he is in Lagos. Some of his friends suggest that these meetings take too much of the President's time, particularly as he is constantly holding discussions with Senators and members of the House of Representatives from his own and other parties. He maintains, however, that they help to keep him in touch with the party outside the legislature. State NPN caucuses also bring some of their problems to him. Nor does he neglect his old friends when they visit Lagos, or delegations of ordinary citizens. Many visitors he himself escorts to the door of his house. Such is his stamina that his informal talks may carry on until two in the morning. There are, too, formal dinners, although nobody supposes that this abstemious man finds much joy in these; he prefers a quiet dinner with friends.

If his visitors allow him, he likes to retire at about 11 o'clock, when he makes the day's last prayers. Then, as he put it in his own account of a Lagos working day, "sleep" – which comes easily to this calm and patient leader whom nobody has seen losing his composure.

Saturday morning he likes to keep free, although once again it is a time for private visitors. On Saturday evening he likes to look at and to work on what is called the "farm" at State House – it is really a garden with some chickens – to play indoor games, or golf on the miniature course laid out in the grounds. Sunday is much the same. Yet he is on duty 24 hours a day, seven days a week, at home or abroad, always ready for crises.

State House, Ribadu Road, is a makeshift group of low buildings – what in West Africa is called a "compound" – near the centre of the city, established out of former ministerial houses by Nigeria's second military Head of State, Gen. Gowon. He preferred this arrangement, possibly for security reasons, to the former President's residence or the Prime Minister's house. Both of these look on to the lagoon which first made Lagos an important slave port. Gen. Gowon called the new complex "Dodan Barracks" – the Brigade of Guards barracks adjoin the site.

Although it has been greatly altered and suitably decorated and is excellently maintained and organised, the compound is confined. The President's own separate house is smaller than many residences in nearby Ikoyi. Major presidential functions have to be held elsewhere. In spite of the addition of a row of dwelling houses which lie outside its perimeter walls, State House cannot provide offices even for all the President's Special Advisers. The Secretary to the Government and his staff also have their offices almost a mile away, in the old Cabinet Office. Further away still some presidential aides work in offices attached to the old, dignified State House, once the residence of governors and governors-general, and then of the first President, Dr Azikiwe.

It had been thought that after his inauguration President Shehu Shagari would move into this residence. It had been lavishly refurbished to accommodate Queen Elizabeth and the Duke of Edinburgh during their state visit to Gen. Gowon – which they never made because of his overthrow. In contrast to the former Dodan Barracks it also has attractive grounds, where presidential garden parties can be held, and an open aspect. This latter attraction, however, has been much diminished by the reclamation from the lagoon of a stretch of land, some 150 yards wide, in front of it which now carries two roads, one a fly-over which spoils the view across the harbour to Apapa docks.

Shehu Shagari decided to follow Gen. Obasanjo and occupy the renamed Dodan Barracks, leaving the former State House to accommodate visiting Heads of State such as the former President of Ghana. For in the years since President Azikiwe lived there, Nigerian External Telecommunication has built on a site next to the old mansion the highest commercial sky-scraper in Lagos, complete with a huge aerial. This completely dominates the house. It is said that the security people were unhappy about this, while the President himself disliked the threat to his privacy which the skyscraper posed. For all their careful preparation for the return to civilian rule, the soldiers had failed to provide a suitable residence for the man who would lead Nigeria under civilian rule.

They could argue, however, that presidential accommodation in Lagos was a somewhat academic matter. Certainly the President himself is more concerned about accelerating the move of the capital to the new Federal Territory of Abuja, in the centre of Nigeria, than he is with the deficiencies of either the old or the new State House in Lagos. He has been more sanguine than either members of the National Assembly or some of his advisers about the possible speed of this move to Abuja. His first journey out of Lagos after becoming President was made to the new capital site, when he was accompanied by a number of legislators.

At Abuja he himself will ultimately be housed in a residence specially designed for presidential purposes. If, however, he moves there next year he will have to live in the Presidential Guest House which is being constructed by an Italian contractor, a prospect which dismays him not at all. When the presidential complex at Abuja is finally complete – nobody can say when – he will be able to have around him all the officials who are his personal advisers. His aim has always been to have the administration and the National Assembly established in Abuja well before the 1983 general election, even if many federal agencies, and perhaps a majority of ministries, will have to stay in Lagos much longer. The legislators might at first have to meet in the conference halls of new hotels or in the conference centre now under construction.

The President has no "Chequers" or "Camp David", an official country retreat. But as well as using his own house at Shagari, or his modest one in the middle of Sokoto old city, for a respite from Lagos – but not from callers or politics – he has inherited from Gen. Obasanjo a presidential "Lodge" in the middle of the 2,240 square kilometre Yankari Game Reserve in Bauchi State. From here there are vast views over the forest and savannah, with no building in sight. The only animals which disturb the presidential calm are the baboons. The rest – lion and other cats, elephant, buffalo, hippo, buck of many kinds, hyenas, crocodiles – are there but may not always be visible. The President's two wives and children, during their stays with him at Yankari, are among the keenest animal watchers. Younger members of his entourage can enjoy swimming in Wikki "warm springs", which supply a pleasant pool near the Lodge.

Shehu Shagari can enjoy a different kind of retreat in a resthouse on the Obudu Plateau, in Cross River State, where it is so cold at night that wood fires are welcome. At either of these two places he can, and at times has, put a ban on callers. A smaller resthouse in Jos is well placed to survey the scenic splendours of Plateau State.

Since becoming President Shehu Shagari has visited every state, some more than once. Such visits are necessarily formal;

but they are also very full. Sometimes, to keep to schedule he has to travel too fast to allow people lining the route to catch more than a glimpse of him and his party. But the visits also allow him to meet a great variety of people and to see a great variety of institutions.

In the early days of his presidency a few governors from parties other than the NPN showed a lack of enthusiasm for such visits, although they, no less than NPN Governors, looked to the federal government for assistance of all kinds. The President himself had publicly to rebuke the UPN Governor, Ambrose Alli of Bendel State, for showing discourtesy towards the presidential office. Governor Mohammed Rimi, PRP Governor of Kano, did not attend the opening ceremony of the major Fiat lorry assembly plant in his capital in April, 1981, which the President performed. Yet in a city suffering from massive unemployment this plant, for which a work-force of 1,800 was envisaged, is particularly important. The UPN Governor of Lagos State, too, Alhaji Lateef Jakande, originally found it inconvenient to join the President on occasions such as the welcoming of visitors at Lagos' Murtala Muhammed Airport. This was only one of the problems raised for a President who had small political support in his own capital – although Lagos citizens have never shown him disrespect.

Patiently Shehu Shagari has emphasised that he is President of all Nigeria, and of all Nigerians regardless of party. It was, perhaps, his highly popular and successful visit to Oyo State, which the UPN dominates politically, which marked a real change. Earlier the President had gone to the state capital, Ibadan, to sympathise with people whose homes had been devastated by floods, and had directed that immediate federal help should be given them. Certainly the energetic UPN Governor of Oyo, Chief Bola Ige, did all he could to make the visit successful, in particular by ensuring that the people of teeming Ibadan had full opportunity to see and to cheer his visitor. He thus earned the commendation even of some of the President's political critics. Nigerians, while often allowing their politics to sour their personal relations, have a keen sense of "good form". They can, and for centuries have done with regard to their chiefs, separate the office from the man, so that even if they criticise the latter they can, and believe that they should, show respect for the former. He is most punctilious about referring to every state governor as "His Excellency" – for himself he claims the title "Mr President", which is often used when he is referred to as well as when he is addressed.

In August 1981 there came, too, the invitation to the President from the Lagos State Governor formally to inaugurate work on the great overhead railway network, which is intended to do for pedestrians what the costly network of flyovers, bridges and motorways has done for vehicles in Lagos. That railway will take a very long time to build, and Lagos State cannot possibly meet the cost itself, and will need Federal help. Alhaji Lateef no doubt had this in mind when issuing his invitation to the President. His personal reconciliation with Shehu Shagari, however, has gone much further.

Ministers are not members of the legislature, but can be and are closely questioned by committees of the National Assembly about the conduct of their departments. Although as the constitution puts it, the President may assign to the Vice-President, or to any minister, "administration of any department", the President is always "Chief Executive" of the Federation as well as Head of State and Commander-in-Chief. The Vice-President and all ministers are, therefore, in the last resort advisory. To some extent indeed, the ministers, among whom there were three women in 1982, one in the Cabinet, constitute a miniature Parliament, since the constitution requires the President to appoint at least one minister from each state. So if the number of states multiplies, this opens daunting prospects. The constitution however, makes no reference to a cabinet, but only "regular meetings" of the President with the Vice-President and ministers. The President, it seems, can himself appoint some ministers to his cabinet while making others "Ministers of State".

It would be ingenuous to see the ministers as purely personal appointees of the President. His party obviously has an important voice in selecting them; but he can and does insist on allocating or changing portfolios himself. This was well demonstrated when the NPN agreed that the NPP, as part of the 1979 "accord" between the two parties, should have six ministerial and junior ministerial posts. There was no question of the NPP naming the portfolios they wanted; and when the accord broke down, the President, in spite of some protests from his party, retained in their offices the NPP ministers who chose to stay with him, notably Dr Ishaya Audu, the Foreign Minister.

The President's ascendancy in the cabinet is shown, above all, by the absence of voting; he alone decides what is the "sense" of a meeting. There is no means of knowing what dissension, if any, there is. Ministers are careful to say publicly nothing to suggest that there is anything but perfect unity.

The President, as chairman, also has direct responsibility under the constitution for decisions of the National Council of State, the National Defence Council and the National Security Council; he has also assumed the chairmanship of the "Green Revolution Council" on which all ministers serve, whose responsibilities have a bearing on agriculture.

The Council of State is the body of "elder statesmen" which advises the President on a variety of matters, including the "prerogative of mercy", certain appointments and, when required, "the maintenance of public order". One says "elder statesmen". The Council, however, includes as well as former Heads of State, Chief Justices and a senior chief from each state, all state governors, the President of the Senate, and the Speaker. It was therefore, something of a triumph for the President to persuade this body to lay down the principles on which new local governments should be created – a very contentious issue. President Shehu Shagari is not a man to manipulate the levers of power; but he has shown that, even if in limited matters, he can find in the Council of State a wide accord which augurs well for national unity. The functions of the other federal bodies of which he is chairman are clear from their titles.

A main issue in Nigerian politics is still "jobs". It is not surprising that the NPN approached it before the election in a wholehearted way. The President has been furnished with what might be called a "bible" to assist him in making appointments. And since in Nigeria now federal government appointments include such exotic jobs as a director for Nigerian National Shrimps, as well as the chairmen and some board members of eleven banks, this is one of the President's major responsibilities.

Each state has produced five suggestions for chairmen of federal or partly federal bodies, and forty for their directors. This gives the President a fairly wide choice, when he refers to the "bible"; but it is still a circumscribed choice. While the principle of spreading the appointments fairly among the states is eminently sound, and is required by the constitution, one wonders whether spreading them more widely politically might not also be beneficial for stability, even if in Nigeria members of a victorious party still expect a monopoly of the spoils.

Some of his friends and supporters express disquiet about the time the President has to spend on the 14-mile road journey in the presidential Mercedes to and from Murtala Muhammed Airport to accompany visiting Heads of State when they arrive and depart. They point to his own experience on state visits abroad. In Washington he went by helicopter from the airport to the White House, to be greeted on the lawn there by President Carter. In Britain, as is customary, he was greeted not at Gatwick Airport but at London's Victoria railway station by the Queen. He then accompanied her in the carriage procession for the one and a half mile drive to Buckingham Palace (he had flown out of Lagos' Murtala Muhammed Airport at 4 o'clock that morning).

African Heads of State also make more frequent state visits to Nigeria, sometimes with "shopping lists", than President Shehu Shagari makes to other African states (in 1981 one visiting President headed his "shopping list" with tanks; another with typewriters). He says, however, that since it is the custom for Nigeria's Head of State thus to greet and bid farewell to his counterparts on state visits (and nearly all their visits are so designated) it would be invidious to single out any particular occasion to discontinue the practice. He can, in any case, himself fly in a helicopter when not accompanying his guest. Some of his friends are also worried about the time the President must spend on receiving the credentials of foreign ambassadors (there are over eighty diplomatic missions in Nigeria) and taking leave of them. As a Head of Government only, a Prime Minister is, in this matter, more fortunate.

There has been too, some criticism in Nigeria of the number of his journeys abroad since he became President. He is, however, one of the few important Third World leaders whose visits create no anxiety among his hosts' security services. Nigerians abroad – and almost every country Shehu Shagari has visited can produce a group of Nigerians, sometimes very large – treat him with respect and courtesy. Nobody has criticised his use of a special Nigeria Airways 707 for his foreign visits. A Boeing 727 is now on order for the President's international travel, at a cost of ₦22m; nobody grudges him this. His own quarters in the adapted Nigeria Airways 707 aircraft were suitably spacious, with an extra-large presidential chair. There were also special quarters for ministers. On his overseas visits, however, the aircraft has always been full of officials and aides of various kinds, as well as of journalists and TV and radio people, who would often have found it impossible to accompany the President by any other means. This will be true of the 727. There is also a permanent "federal flight unit" consisting of smaller aircraft, including an executive jet ordered by Gen. Obasanjo.

The President of Africa's most populous country cannot avoid attendance at continental and regional conferences, such as those of OAU and its committees, of some of which he has been chairman, or ECOWAS, or such international gatherings as Commonwealth Prime Ministers' conferences, or the Cancun "Summit" on the Brandt report. He must also accept some, at least, of the invitations he receives to visit individual countries, particularly in Africa, if Nigeria is to avoid the accusation of arrogance.

Shehu Shagari, in short, is the "Mr Africa" whom many

international magazines have identified. It is a role which he does not accept, but which he cannot avoid.

One of the shrewdest assessments of the President comes from an unexpected source, *Choice*, a publication of the US Association of College and Research Libraries. A reviewer in that publication, writing about *My Vision of Nigeria*, the collection of Shehu Shagari's speeches as President, published in 1981, says that they are "informed, careful, cautious and thoughtful; they teach, but do not lecture; they are political but not blustering". The President, says *Choice*, is "clearly concerned with promoting constitutionalism, law and order, public welfare, economic development, and reconciliation in a nation once tragically torn by civil war, ethnic hostility and bureaucratic corruption. On the national level he tends towards conservatism, urging administrative efficiency, budgetary reforms, and prosperity linked to productivity. At the international level he predictably advocates the end of apartheid in South Africa, promotion of the New International Economic Order, and opposition to external interference in Pan-African affairs". This, says *Choice*, is not the empty "rhetoric of a self-serving politician, but the patient deliberation of a dedicated public servant". That is Alhaji Shehu Shagari's position.

POSTSCRIPT

A NEW BEGINNING?

For Nigeria the return to civilian rule in 1979 represented a more fundamental political change than had independence itself. In 1960 the parties in power in the Regions were already exercising virtually complete sovereignty, which they continued to exercise. Independence could only entrench them more solidly. The final removal of Britain's veto power at the centre did not significantly change the nature of the government of Sir Abubakar Tafawa Balewa. The Northern Region was no less able than before to dominate the Federation's politics, and the NPC to dominate the Region. A fourth, small, Region, the Mid-West, was to be created in 1963, and the apparently impregnable Action Group government of the Western Region was to split and lose power. Yet the pattern of politics seemed set, at least for some years. Independence meant continuity.

In 1979, however, the transformation was radical. After over thirteen years when parties had been formally banned, power was being transferred to the parties. The former big Regions had been broken up into states by the soldiers. Yet, since the states' military governors were appointed by and were answerable to and removable by the Supreme Military Council, the state governments enjoyed only such powers as were devolved to them by the Federal Military Government, and had no independent authority. Under military rule Nigeria had, in fact, not been a true federation at all. In 1979 however, the states assumed an autonomous jurisdiction under their elected governors. The political significance of the break-up of the big Regions could now be really tested.

Above all Nigeria was to operate a presidential system which was essentially different not only from military rule, but from the parliamentary system in operation before and after independence. The President himself, although his power is circumscribed by the constitution, by the courts, by the federal legislature and by the autonomy of the states, occupies a position such as no Nigerian has previously occupied. In practice a Prime Minister can, while sheltering behind a constitutional fiction, be as powerful as any President. He can, however, never seem to the mass of his countrymen to be as powerful. His continuation in office depends from day to day on the possibly fluctuating votes of his supporters in parliament, and in theory his government can at any time be turned out. Nigeria's only Prime Minister was, and was known to be, inside his own party subordinate to its leader, the Sardauna of Sokoto. As was shown by the 1964 dispute between Sir Abubakar and President Azikiwe after the general election, the separation of the offices of Head of State and Head of Government could produce confusion in a country where constitutional conventions were uncertain.

By contrast the President now has what the Constitution Drafting Committee (CDC) called an independent right to govern because he is directly elected by all eligible citizens. No defeat for his measures in the legislature can lead to loss of his office. He can be removed before the end of his four-year term only by the complex process of "impeachment".

His lack of an assured majority in the National Assembly, however, has made it difficult for President Shehu Shagari to display the "energy and despatch" in all matters which the CDC hoped the Chief Executive would be able to show. The CDC expressed apprehension that a President "armed with the organised forces of the State" could, in the last analysis, "dismiss the Legislature which, as an institution has no organised force under its control and no machinery for preventing usurpation of power by the executive". The possibility of President Shehu Shagari attempting such a usurpation has never been mentioned or imagined. He is devoted to a constitutional course, whatever the consequences for himself.

265

Historians may see his championship of the constitution as his greatest service to the Federal Republic.

The President is more powerful than was the Prime Minister for another reason. He chooses his ministers – as well as his Presidential Advisers and Assistants – from outside the legislature, so that they depend entirely on him. He does not have to worry about conciliating a powerful minister because of the following he may command in the legislature. This could mean that many people of calibre will not seek election to the legislature, as that would exclude them from ministerial office; or that too many ministers are people who failed to win an election. In practice, however, the power of the legislature, particularly the Senate, under the new constitution can attract ambitious politicians. And although in practice, too, President Shehu Shagari has been limited in his choice of ministers to those party or "alliance" people who can claim political rewards, in theory he could turn to independent people who would not dream of standing for election.

Whether Shehu Shagari is the NPN presidential candidate in 1983, and whether, if he is, he will again win, are questions beyond the scope of this work. But the 1983 general elections, and in particular the security arrangements for them, will be one of his own major responsibilities as President; and they will be a very exacting responsibility.

The CDC decided, like Bagehot, that "party organisation is the vital principle of representative government"; it completely rejected the tentative proposal of the military regime that it should consider the possibility of "no-party" government. Nigerian newspapers of all political persuasions expressed disquiet at Mr Robert Mugabe's advocacy of one-party government for Zimbabwe. There was, too, general condemnation in Nigeria of the overthrow of civilian government in Ghana at the end of 1981. Yet if the parties are vital for the maintenance of Nigeria's representative government, they are also its main problem.

There were many allegations of malpractice during the five stages of the 1979 elections. Yet since none of the five parties contesting the elections was in office, and they were thus

unable to influence the results through control of the election machinery, the force of the allegations was tempered. The soldiers, it was also alleged, wanted an NPN victory. Few, however, accused them of rigging the results. In spite of the widespread belief, both in Nigeria and abroad, that they might in the end be reluctant to relinquish power, the soldiers were generally regarded as playing the role of "umpires", to use Gen. Obasanjo's word; even if the analogy he made between the politicians and "players" would not be so readily accepted. At the next general election there will be no such umpires. State and local government officials will be largely responsible, under the direction of the Federal Electoral Commission (FEDECO), for conduct of national and state elections; and – which was not the case in 1979 – the political allegiance of each state government will be clear.

The National Assembly's long consideration in 1981 and early 1982 of the proposed new Electoral Law, under which not only the 1983 general elections but over fifty by-elections and the already overdue local government elections would be held, showed considerable suspicion between the parties about the possibility of malpractices by their opponents in 1983. The chairman of FEDECO, however, Mr Justice Ovie-Whisky, has warned Nigerians that the excessive time and numerous stages proposed by the legislature for hearing of election petitions could virtually deprive Nigeria of a government after the 1983 elections.

More serious is the growth of political thuggery, a feature of pre-1966 Nigerian politics, about which the President has warned leaders of all parties, including his own. The rewards of political victory in Nigeria are still such that the politicians will go to great lengths to achieve it.

There is, too, much concern about the widespread smuggling of arms into Nigeria. The smugglers are not thought to be those who propose to use the arms. They enrich themselves by selling arms to people who seek protection either against armed robbers or against future political opponents. The dangers of violence in the 1983 elections should not be minimised. A narrow victory in the presidential election of the kind

Shehu Shagari won in 1979 may also not be so readily, if grudgingly, accepted by his opponents.

At the end of his first term as President Shehu Shagari might leave a particularly important piece of unfinished business. At the beginning of 1982 it was still doubtful whether a new and reliable census could be organised and completed before this term ends. If a census is not completed this will be recorded as one of his failures – as it was of the years of military rule. Accurate census figures are essential for the allocation of federally-collected revenues among the states. They also affect delimitation of constituencies for the legislatures, and the allocation of seats in the House of Representatives and the state Houses of Assembly. In the 1979 elections all parties agreed to accept the Federal Military Government's decision, enshrined in the present constitution, that until a new census is held the disputed 1963 figures hold the field. In 1983 disappointed parties may not be so ready to accept figures which they can claim lack validity. The constitution itself recognises the controversial nature of Nigerian censuses, by providing that the Council of State can recommend to the President rejection of a population count if the Council concludes that the figures are inaccurate or that the results are "perverse".

Under the constitution political parties can be registered by FEDECO to contest elections only if they match up to rigorous tests. There was much controversy in 1978 when FEDECO rejected such parties as the Nigerian Advance Party and the Whig Party of Nigeria. In FEDECO's view these failed to establish their "federal" credibility and their nation-wide organisation. For 1983 FEDECO will face the testing task of deciding whether the "Rimi faction" of the PRP, which will no doubt still appear to control both the Kano and Kaduna state governments, has a federal organisation. The same problem will arise over the break-away faction of the GNPP or over the GNPP itself, which also controls two state governments.

President Shehu Shagari's NPN, fortuitously to some extent, emerged from the 1979 election as the most truly national of any party Nigeria has known. By contrast Chief Awolowo's UPN, the runner-up, was based solidly on Yoruba areas and had little support elsewhere. Dr Azikiwe's NPP was hugely successful in Ibo areas, but it also won Plateau among the states in the north. The other two registered parties – PRP and GNPP – each found their support only in two states. This pattern may persist in the 1983 elections.

Whether the former identification of present parties with those which operated in Nigeria before 1966 will persist is uncertain. The election results certainly answered the accusation that the NPN is a revived NPC, since the party lost heavily in NPC strongholds such as Kano and Borno, but won handsomely in areas, notably Cross River, Rivers, and Benue states, where the NPC did not operate or was strongly opposed. Yet Nigeria's parties are still, with the exception of the NPN, ethnic or particular, not universal, in their support, or depend chiefly on an individual leader for their appeal. In spite of the use of the term "progressive" to describe themselves by the NPN's opponents, all the registered parties tend to represent "interests", and with the partial exception of Kano, to bring together the privileged and powerful in the areas where they have support.

The great immediate test for Nigerian democracy, however, is whether, having been re-established by a general election ultimately supervised by the soldiers, it can now prosper in a general election organised and supervised by civilians. This is more important for Nigeria than the oil price, the problems of Chad or the Western Sahara, than the development of the steel industry or the method of allocating federally-collected revenue. President Shehu Shagari is dedicated to the strengthening of Nigerian democracy. It is by his success in this endeavour that history will judge him. So far the judgment can only be favourable. Whether Nigeria will continue to set a democratic example is, however, still uncertain. Her continued attachment to multi-party democracy, to which her President is totally committed, could affect significantly the balance of world forces.

BIBLIOGRAPHY

My Vision of Nigeria: Shehu Shagari edited by Aminu Tijjani and David Williams (Frank Cass, 1981)

Uthman dan Fodio by Alhaji Shehu Shagari and Jean Boyd (Islamic Publications Bureau, Lagos, 1978)

The Fulani Empire of Sokoto by H. A. S. Johnston (Oxford, 1967)

The Hausa Factor in West African History by Mahdi Adamu (Ahmadu Bello and Oxford, 1978)

My Life: the Autobiography of Sir Ahmadu Bello, Sardauna of Sokoto (Cambridge, 1962)

Nigeria Speaks: Speeches of Sir Abubakar Tafawa Balewa (Longmans, 1964)

Nigeria by Thurstan Shaw (Thames and Hudson, 1978)

Nigerian Perspectives by Thomas Hodgkin (Oxford 1960)

Central Administration in Nigeria 1914-1948 by Jeremy White (Irish Academic Press and Cass, 1981)

Education in Northern Nigeria by Albert Ozigi and Lawrence Ocho (Allen and Unwin, 1981)

Awo: the Speeches of Chief Obafemi Awolowo (Cambridge, 1960)

Zik: the Speeches of Dr Nnamdi Azikiwe (Cambridge, 1961)

The Politics of Tradition by C. S. Whittaker Jr (Princeton, 1970)

Politics and Crisis in Nigeria by B. J. Dudley (Ibadan, 1973)

The Story of Nigeria by Michael Crowder (Faber and Faber, 1978)

Nigerian Government and Politics edited by John P. Mackintosh (Allen and Unwin, 1966)

The Nigerian Civil War by John de St Jorre (Hodder and Stoughton, 1972)

Soldiers and Oil edited by Keith Panter-Brick (Cass, 1978)

Nigeria Returns to Civilian Rule by Okion Ojigbo (Tokion (Nigeria), 1980)

The Nigerian 1979 Elections edited by Oyeleye Oyediran (Macmillan Nigeria, 1981)

Nigeria since 1970 by Anthony Kirk-Greene and Douglas Rimmer (Hodder and Stoughton, 1981)

270

INDEX

Abubakar, Alhaji Sir, *see*
Balewa, Alhaji Sir Abubakar
Tafawa
Abubakar, Sir, Sultan of Sokoto,
see Sokoto, Sultan of
Abuja, xix, 149, 155, 186, 187,
256-7
Action Group, 48, 70, 75, 150,
163, 167, 171, 204
Afghanistan, 203, 205-6
"African Common Market", 53,
226
African, Caribbean and Pacific
Countries (ACP), 206
African Development Bank
(ADB), 54-5, 124, 207, 226
agriculture, xix, xxiv, 5, 49, 87,
113-15, 181, 218, 219-220,
223-4, 226-7; in Sokoto State,
10-12, 20
Aguiyi-Ironsi, General, 79, 80-6
Ahidjo, President, 210-11
Ahmadu-Suka, Alhaji Osman,
249
Ahmed, Alhaji Mohammed
Buba, 248
Akinjide, Chief Richard, 170
Akinloye, Chief Adisa, 74, 150,
165
Akintola, Chief S. L., 69, 70, 74,
79
Aliyu, Alhaji, *see* Bida, Alhaji
Aliyu, Makaman
Aloba, Abiodun, 246, 248-9

Amin, General, 125-6, 215
"Amirul-Hajj", Shehu Shagari
as, 230-3
Ani, Chief Michael, 62, 64, 168
Angola, 203-5, 214
anti-Ibo riots, 84-5, 96-7; *see also*
Ibo
Archibon-Omon, Archibong,
248
Argungu raid on Shagari, 12-13
Argungu Senior Primary
School, Shehu Shagari as
headmaster of, 29-30, 40-1
armed forces, and Cameroon,
210-11; in Chad, 209-10;
composition of, 92, 146;
control of, 73, 180; and Kano
riots, 239-40; as political force,
174, 191-2, *see also* military
rule; as relief workers, 112;
size of, xix, 173, 191-2, 207;
training of, 64
Audu, Professor Ishaya, 165,
204, 260
Awolowo, Chief Obafemi, 48,
105, 115-17, 120, 138, 150, 151,
198; as presidential candidate,
115-16, 164, 166, 167, 169-71,
174, 175, 179; release from
gaol, 97, 115; on trial, 62, 65,
70; *see also* Action Group,
United Party of Nigeria
(UPN)
Ayida, Allison, 108, 116, 117

271

272

INDEX

economy, xxiv-xxv, 49-57, 87,
112-24, 139-40, 152-3, 181,
216-27; *see also* "African
Common Market", ADB,
agriculture, ECOWAS,
election manifestos, industry,
National Development Plans,
oil, revenue
education, xxv, 5, 16-30, 87,
90-3, 102, 114, 121, 139, 181,
185, 190, 195-6, 207, 219, 224,
225-6, 235, 243
Egypt, Shehu Shagari visits,
65-6
Ekwueme, Dr Alex, 163, 164-5,
254
election manifestos, 70, 165,
171-9, 190, 193, 216, 219-20
elections, 34, 65, 74, 142, 145-6,
154; 1951-2: 34, 39, 40; 1954:
42-3, 44; 1959: 47-8; 1964:
69-74; 1976 (local): 136-7; 1979:
13, 37-8, 42, 115-16, 151, 154,
157-79, 216-17, 266-9; 1983:
183, 196, 198, 216-17, 266-9
electorate, viii, xix, xxii, 42, 47-8,
70-1, 167-9, 216-17
emirates, 2, 4-5, 8-10, 35-8, 70,
87, 136, 153-4, 178, 192-4
Enahoro, Chief, 65, 97, 163
Equatorial Guinea, 213
Ethiopia, 54, 206, 215
European Economic Community
(EEC), 54, 55-7, 206

Federal Electoral Commission
(FEDECO), 65, 71, 154, 155-6,
161, 166, 267, 268
Federal Scholarship Board,
Shehu Shagari on, 44-5, 57
France, 50-1, 54-7 *passim*, 104-5,
111, 133-4, 205-11 *passim*
Fulani, xxi, 3-6, 10-11, 20, 37,
210

Gaddafi, Colonel, 215, 238-9; *see
also* Libya

Ghana, xvii, xviii, 10, 32, 87,
155, 211-13, 217, 218, 219, 266
Goukhouni, President, 209, 210,
215; *see also* Chad
government, local, xix, xx,
xxv-xxvi, 87, 102-3, 136-7,
146-9, 180-6, 192-4, 260; *see
also* chiefdoms, emirates,
revenue, states
Gowon, General Yakubu, xviii,
xx, 96-7, 105-9, 115-27 *passim*,
190-1, 207, 230, 255-6
Great Nigerian People's Party
(GNPP), 13, 153, 154, 155,
178-9, 186, 187-8, 268, 269; *see
also* Ibrahim, Alhaji Waziri

Hajj, 228-34
Hausa, xx-xxi, 2-5, 10
Houphouet-Boigny, President,
104; *see also* Ivory Coast

Ibo, xx, xxi, xxii, 63, 70, 81-90
passim, 96-7, 112, 162-3, 165,
179; *see also* Biafra
Ibrahim, Alhaji Waziri, 13, 81,
153, 164, 169, 171, 179; *see also*
Great Nigerian People's Party
Igoh, Charles, 246, 247
independence, 31-2, 35, 47, 51,
57-61, 87, 192, 264
industry, xxv, 114, 119, 132-4,
195, 216, 220-2, 224-5, 253,
269; *see also* Kainji dam, oil,
trade unions
"intellectual radicals", 197-8
Israel, 66, 174
Italy, 55, 57, 105-6; *see also*
Vatican
Ivory Coast, 104, 155, 217, 218

John-Paul II, Pope, xxiii, 194
Johnston, H. A. S., 28, 33, 34

Kaduna College, *see* Barewa
College
Kainji dam, 50-1, 52, 87, 113

273